The Old Tracks through the Cheviots

Discovering the Archaeology of the Border Roads

David Jones with
Coquetdale Community Archaeology

First published in the United Kingdom in 2017 by Northern Heritage Services Limited

Northern Heritage Services Limited
Units 7&8 New Kennels, Blagdon Estate, Seaton Burn,
Newcastle upon Tyne NE13 6DB

Telephone: 01670 789 940

www.northern-heritage.co.uk

See our full online catalogue at www.northern-heritage.co.uk

ISBN: 978-0-9957485-0-7

Typeset in Gill Sans

Design and layout by Ian Scott Design

Printed and bound in Malta on behalf of Latitude Press Limited

This book has been produced using paper from sustainable
forest sources and environmentally friendly inks

British Library Cataloguing in Publishing Data
A catalogue record for this book is available from the British Library

Front cover illustration:
The fort on Moat Knowe in Roxburghshire.

Back cover illustrations are from top:
An excerpt from Mercator's map of Northumberland of 1595.
The abandoned farmhouse of Seefew between Hownam and Belford.
A standing stone above Hownam with Tronshaw Hill in the background.

This book was produced with the help of funding from the Heritage Lottery Fund and
Northumberland National Park.

Contents

List of Maps

Foreword

We often do not think about roads. They are commonplace, everyday 'things' we use to get to and from places. But when you drill through the history of a road you will often find them intimately bound with the histories of villages, towns, regions or even nations. People, ideas, politics, religions – everything a society and a culture has to offer – have moved along them, sometimes for centuries or even millennia. They are also often the most stable and long-lived elements of the historic environment. While entire ways of life change around them, roads offer a continuity of movement between places which seldom changes, even though everything else does. And it is this long-lived 'between-ness' that makes roads particularly special. They are persistently transient, liminal spaces that offer connection, but are in themselves the places where culture moves and changes the fastest. People and their ideas meet along roads, and new ways of thinking are formed. A famous movie once said 'where we're going, we don't need roads'. Well, this is not the case. Without roads we go nowhere in both the literal and figurative senses.

So it is with this in mind that I am delighted to introduce you to this book on the Border Roads. Routes such as Dere Street and Clennell Street are roads with deep and profound stories to tell. Not only do they navigate a difficult, transitional landscape through the Cheviots linking England with Scotland, they are historical landmarks in their own right. Many are undoubtedly prehistoric in origin, though there is very little hard archaeological evidence to prove this. They once connected Neolithic, Bronze and Iron Age societies on both sides of the Cheviot massif, and continue to do so into the present. These connections have broadened the prospects of these 'Borderers' as a result. From the earliest times the roads provided access to resources in the hills and between the lower lands on either side of the Cheviots. For millennia farmers and herders have used the roads to transport goods and stock to summer fields and pasturage, to markets and to fairs. But the roads were also political and military assets. There is a reason why the northern Cheviot ridge contains dozens of Iron Age forts along the route-ways to the Merse, the rich farmland between the Lammermuirs and the Tweed, or why Dere Street was upgraded by the Romans during their occupation north of Hadrian's Wall, or indeed why the Otterburn Training Camp was created in 1911. These roads hosted British, Northumbrian, English and Scottish armies as well as their proxies; March wardens, reivers and worse still … tax collectors. But throughout history, the most important users of the roads were the people who lived near them; the communities on both sides of the artificial border who have always had more in common than they had differences.

As this book will show, the history and archaeology of the Border Roads is critical to an understanding of the Border lands themselves. But there is still much we do not know about them. Future archaeologists may be able to date them, accurately map their various braided paths, even tell what and who travelled along them, and why. This book offers a glimpse of this exciting and rich seam of research. I hope it encourages you to make your own journeys along them.

Dr. Christopher Bowles
Archaeology Officer, Scottish Borders Council

Preface and Acknowledgements

Coquetdale Community Archaeology (CCA) was founded in 2007 as a spin-off from a community project run by the Northumberland National Park Authority, working mainly in the upper Coquet valley and the surrounding areas.

In 2014, we started researching and documenting the archaeology along the old tracks through the Cheviots. We anticipated that the project would provide opportunities ranging from research to excavation, and would allow us to blend archaeology with local history. This book is one of the results of that project.

There are many groups and individuals without whom this work would not have been possible, and we would like to take this opportunity to express our appreciation.

Firstly, we thank the Heritage Lottery Fund and the Northumberland National Park Authority for providing generous funding.

Then there are the members of Coquetdale Community Archaeology and others who variously dug, drew, walked, photographed, researched, worked with schools, proofread, advised, managed, directed and wrote:

Lorna Aiken, Caroline Allott, David Astbury, David Bradbrooke, Sue Braithwaite, Charlotte Boxall, Michael Boxall, Sue Brophy, Dave Brummit, Barry Butterworth, Chris Butterworth, Alison Chapman, Ian Colquhoun, Keith Cooper, Andy Curtis, Margaret Cutts, Jeanette Dagg, John Davies, Emma Delgaty, Gillian Dick, John Dryden, Barbara Esslemont, Pat Fenwick, Janet Fenwicke-Clennell, Ian Filtness, Irene Foggett, Jan Frazer, Keith Gray, Bridget Gubbins, William Gubbins, Ted Hall, Janice Henney, Peter Henney, John Herbert, Lizzie Herbert, Johnnie Heywood, Lyd Heywood, Elanor Hillier, Mike Hodgson, Dieter Hofmann, Pat Holliday, Michael Hutchinson, Bob Jackson, Chris Jackson, Cathy Jenkins, Marc Johnstone, Anne Jones, Ben Jones, Chris Jones, Mike Jones, John Lazarus, George Martin, Barbara McCabe, James McQuillen, David Millward, Karen Millward, Roger Miket, Gordon Moir, Krissy Moore, John Nolan, Christine Ogg, Mike Parsons, John Pearson, Jessica Plane, Cheryl Rayner, David Robinson, Jonne Robinson, Peter Robinson, Glyn Scott, Margaret Scott, Barbara Sexon, Sue Shaw, Ian Spencer, Margaret Steward, Gemma Stewart, Jen Teulon, Ellie Thompson, John Tribe, Dave Tuck, Jenny Vaughan, Heather Waldron, Natalie Ward, Jess Watkins and Tony Williams.

There are people and organisations who supported, encouraged and facilitated the project in many different ways. Without their help we could not have achieved what we have.

These include:
Chris Burgess of Northumberland County Council and Chris Bowles of the Scottish Borders Council for their encouragement and support and the latter for writing the foreword for this book; Jacqui Huntley of English Heritage (later Historic England) for technical advice; Phil Abramson and Chris Livsey for the Ministry of Defence, which owns the land where we excavated and a lot of the territory we walked over; Chris Jones and Ruth Dickinson for the Northumberland National Park; Christopher Hunwick, the Head Archivist at Alnwick Castle; Ian and Eunice Tait for providing food, looking after equipment, and encouraging investigations on their farm; the

Northumberland Archaeological Group for the loan of equipment; Kirsty McCarrison of Durham University who helped us work with schools; Simon Gray for facilitating access to Uswayford and Tom and Richard Mason for bringing digging machinery both to open and backfill trenches. Last but not least we owe much to Beryl Charlton, whose work in the area acted as the foundation for so much that has followed, to Richard Carlton of the Archaeological Practice whose studies for the Northumberland National Park provided the impetus for this project and who directed some of our fieldwork, and to John Nolan and Jenny Vaughan who directed the rest.

Our apologies if we have overlooked anyone. It was not intentional, but over the years we may occasionally have lost track of individuals who contributed.

Readers should note that the maps, which were drawn by Marc Johnstone, have been designed to help them locate sites near the Old Tracks, rather than be complete representations of the landscape. Ordnance Survey maps should be used to understand the latter.

On a different topic, we should explain our approach to units of measurement; throughout this book we use the Imperial system for distances. While we understand that this would not be correct for an academic publication, miles, yards and feet are still deeply ingrained in our everyday language and we felt their use was appropriate here.

Staying with measurement, on occasions we give examples of the valuations attached to old inventories of farms or estates. Rather than estimate what they would be worth today, we sometimes offer a comparison with the worth of other people in the area; this provides an indication of whether these were particularly wealthy or impoverished individuals. We do this because estimating the current value of an historical sum of money is a complicated procedure; it depends, for example, on whether the objective is to assess its purchasing power, or whether it is to gain some understanding of the economic status of the person in question. For example, the purchasing power of a £200 legacy in 1650 would be about £25,000 in modern money. However, the prestige value of that sum – the standing it conferred on its owner in comparison with other individuals in society – would make it worth about £1.1 million. This sort of spread makes such conversions almost meaningless unless they are accompanied each time by an explanation. A website that covers this subject in more detail is www.measuringworth.com.

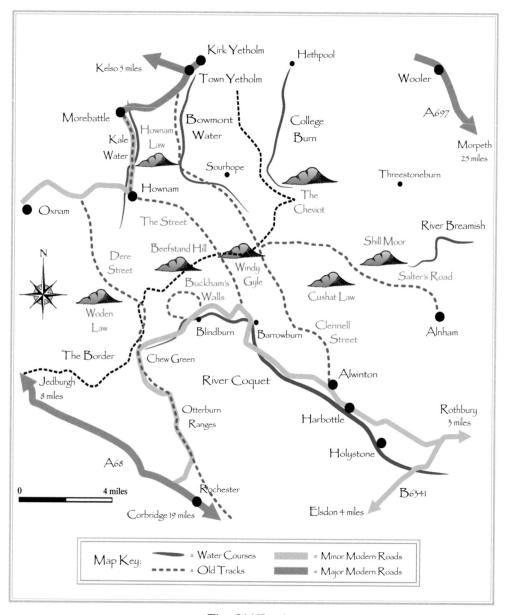

The Old Tracks

Introduction

Some 300 years ago, the man who wrote Robinson Crusoe – arguably the first English novel – was hauled up the Cheviot on horseback. Clearly terrified, Daniel Defoe later described frightful heights, failing hearts and fears that the top, if reached, would be a pinnacle *with a precipice every way round us'*. He need not have worried.

The Cheviots are indeed one of the major landmarks of the border country, but in reality they consist of rolling summits with no rugged peaks or crevasses and few distinguishing features. Outlying ridges extend south into Northumberland and north into the old Scottish county of Roxburghshire; these ridges are exploited by ancient routes, all with their origins deep in prehistory. As well as just being ways to pass through the countryside, they have been used for activities as disparate as trading, driving livestock and moving troops – as well as smuggling and raiding.

These are the Border Roads. They are the relics of connections between England and Scotland that existed well before there was any concept of the two countries. Joining up with networks of lowland tracks that have often either disappeared or been subsumed by modern roads, they show how people negotiated the landscape for thousands of years. Although marked on modern maps as specific paths, they were not always thus. Even relatively recent maps show alternate routes that drop off the ridges where the access is easiest to link up with individual settlements. In their heyday the roads may actually have been thought of as a broad sense of direction across the hills, part of a network of hill trails that linked remote places with the outside world.

The country the roads pass through is now largely moorland, grazed by sheep and crossed by walkers, but in the past it was used more intensively. The Cheviots are scattered with the remains of upland farms and dwellings that date from the Bronze Age to medieval times and later. Some of the land was cultivated, but sheep farming was ever present and at the heart of many businesses – milking and cheese making, spinning wool, weaving yarn and fulling cloth. This meant there was much more going on – and many more people – in the uplands. Such activity reshaped the landscape and left its mark.

Developments and changes have rarely destroyed the signs of this earlier presence. This means you can walk for just a couple of hours and, if you know what to look for, see Bronze Age hut circles, Iron Age camps, Romano-British settlements, medieval field systems, nineteenth-century whisky stills and signs of even more recent agriculture. The landscape has captured its history – but this is not a history where you need expensive equipment to see what's gone before. All you need to know is where to look. It is an unspoilt landscape.

Archaeology helps people understand human history, culture and behaviour through the artefacts and structures of past generations, and that understanding is enriched if there are links to historical records. This book takes readers along the Border Roads, paints a picture of their history and explains the role of the mounds, the earthworks, the ruins and the patterns in the landscape that people might otherwise just walk past.

This is not a complete gazetteer of all the archaeological sites in the Cheviots. Rather, we have selected the major roads and then described the history and the remains of interesting sites along them. Sometimes there is quite a lot of history, and only a few remains; sometimes it's the other way round – and with luck there are both.

And we say 'along' the roads, but we use that word liberally. Sometimes the path goes right by a site, in which case the selection is easy, but sometimes the remains are a little way away. We have based decisions about inclusion on the rules that the Michelin Guides once used: if a restaurant is a bit off the beaten track is it worth a detour or, if it's further away, is it worth a journey? We don't want to send people up long steep hills just to see a small cairn. In broad terms, if you can see a site from a road – and it's interesting – we will describe it.

This is not a book to take out on the hills, although the interested reader can clearly select some of the sites we describe and plan a walk to visit them. However, as companions to this book we are developing a comprehensive website and a guide that covers walks of varying degrees of distance and difficulty. More information on these is in the Afterword.

The book covers five principal roads or routes.

Clennell Street: this starts from Alwinton and heads north, passing Kidland and crossing the Usway Burn near Uswayford just south of the border. Once over the ridge, it drops down to Cocklawfoot and then follows a modern road north to Town Yetholm.

Salter's Road: a route that heads broadly north-west from the ancient village of Alnham up to the border, where it joins Clennell Street.

The Street: a route that starts at Barrowburn, on the Coquet upstream from Alwinton. It follows the river to Slymefoot, where it turns north up a ridge to the border. After that it heads north-west to Hownam and then north towards Morebattle.

Buckham's Walls: further upstream again this is a series of tracks in an area rich in archaeology north of the Coquet and close to paths that cross the border to Raeshaw Fell and beyond.

Dere Street: part of a more extensive Roman road, the section we describe starts at Rochester. With its origin further south than our other roads, the track heads north across the fells, past the source of the Coquet near Chew Green and thence into Scotland to Pennymuir and Whitton Edge.

We focus on the stretches of these routes that cross the Cheviots, describing areas that are not only accessible to people who use the hills but also, on occasions, road cyclists and drivers.

The first three chapters cover what the roads have in common: the geology, the climate, the agriculture and the records and structures that people have left behind them. Many of the roads share archaeological features; four of them, for example, pass by hillforts or palisaded settlements. The common characteristics of structures like these are covered in the early chapters, leaving us to focus on what's special about the particular sites when we describe the individual roads, and each of these has a dedicated chapter. At the end of the book, there's a glossary of common terms as well as an index to the key sites described.

People sometimes expect archaeology to be an exact science, but mostly it isn't. On occasions, something unarguable can be established, but very often it consists of stories, opinions and observations that make the best possible sense out of evidence that is either limited or inconsistent. So what follows is neither true nor false, but what we know. We hope you enjoy it.

Sheep have always been a key part of the Cheviot economy.

Chapter 1

A Brief History of the Cheviots

This chapter describes how the Cheviots were formed and outlines the history of human activity in the area. We explain the role of climate in the uplands and how it influenced the plants and animals that lived there. All this created the context in which the Border Roads came into existence and the nature of the landscape they cross.

The next two chapters look at the ways people have left their marks on that landscape, from the records they made to the traces they left behind them, with activities that ranged from farming to warfare. Then we look at each Border Road in turn.

The Geology

Although the story of the Border Roads goes back for several thousand years, the Cheviots themselves are much, much older.

Looking at them today, with their rolling outlines cut through by rivers and streams, it's hard to think of them as volcanoes – but that's what they were. Some 400 million years ago two continental plates, one carrying what is now Scotland and the other England, collided. In doing so they closed up the body of water that had separated them, known as the Iapetus Ocean; the fault line that resulted, the Iapetus Suture, runs today from the Solway Firth to Lindisfarne.

The collision may have lasted for as long as 20 million years and resulted in violent volcanic activity, followed by massive outpourings of a sticky lava consisting mainly of andesite, a rock that is named after another mountain range on the edge of a continental plate – the Andes. The volcanism was followed by the intrusion of a large granitic magma plug which slowly crystallised and now forms the Cheviot itself and Hedgehope Hill.

North of the Cheviots, the foundations of the Scottish Southern Uplands consist of rocks called shales and greywackes. These were formed from oceanic sediments that were piled up on the edge of the Scottish continental plate as the collision with England progressed. Similar rocks from this time can be seen in the bed of the River Coquet near Makendon, a mile or so downstream from its source.

We don't know what the young Cheviots looked like or how high they were, but modern andesite volcanoes are typically steep-sided peaks. This contrasts with those formed from more fluid lava, such as those in Hawaii, which have much shallower slopes.

As the volcanic activity died away, cycles of faulting, deformation, erosion and deposition caused further changes in the Cheviot landscape. The Breamish and Harthope valleys, for example, are the sites of fault lines, while the agricultural land that lies on both sides of the Cheviots is the result of erosional deposition. The fell sandstone which forms the Simonside Hills in Northumberland as well as other crags and fells is the result of thick fluvial deposits of sand.

Finally, after millions of years of erosion, principally caused by successive ice ages, we get what we have today – some exposed andesite and granite, the hills with their peaty tops covered with heather and cotton grass and the more fertile slopes and valleys, homes for differing types of grassland with pockets of bracken and gorse.

Timelines and human history

The ice last left the Cheviots over 12,000 years ago; if there was any human activity in the area before that, then no trace of it has been found. People seem to have returned to Britain shortly afterwards, although periodic cold spells may have made their stays intermittent. This period is the final part of the Palaeolithic, and worked flints identified at Howburn, some 70 miles to the north-west of the Cheviots, suggest that early hunting groups were active in that area. The flints are of a type associated with finds in northern Germany and it seems likely that the people who made them were exploiting warmer weather to move across the land now covered by the North Sea. Following river valleys like that of the Tweed, they may have been hunting animals such as reindeer fattened by summer grazing.

Somewhat later, around 8000 BC, the climate stabilised at a warmer level; this is the start of a period called the Mesolithic and hunter-gatherers were found everywhere in the British Isles. We don't know how much of their time was spent on the move, but they left their traces in the form of worked flints on and around the Cheviots, and the remains of a circular building have been found at Howick on the Northumberland coast. Dated to 7600 BC, it seems to be a house that was used for about 100 years, implying permanent or at least regular seasonal settlement.

Farming arrived in these islands around 4000 BC, and with it the period we call the Neolithic. As with most of the dates that follow, this classification is dependent on geography; for example, the same period started very much earlier in the Middle East.

Early Neolithic structures are common in England and Scotland, ranging from burial barrows and enclosures to the stone houses found at Skara Brae in Orkney. The later Neolithic, after 2900 BC, is perhaps best known for the appearance of henges, circular or oval-shaped earthworks often associated with wooden or stone circles such as those at Stonehenge and the Ring of Brodgar. There is some evidence of late-Neolithic activity in the Cheviots; for example, two burial pots were found in a grave-pit on Wether Hill above Ingram and stone circles at places like Hethpool in the College valley and Threestoneburn may date from that period. There is no evidence that there were Neolithic farms in the area, but any remains might well have been destroyed by later activity.

At the end of the Neolithic, around 2200 BC, metalworking skills arrived in Britain – first with the use of copper and then the much harder bronze, an alloy of copper and a small amount of tin. The Bronze Age lasted for some 1,500 years and the people left their mark across the area. At least one lowland settlement has been identified to the north of the Cheviots in the Milfield basin, while as part of a project starting in 2006, students and local archaeologists excavated a turf-walled roundhouse in Kidlandlee Dean, next to Clennell Street. Elsewhere, cairns of the period abound and in 1837 two late Bronze Age shields were found at Yetholm, at the northern end of Clennell Street.

Around 750 or 700 BC, iron started to replace bronze as the metal of choice. The new technology was not adopted overnight, and as with all the dates in this chapter the actual boundaries of the Iron Age are somewhat blurred, with the metal maybe coming into common use rather later in the north than in the south. Trade probably brought iron artefacts to remoter areas before the arrival of technologies such as smelting and forging.

The most striking Iron Age structures in the Cheviots are the hillforts or camps, which were probably preceded by palisaded settlements, some of which may date from the late Bronze Age. The camps that have been dated were mostly built in the late Iron Age and some may have stayed in use after the arrival of the Romans. Traces of upland cultivation are sometimes found nearby; these are known as cord rig and, like the other structures mentioned, are described in more detail in Chapter 3. Elsewhere, remains of unenclosed roundhouses that date from the same period are common.

After two earlier brief visits, the Romans arrived in force in Britain in AD 43. This is generally accepted as the end of 'prehistory' but at the risk of repetition, the transition from the Iron Age to the Romano-British period is also indistinct. The Cheviots, for example, probably didn't see much Roman activity until around AD 79, when Agricola, the governor of Britain, launched a campaign in the north. But even then, the relationship between the Romans and the local population differed greatly between the north and the south. In the latter there was clearly a considerable degree of cultural integration, with Roman civilians living in towns and country villas and powerful figures in British communities copying their habits and lifestyle.

It wasn't like that in the north. Here the Roman presence was almost entirely military – the most northern known villas are in North Yorkshire – and while there must have been trade with the local population it is probable that there was less cultural assimilation. So some Iron Age customs and lifestyles would have continued; in the north of Scotland it's fair to say that the period lasted for another 400 years or so.

The Medieval period, or the Middle Ages, followed the Roman departure around AD 410 and covers over a thousand years. The first part of it, the Early Medieval, consisted of what are sometimes called the Dark Ages and lasted until the end of the first millennium. In the British Isles, the period was dominated by incursions and immigration from Scandinavia and north-eastern Europe; little tangible evidence of this activity has been found in the Cheviots themselves, although traces of it are found in some place names. At Yeavering, north-west of Wooler, large buildings and other structures that dated from the sixth and seventh centuries were excavated by Brian Hope-Taylor in the 1950s. Bede, a monk and a scholar from the monastery at Jarrow, mentioned the site under the name *Ad Gefrin*. It may have played an important role in a royal estate in the kingdom of Bernicia.

The High Medieval, or the High Middle Ages, followed. The name is somewhat unusual; it is often claimed that it refers to the flowering of European culture with the construction of castles, cathedrals and universities, but it's also a neat way of avoiding the term 'Middle Middle Ages'. Be that as it may, while there are no cathedrals or universities in the Cheviots, there are castles dating from this period, such as that at

Harbottle, together with documentary records of major landowners and the remains of their estate boundaries, farms and mills.

The final part of the medieval period, the Late Medieval, starts by convention at around AD 1300. From an English perspective it is often accepted, albeit somewhat arbitrarily, that it concludes with the accession of Henry VII in 1485, although some commentators describe the battle of Flodden in 1513 as the last great medieval conflict on British soil. In the Cheviots this period was mainly marked by Anglo-Scottish guerrilla warfare, with parties of reivers moving to and fro across the border stealing stock, capturing people and burning buildings and crops. Communities on either side of the border took advantage of the general mayhem to attack each other as well, so the men of Redesdale would raid Coquetdale, and *vice versa*. The result was that the area was substantially depopulated; landowners complained to the Crown about still having to pay taxes, and the situation was made worse by spells of famine and by the Black Death in 1349.

Perhaps predictably, archaeologists generally refer to anything after the Medieval period as Post-Medieval. Some people only use this term for dates up to 1750 or so, after which the Modern period begins. In practice, however, we'll see that more recent objects and structures are often easier to date more accurately, and so they are usually referred to by their century – such as seventeenth or nineteenth.

How dates are derived

Archaeologists are often asked 'How old is it?' or 'When did that happen?'. Fortunately, there are several ways of providing an answer.

First, on a dig, you can usually get an understanding of relative ages by establishing where things are found. Put simply, if one object is underneath another, it's probably older. If a piece of pot that looks as if it's from the thirteenth century is on top of a floor, the chances are the floor is earlier. Of course, it can be more complex than that; the object may have been somewhere else for a long time and then dropped on the floor, so human activity may cause confusion, as can burrowing animals that occasionally move things. And it can be more difficult to understand the relationship between two objects if they are not close together – but the principle is valid.

Specialist knowledge can usually help identify the age of an artefact, such as a piece of pottery or jewellery. Styles, creative skills and manufacturing techniques all change with time, so an expert will be able to provide a rough date for what's been found. Objects such as coins can provide more precise dates, although they may have been in circulation for some time before being dropped or buried, while fragments of clay smoking pipes can be very useful. These were the precursor of the modern cigarette; the shape of the bowl and the size of the bore are indicative of age (Figure 1.1), but the manufacturers were usually thoughtful enough to stamp them with their name or initials. If these can be identified, then an archaeologist can determine when and where the pipe was made. Given that they probably didn't last very long, this is a good indication of when they were discarded, and this helps date sites from the seventeenth century onwards, when tobacco was first imported from Virginia.

Dating objects by their appearance depends on reference to other similar objects whose date is actually, or at least better, known; archaeologists apply the same process

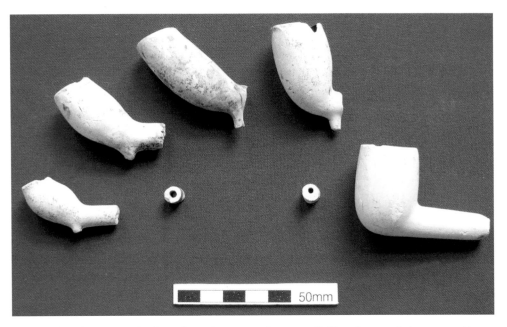

Figure 1.1 Clay pipe styles from the mid-seventeenth century (left) to the twentieth century. Also shown is the change in pipe bore – wider around 1700 than in the nineteenth century.

to larger structures as well. For example, hill forts or camps surrounded by ramparts and ditches are usually thought of as belonging to the late Iron Age. This is not because they have all been excavated and examined; they haven't, but finds from those that have indicate that these structures were built then.

But there are ways of getting more precise, and usually more accurate, dates. One such is dendrochronology – the use of tree rings. Different weather conditions lead to different annual rates of growth in trees, resulting in distinctive patterns in the rings on a cross-section of timber (Figure 1.2). Reference sets of these patterns have been established for different regions over long periods of time, and timber finds can often

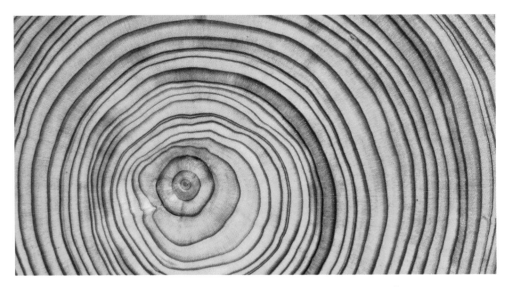

Figure 1.2 Tree rings: thick rings indicate years of good growth.

be matched against them. If the cross-section of the wood is complete – if it shows bark or the distinctive wood near it – then its felling date can be established with extraordinary precision. Using this technique in a different part of the country, it is now known that the Sweet Track, a Neolithic timber causeway in the Somerset Levels, was built in either 3807 or 3806 BC.

Radiocarbon dating is another common technique. Carbon is an element found in all living material, and a small fraction of it is in a form that is slightly radioactive. While carbon is in a living organism, perhaps a piece of wood or bone, then that radioactive fraction is continually refreshed from the natural environment; but when the tree is cut down or the animal dies, then that absorption stops and the radioactive fraction starts to decay. At a later date, a measurement of how much of it is left will generate an estimate of when the living object died and the decay started. Modern analytical techniques can usually provide dates for organic objects to within 100 years or so.

This specific approach only works for objects less than 50,000 years old; beyond that there simply isn't enough radioactive carbon left to be measured accurately, but there is similar decay behaviour in other elements that can extend measurements back for millions and even billions of years.

Other dating technologies have emerged in recent years. For example, it's now possible to find out how long ago certain soils were last exposed to light, or how long it is since objects such as ceramics were last heated above 500° Celsius. And a technique called archaeomagnetic dating allows scientists to ascertain the orientation of any trapped magnetic field in objects that have been heated; this means they can determine the location of the Earth's magnetic poles when that heating last occurred. Over time, these poles have wandered in a known pattern, so the direction of these fields can provide a date for that heating. But such techniques are beyond the scope of this book (which is one way of saying we've never been able to afford them).

Finally, if something happened within the last 2,000 years or so, then there may be written records that describe it. We look at different types of these in the next chapter.

Climate

With the future of the world's climate a subject of intense discussion and argument, there has been a growing interest in the study of past climatic conditions. Scientists use several ways to assess these, such as analysing cores drilled from places like the Greenland icecap and studying tree rings and pollen samples taken from deposits in soils and bogs.

The emergence of the Northern Hemisphere from the last Ice Age was not altogether smooth. After a period of gradual warming, around 10900 BC there was a sudden downturn in temperature of between two and six degrees Celsius which lasted for about 1,000 years. This cooling was sudden and there are several theories as to what caused it, ranging from meteoritic impact to the disruption of warm Atlantic currents by glacial meltwater.

This hiatus would have certainly affected the human recolonisation of Northern Europe, but once it was over, in broad terms the climate settled down to a long period of warming before plateauing for some four millennia at temperatures that were probably about two degrees Celsius above those of the twentieth century. This is sometimes called the climatic optimum. In fact, conditions that favoured upland settlements lasted into the Bronze Age, but were followed by a gradual decline in temperatures that continued until the nineteenth century.

These changes, however, were not smooth and the equilibria were not uninterrupted. Around 6200 BC, the Northern Hemisphere experienced a cold period of between two and four hundred years, probably caused by the collapse of giant meltwater lakes in North America disrupting Atlantic currents. Later, in the Neolithic, analyses of lake levels and vegetation patterns suggest phases of cooler, wetter weather. From the late Bronze Age onwards, there seem to have been intermittent periods of warming embedded in an environment that was getting wetter and cooler, particularly in the early Iron Age. The climate was probably warmer again during the Roman occupation, but subsequently cooler until the Medieval Warm Period, which lasted from around AD 950 to AD 1250. With temperatures perhaps slightly warmer than those of the twentieth century in Northern Europe, the Vikings took the opportunity to colonise Greenland and visit North America, but research has shown that some other parts of the world were substantially colder. The period known as the Little Ice Age that followed may have been at least partly due to a reversion to the original cooling trend. This trend halted in the mid to late nineteenth century and the climate has been getting warmer ever since.

It is hard to say what precise effects these continental-level changes would have had on the Cheviot uplands. Cooler and wetter weather, for example, may have led to the formation of peat deposits, but as we explain below, the clearance of trees and scrub by early farmers would have had a similar effect. Life in the hills, however, would always have been difficult, with changes in the climate having an effect on the crops that could be grown and on the animals that could be reared. And among the general trends that might be decades or centuries long, there was always the risk of a sudden disaster. The Cheviot volcanoes might have been extinct for hundreds of millions of years, but others hadn't. Ash clouds from the eruption of Mount Tambora in Indonesia caused the best-documented recent catastrophe – the 'Year Without a Summer' of 1816 – which resulted in famine across much of Western Europe. There was a snowstorm in the Cheviots on 11th May, killing three-quarters of that year's lambs[1]. 500 years earlier, it's been suggested that the succession of cold wet summers and crop failures that started in 1315 was due to the eruption of Mount Tarawera in New Zealand. The result of this was the Great Famine; millions of people died in Europe, and a contemporary chronicler recorded that people in Northumbria were reduced to eating *dogs and horses and other unclean things*.

Although no volcano was involved, in the 1430s cold weather and crop failures meant that in some years Durham tithe receipts were halved. Things were even worse in Scotland; the winter of 1432-3 was so cold that wine and ale reportedly froze, was sold by weight and had to be melted by the fire before drinking.

Flora

At the end of the last Ice Age, the Cheviot landscape would have been completely devastated. However, the damage was only temporary; as we are seeing today with

---

[1] It wasn't just in the Cheviots. In Newcastle the radical lawyer and reformer, James Losh, noted in his diary *We had today, for two hours, the heaviest fall of snow I ever recollect to have seen at any season*.

Figure 1.3 A late summer tundra landscape in northern Canada. The low red shrubs are arctic willow.
(© Geo. Swan under Creative Commons Attribution 2.0 licence).

the retreat of Arctic land ice, tundra vegetation is swift to establish itself, first with growths of moss and lichen and then sedges and grasses. Figure 1.3 shows what things might have looked like.

Shrubs with root systems would have followed; radiocarbon dating of pollen extracted from Din Moss, which is about three miles north-west of Kirk Yetholm, shows that evergreens such as pine and juniper had appeared by around 8000 BC, with deciduous birches and hazels not far behind. Pollen analysis like this is almost the only way to determine what plants populated the prehistoric landscape. The Din Moss work was carried out in the 1970s by two scientists from Cambridge; since then we are fortunate in that Richard Tipping, from the University of Stirling, has done extensive work in the Bowmont Valley, which runs south from Kirk Yetholm to within three miles of the border.

The major deciduous tree varieties, such as oak and elm, had populated the valleys and the Cheviot slopes by between 6000 BC and 5000 BC, but shortly thereafter there are indications that numbers of open areas were appearing in the woodland, with fire being the most likely cause. It's been suggested that this is indicative of land management by Mesolithic hunters – attracting grazing animals such as deer by clearing areas and encouraging the growth of grasses.

While there were finds of earlier cereal pollen at Din Moss, more substantial land clearance for farming started in the Neolithic period at around 2500 BC. This shows up both in pollen studies and also in analyses of increased sediment deposits in waterways downstream, which are symptomatic of erosion following reductions in woodland. These clearances continued through the Bronze Age and the Iron Age, despite the deteriorating climate. Indeed, cooler conditions might have encouraged development of additional farmland to compensate for reduced yields, but continued clearance of trees and shrubs would have further reduced soil stability and hastened erosion.

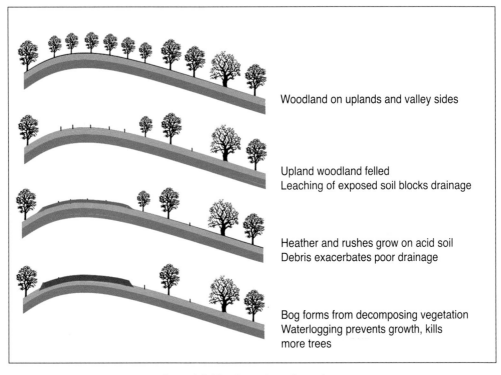

Woodland on uplands and valley sides

Upland woodland felled
Leaching of exposed soil blocks drainage

Heather and rushes grow on acid soil
Debris exacerbates poor drainage

Bog forms from decomposing vegetation
Waterlogging prevents growth, kills
more trees

*Figure 1.4 **The formation of peat bogs.***

Over time, this activity would have given rise to one of the defining characteristics of the modern Cheviots, the peat bog. As exposed soil erodes and leaches, it becomes more acidic and less productive and some of the material is washed out and deposited downhill; this blocks natural drainage and rainwater accumulates behind the obstruction. As the farmers move on, so heathers and rushes grow on the abandoned areas; when they die their debris decomposes slowly and layers of peat start to accumulate in the wet ground, resulting in a blanket bog that may be many feet deep (Figure 1.4).

It seems likely that the Cheviot landscape at the end of the Iron Age was very much like the one we know today. In warmer weather medieval farmers came back to the uplands and ploughed the land for arable crops, but the continuing grazing of the hills by sheep and the occasional feral goat – probably descended from medieval domesticated animals that were replaced by more profitable sheep – has prevented the regeneration of anything woody. So we now have heather and cotton grass on the tops, with white grass, moor-grass and bent grass lower down and fescues in the valleys – with growths of bracken and gorse both there and on the slopes.

Fauna

While many of the wild animals that we now see in the Cheviots and the countryside around would have been familiar to our ancestors, there are some that have appeared relatively recently, while others that they knew well have become extinct.

Probably the earliest import was the goat. They may have been introduced to the country during the Neolithic with stock descended from wild goats or ibexes native to the Middle East. They are discussed in more detail in the section on farming in Chapter 3.

Also not widely appreciated as a non-native species is the rabbit. The Romans imported these as a food supply, but they seem not to have become established in the wild until the twelfth or thirteenth centuries. Much later, the mink was brought over from Canada in the 1920s to populate fur farms[2]; unsurprisingly, some escaped – probably to feed on the rainbow trout that someone had thoughtfully imported from North America about 30 years earlier.

As well as the rabbit, the Romans may well have introduced the pheasant, which by the Middle Ages was an essential part of any nobleman's feast. In 1465 the inauguration banquet for Neville, Archbishop of York featured no fewer than 200 pheasants, as well as 12 porpoises and seals, 104 peacocks, 400 swans, 500 stags, 2,000 geese, 4,000 ducks and six boars. Imports of exotic pheasant varieties such as the Chinese Ringneck started in the eighteenth century; most modern pheasants have a fairly mixed heritage but none of them has yet worked out how to handle traffic.

Although there are still red squirrel strongholds in the Cheviots, the grey squirrel is probably the best known of the new arrivals. These were first released in the British Isles in 1876 in Henbury Park in Cheshire, apparently as an exotic novelty. With further such introductions around the country they spread rapidly and within 25 years greys had reached as far north as Scotland, establishing colonies in areas ranging from Argyll in the west to Stirling in the east.

Other animals have vanished, sometimes in the depths of prehistory. Elk, one of the largest members of the deer family, seem to have disappeared from the British Isles about 4,000 years ago, while aurochs, the ancestors of modern cattle, probably died out about 1,000 years later. DNA evidence from bones found in mainland Europe suggests they interbred with domesticated Neolithic cattle before they vanished.

Other animals held on for longer, in spite of human hunting and farming. There are no records in the Cheviots of lynxes or bears, but their bones have been recovered from caves at Inchnadamph in north-east Scotland. Lynxes prefer woods and forests to hills and may have survived into Roman times, while brown bears are somewhat more flexible in their choice of habitat and may have lasted a little longer.

Until recently, it was thought that beavers died out over 1,000 years ago, but in 2014 a piece of wood was found in the bank of the Scaup Burn in the Kielder Forest that had clearly been gnawed by one. Carbon dating showed the wood dated from the

---

[2] At around the same time, there was a proposal to establish a fur farm in the College Valley in the northern Cheviots, a venture that would have included breeding skunks. Fortunately, this never happened.

fourteenth century; because beavers like wood they would probably have retreated from upland sites as the trees there vanished, but they could have survived into late medieval times in rivers in the Cheviot valleys.

Wild boar are happiest in dense forest and may have been found near the Cheviots at around the same time. It's very hard to determine when the native population finally disappeared, because hunting them was very popular and as early as the seventeenth century there were several attempts to reintroduce stock from places like Germany.

Wolves were once common in the British Isles; there were reports that in the seventh century they were so numerous that owners of large sheep flocks found protection almost impossible. Even hundreds of years later, they must have made shepherding in the Cheviots a challenging job. Records from 1235 show that the monks of Melrose reached an understanding with Alexander II, the king of Scotland, about hunting and trapping them; at around the same time the monks of Newminster Abbey agreed with the local landowners, the Umfravilles, that they had hunting rights for wolves and foxes in the lands ceded to them on the southern flanks of the Cheviots.

No-one knows for certain when and where the last wolf died. Many places claim that distinction but it's unlikely that it was in the Cheviots, even though there is a local legend attached to a field called Wolfer's Law, near Harbottle. In England they finally disappeared from places like Lancashire's Bowland Forest and the Yorkshire Wolds as late as the fifteenth century, while in Scotland the last recorded wolf was killed in Perthshire in 1680, although there were reports of them in the next century. One of the last documented instances of wolves in the Borders was in 1458, when Gilbert Home earned five shillings for killing ten wolves in Cockburnspath in Berwickshire.

The golden eagle disappeared from the Cheviots even more recently. Although there is still the occasional report of a sighting, they seem to have generally stopped nesting here in the latter part of the nineteenth century[3]. But as we shall see in the chapter on Clennell Street, they still live on in place names.

---

[3] Descriptions of eagles suffer from the same exaggerations as those of fish. In 1769 the historian John Wallis wrote that in 1735 a golden eagle had been shot in Warkworth and that its wingspan had been measured at 11¼ feet. That's some three feet more than any golden eagle found in the world today.

An extract from Matthew Paris's map of Britain, dating from the 1250s.

Chapter 2

Archives and Archaeology

If archaeology can be linked to written material, then it's a powerful way of generating information, ascertaining dates and checking stories. Throughout this book we have tried to supplement what can be seen on the ground with material culled from archives and other sources.

The earliest reference to Britain comes from a Greek explorer called Pytheas, who probably circumnavigated the British Isles in around 325 BC, describing the Cornish tin trade and mentioning places like Kent and the Orkneys. Starting from southern France, his expedition may have taken him east to Scandinavia and as far north as Iceland. Some 350 years later, another Greek called Strabo reported on the country in greater detail, listing its exports and describing the way people lived – in huts inside enclosures with wooden ramparts.

The first Roman to write about Britain was the historian Tacitus. In AD 98 he published a short book entitled *On the life and character of Julius Agricola*. Agricola had governed Britain for eight years from about AD 77 and was the general responsible

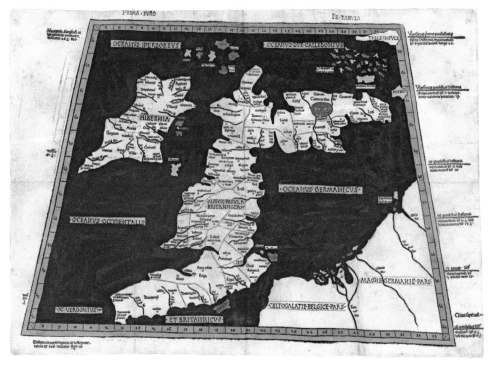

Figure 2.1 There are no surviving originals of Ptolemy's maps, and this is a medieval interpretation of his work on the British Isles. Bremenium is marked where Scotland starts its rather alarming lean to the east, just to the left of the river running north-south, which is the Tweed.

for the first Roman campaigns in the far north of England and Scotland. The book described this activity and was very complimentary about Agricola's achievements and behaviour, possibly because the author was his son-in-law.

Another Greek, Ptolemy, lived in Alexandria but provided the first reference to a specific place with which this book is concerned. Writing in about AD 140, his *Geographia* was essentially a gazetteer of Great Britain, although he never came here and borrowed most of his material. He mentioned Bremenium (modern Rochester in Northumberland – Figure 2.1) and listed the various native tribes who lived in the north of England and Scotland.

After that, most Roman historians just mentioned Britain in passing. The only useful material (for us) are the Antonine Itineraries, a register of Roman locations and distances along roads throughout the Empire. Probably written around the beginning of the third century AD, the British section, the *Iter Britanniarum*, consisted of 15 routes, the first of which started at Bremenium.

Of more interest, however, are the vernacular records left by Romans who lived here. The best known are the Vindolanda tablets; written in the years around AD 100, these are letters that give a unique insight into the personal and military matters that engaged the people living around Hadrian's Wall. Although fewer in number, of equal interest are the various stone inscriptions left behind by Roman soldiers and their relatives both around the Wall and further north (Figure 2.2). An analysis of those found at Rochester and at places like Cappuck near Jedburgh, provides an insight into the types and numbers of troops in the area and the work they carried out.

Figure 2.2 A Roman inscription now in Elsdon church. It commemorates Rufinius, about whom there are more details in Chapter 8.
(Image © Lorraine Kerr Photography).

In the centuries after the Romans left, sources of material that provide any information about the border area are very limited. One exception is the *Ecclesiastical History of the English People*, written about AD 730 by the Venerable Bede, a monk at the monastery at Jarrow. But this provides only sketchy geographical information; it concentrated on political and religious matters, as did a second source, the *Anglo-Saxon Chronicle*.

Matters improved once the Normans arrived. Although the

Domesday Book did not extend as far north as Northumberland, the king's supporters were granted large land holdings and estates in the county. The records of these, and the religious houses that were founded in places like Morpeth, Kelso and Melrose, provide considerable insight into the ownership of various assets. We get details of boundaries and disputes, leases and payments, trade and taxes. Among the affairs of Newminster Abbey in Morpeth, which was founded in 1137 and which held land in the Cheviots from 1181, there is one of the first references to a non-Roman route through the Cheviots, with Clennell Street being referred to as *Hernespeth* or *Yarnspeth*.

Official records

The records of medieval government also provide useful information. Then as now, raising money was a major concern and surviving tax records offer insights into contemporary society. They can tell us who owned land, how many people lived in different communities and how wealthy they were. Tracking changes in taxation levels helps us estimate how external events shaped society.

When a person of some standing and wealth died, there would be a process called an inquisition *post mortem*. Somewhat analogous to the modern assessment of death duties, this was an inquiry into the deceased's affairs in order to ascertain what assets were due to the Crown. In a still feudal society, most land at least theoretically belonged to the monarch and if no heir had been specified, then the estate reverted to him. This tax was clearly not popular, and landowners would go to considerable lengths to avoid it, some of which were remarkably similar to the ways people try to avoid death duties today.

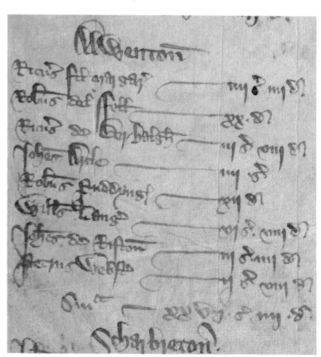

Figure 2.3 *The 1336 Lay Subsidy Roll for Alwinton.*
Eight people paid a total of 27 shillings and four pence.
(Image courtesy National Archives).

Less wealthy people paid periodic taxes called Lay Subsidies which were raised by Parliament when the monarch needed money, typically for a war (Figure 2.3). The poor and the clergy were excluded (the clergy paid other taxes) and local assessors would estimate the value of an individual's assets and levy a payment that was a fraction of that value – often a tenth. Towns and the countryside were usually taxed at different rates and they also had different exemptions – in the towns these might include beds and some clothing, while country people paid no tax on their animals or the tools of their trade. Knights could claim exemption for armour, horses, jewels and items of gold or silver.

Almost everyone paid Poll Taxes. Three of these were raised between 1377 and 1381, the first two at a rate of four pence per head and the third at 12 pence. Applicable to everyone apart from beggars and children under 14, they were an even less popular way of raising money, which is why they culminated in the Peasants' Revolt. However, surviving records are useful because they list, by name, most people in a parish or district and give a good assessment of adult population numbers.

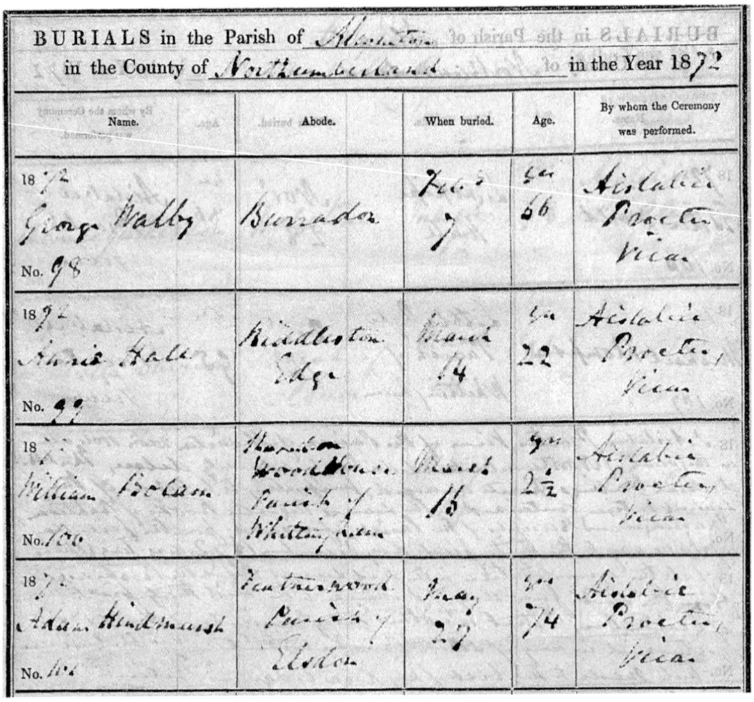

Figure 2.4 An excerpt from the parish records of Alwinton showing burials in 1872. One person has come from Featherwood on Dere Street, in the parish of Elsdon.

As well as tax records, there are many other sets of state documents that shed light on medieval and post-medieval affairs in Northumberland and Roxburghshire. These include royal letters, charters and other state papers that relate to both England and Scotland. Very often their focus is on military matters and disputes over land and other assets, but there are occasional references to mundane crimes and the activities of officials called the Border Wardens who tried to maintain order in the area. The originals of these records are held in the National Archives, but we are fortunate in that many of them were transcribed and published by antiquarians in the nineteenth century, at a time when writers such as John Hodgson and Eneas Mackenzie were producing their histories and guides to our area.

After the fifteenth century, there are ever-increasing numbers and types of records to consult. From 1538 English churches were obliged to keep registers of all births, marriages and burials among their congregation (Figure 2.4). Few of these early records survive, but on both sides of the border there are several that date from the seventeenth century. Although the priest was only obliged to record basic information, they sometimes included additional material and this allows researchers to track farm names, family relationships and people's occupations, all of which help build a picture of the society of the time. Around the start of the nineteenth century non-conformist chapels appeared; they also maintained records, and these can be very helpful because they often contain more detailed information.

From the seventeenth century or so, local court records from Quarter Sessions have often been preserved and these can furnish insights into the less well-behaved members of society, with details of cases involving disputes over property, crimes such as robberies and quite a few murders. Sometimes you can trace an entire criminal career, and the details provided can help the lucky researcher track down the location of long-deserted dwellings. There is an example of this in the chapter on Clennell Street.

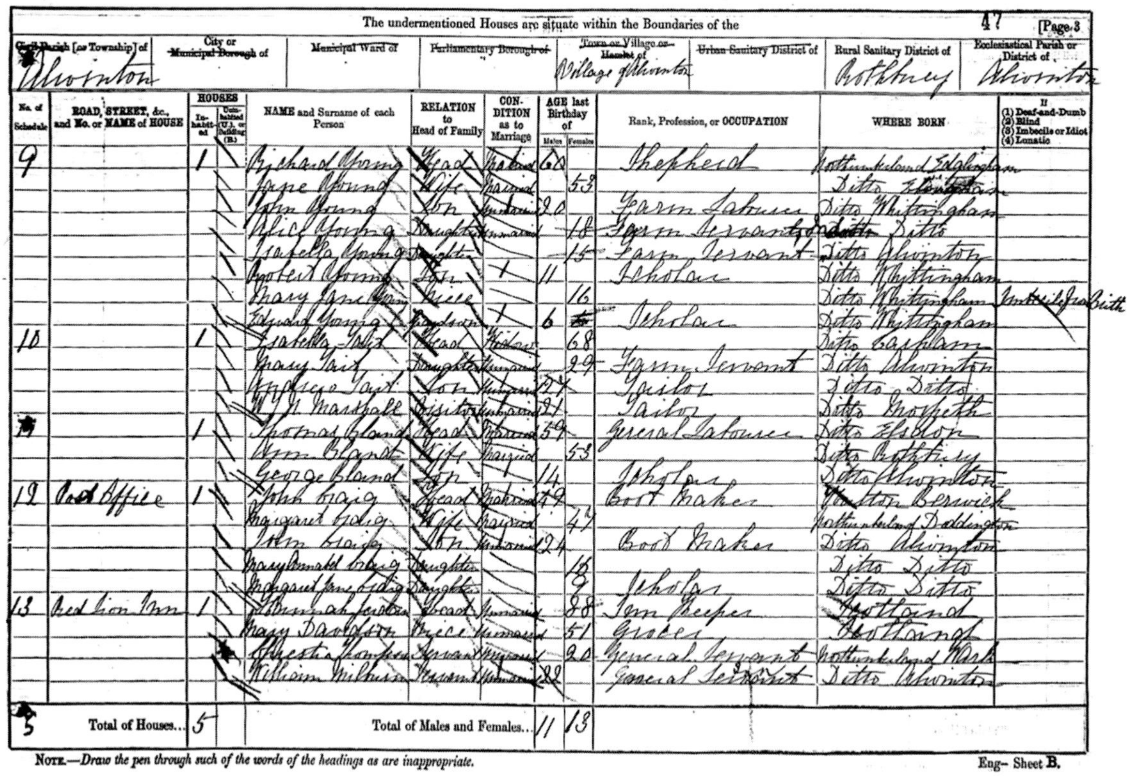
The undermentioned Houses are situate within the Boundaries of the 47 [Page 3

Civil Parish [or Township] of	City or Municipal Borough of	Municipal Ward of	Parliamentary Borough of	Town or Village or Hamlet of	Urban Sanitary District of	Rural Sanitary District of	Ecclesiastical Parish or District of
Alwinton				Village of Alwinton		Rothbury	Alwinton

No. of Schedule	ROAD, STREET, &c., and No. or NAME of HOUSE	HOUSES Inhabited	HOUSES Uninhabited (U.), or Building (B.)	NAME and Surname of each Person	RELATION to Head of Family	CONDITION as to Marriage	AGE last Birthday of Males	AGE last Birthday of Females	Rank, Profession, or OCCUPATION	WHERE BORN	(1) Deaf-and-Dumb (2) Blind (3) Imbecile or Idiot (4) Lunatic
9		1		Richard Young	Head	Married	60		Shepherd	Northumberland Edlingham	
				Jane Young	Wife	Married		53		Ditto [illegible]	
				John Young	Son	Unmarried	20		Farm Labourer	Ditto Whittingham	
				Alice Young	Daughter	Unmarried		18	Farm Servant	Ditto Ditto	
				Isabella Young	Daughter			15	Farm Servant	Ditto Alwinton	
				Robert Young	Son		11		Scholar	Ditto Whittingham	
				Mary Jane Young	Niece			16		Ditto Whittingham	Imbecile from Birth
				Edward Young	Grandson		6		Scholar	Ditto Whittingham	
10		1		Isabella Tait	Head	Widow		68		Ditto Eglingham	
				Mary Tait	Daughter	Unmarried		29	Farm Servant	Ditto Alwinton	
				Andrew Tait	Son	Unmarried	27		Tailor	Ditto Ditto	
				W. J. Marshall	Visitor	Unmarried	21		Tailor	Ditto Morpeth	
11		1		Thomas Bland	Head	Married	59		General Labourer	Ditto Elsdon	
				Ann Bland	Wife	Married		53		Ditto Rothbury	
				George Bland	Son		14		Scholar	Ditto Alwinton	
12	Post Office	1		John Craig	Head	Married	49		Boot Maker	Norham Berwick	
				Margaret Craig	Wife	Married		47		Northumberland Doddington	
				John Craig	Son	Unmarried	24		Boot Maker	Ditto Alwinton	
				Mary Ann Craig	Daughter			16		Ditto Ditto	
				Margaret Jane Craig	Daughter			9	Scholar	Ditto Ditto	
13	Red Lion Inn	1		Hannah Jordan	Head	Unmarried		88	Inn Keeper	Scotland	
				Mary Davidson	Niece	Unmarried		51	Grocer	Scotland	
				Alethea Hanson	Servant	Unmarried		20	General Servant	Northumberland Wark	
				William Milburn	Servant	Unmarried	22		General Servant	Ditto Alwinton	
5	Total of Houses...	5		Total of Males and Females...			11	13			

NOTE.—*Draw the pen through such of the words of the headings as are inappropriate.*

Eng– Sheet B.

*Figure 2.5 **A page from the 1881 census for Alwinton, with the Post Office and the now defunct Red Lion Inn. Each entry gives a person's name, marital status, age, job and birthplace. It also records certain disabilities.***

Although national censuses started in 1801, those before 1841 contain relatively abstract information, such as the number of people in a parish and the number of inhabited and uninhabited houses. Not all of these returns still exist, with the survival rate in Northumberland being particularly low. From 1841, however, detailed information was recorded about individuals and where they lived; the law allows this material to be made public after 100 years, and so there are almost complete records about people and communities available up to 1911 (Figure 2.5). For the Border

Roads we can, for example, see which families were living in outlying farms and settlements and look at their occupations and trades.

In a similar vein, county archives often have management records and diaries from schools dating back to the nineteenth century, providing anecdotes and local information about rural communities that have changed out of all recognition, or even disappeared completely.

Maps

Among the most interesting sources of documentary evidence are maps; ranging in coverage from the entire country down to an individual estate or parish, these can track the appearance and disappearance of buildings, identify field systems and their owners and show old routes and thoroughfares.

Early maps of the British Isles show few details in the area covered by this book, the main exception being the presence of Harbottle. An early appearance was on the Gough map of Britain, dating from around 1360, where is is shown as *hbotell*, south of the Cheviot and the surrounding hills (*mons cheivioth*). The castle gave Harbottle some status; in George Lily's 1546 map *Harbotel* is one of only six places shown between the Tyne and the Tweed, the others being Newcastle, Tynemouth, Alnwick, Bamburgh and Norham.

The first detailed maps date from the late sixteenth century, when cartographers such

Figure 2.6 Part of Mercator's 1595 map of Northumberland.

as Timothy Pont drew them at a large scale for specific areas in Scotland, and Gerard Mercator of projection fame produced maps of entire counties. These are things of beauty, as his depiction of Northumberland in Figure 2.6 shows.

Apart from the beauty, there is the occasional error, so Windy Gyle (*Windgnyle*) is placed midway between the border ridge and the Usway Burn, whereas it should be on the ridge itself. However, on the positive side it's unusual in that it shows '*Hexpathgate*', a place of historic interest that will be described in the chapter on Clennell Street.

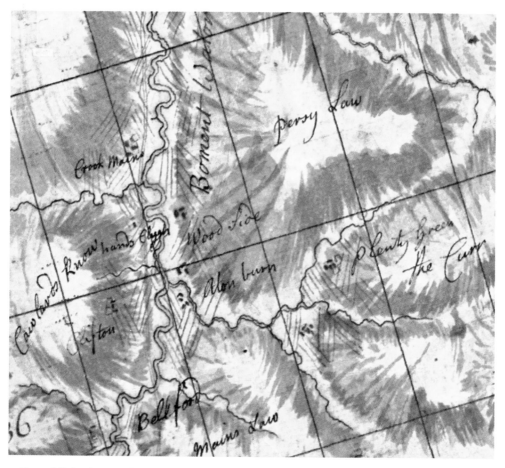

Figure 2.7 Roy's map of Bowmont Water north of Belford, showing Clennell Street running parallel with the west bank. The map on the inside cover shows whereabouts this is.

The quality of cartography in both England and Scotland improved with the years, but it was still not good enough for some people. In the Scottish campaigns that followed the Jacobite rising of 1745 the British Army found itself '*greatly embarrassed for the want of a proper survey of the country*', and a new one was commissioned. The work was undertaken by William Roy; initially a civilian he worked on a survey for eight years, producing a map of such strategic value that it was kept in London and not fully published until the next century. With an eye for the landscape and the structures in it, he recorded things that would not appear on other maps until well into the twentieth century (Figure 2.7). As a result of his work he joined the army, rose to the rank of Major-General and laid the foundations for the Ordnance Survey. Excerpts from his maps first appeared in his book on Military Antiquities, published posthumously in 1793.

The eighteenth and nineteenth centuries saw the publication of increasing numbers of maps, with cartographers such as John Ainslie and Aaron Arrowsmith north of the border. To the south there were family concerns – Andrew and Mostyn Armstrong (father and son) and Christopher and John Greenwood (brothers). Such mapmakers used a variety of techniques to produce their material. The most diligent embarked on their own surveys, but they certainly borrowed heavily from earlier maps and also relied on descriptions of remote areas produced by local contacts. This meant they never visited some of the places they drew, so errors would appear and then be propagated for several generations; there was at least one instance of an early map maker being taken to court for blatant plagiarism.

Figure 2.8 The 1863 1st edition OS map of the area east of Hownam in Roxburghshire. Note the 'Druidical Circle (Supposed)' on the right.

In 1850, the cartographer Henry MacLauchlan was commissioned by the Duke of Northumberland to survey Dere Street up to the Scottish border, and his map at a scale of two inches to the mile and its accompanying commentary are a very useful source – even if there are omissions and the occasional inconsistency. While detailed estate maps sometimes survive for specific local areas from the seventeenth century, and enclosure and tithe maps from rather later, the first reliable large-scale sets of maps of both England and Scotland were those produced by the Ordnance Survey. Maps at a scale of one inch to the mile for parts of southern England were first published in 1801, but work at the larger scales only started on the British mainland in 1854. The first maps of Northumberland and Roxburghshire at six inches to the mile were published in the 1860s, with a second edition some 30 years later. Their accuracy is unquestioned, but the surveyors often excluded ancient structures, and if they did record them they sometimes succumbed to the temptation to attribute them to the Druids (Figure 2.8).

Books

One of the first books that described the antiquities of the border area was William Camden's *Britannia*. Written in Latin and published in 1586, the first English translation appeared in 1610. His coverage of Scotland was regrettably thin, although he did discuss inscriptions found near the Antonine Wall. In Northumberland he similarly focused on those from Hadrian's Wall, but he also mentioned some from Rochester, and identified the camp there as Bremenium.

John Wallis's 1769 guide, *The Natural History and Antiquities of Northumberland*, contains very little about the Cheviots, but Eneas MacKenzie's *Historical, topographical, and descriptive view of the county of Northumberland* from the 1820s is more helpful, as is John Hodgson's slightly later *History of Northumberland*. North of the border, there is Alexander Jeffrey's *History and antiquities of Roxburghshire and adjacent districts*, written in 1855, while the Scottish *Statistical Accounts*, published in the 1790s and in the 1830s, provide rich and detailed parish reports on a wide range of topics.

William Roy's more focused *Military Antiquities of the Romans in North Britain* covers both England and Scotland and was published posthumously in 1793. In North Northumberland, the best known author is probably David Dippie Dixon, whose book *Upper Coquetdale* was written at the start of the twentieth century. Finally, designed to continue Hodgson's work, there is the comprehensive *History of Northumberland*. The first volume of this appeared in 1893 but the fifteenth and final one, which covered Alwinton and Kidland, only saw the light of day in 1940.

The section on Further Reading at the end of this book contains recommendations on other written sources and records.

Photography

As well as maps, over the last 100 years other techniques have been developed that help us see and understand the landscape, and there are examples of these in this book.

One of them is aerial photography. The first serious application of this was during the First World War, when it became a vital tool for understanding enemy operations. In 1918 alone, the RAF took some 2.5 million aerial photographs.

After the war, pioneers such as O. G. S. Crawford adapted the technology for archaeological purposes, discovering what researchers still find valuable today. Not only does aerial photography improve the understanding of large landscape features, but the images show details that are almost imperceptible at ground level. The shadows cast by a low sun accentuate small height differences on the ground, which also show up better with a light dusting of snow. Even buried features become visible. Depressions retain more moisture than objects like concealed walls, causing changes in vegetation patterns on the surface. Frost can behave in the same way, with structures below ground holding water in different ways, resulting in correspondingly different marks above them.

In recent years, satellite photography has also become very important – especially in areas that are otherwise hard to access. Initially the province of the military, there are now commercial firms offering a range of imaging resolutions down to one foot. A widely available software package – Google Earth – makes a blend of aerial and satellite images available to anyone with a computer, a tablet or a smartphone.

There are also applications, many outside archaeology, that use images captured at wavelengths outside the visible spectrum. Because of these advances, other aerial techniques have emerged.

One of these is LiDAR – or Light Detection and Ranging. This works by bouncing pulses from a low-powered airborne laser off the ground; monitoring the reflection time and intensity helps build a 3-D map of the terrain below. Height differences of an inch or so can be identified with the right technology, and there are techniques that enable the reflections from vegetation to be filtered out, so that structures under tree cover can be readily seen.

Place names

The study of place names – their meaning and their origin – is a complicated subject. Whole books have been devoted to it; we do not have the space here to enter into it at length, but it's worth describing just some of the more common terms that are found in the Cheviots.

As might be expected, the most common terms are those that define hills. These include *Craig, Dod, Edge, Knowe, Law, Kipp* and *Rig*. These are not necessarily interchangeable. For example, *Law* is often used if the hill comes to a point at the top or if it stands apart from others. *Craig* is more common where there are cliffs or rocky slopes, while *Knowe* is a small hill and *Rig* is a ridge. *Muir* is usually a moor.

Where there are hills there are valleys, so we have *Cleugh* (or *Cleuch*), *Dale, Dean, Haugh, Heugh, Hope* and *Howe*. *Hope* is generally used to refer to the upper part of a valley, while *Howe* is more of a hollow. *Haugh* refers to flat land next to a water-course, while *Heugh* often means a steep-sided valley with projecting rock – as do *Cleugh* and *Cleuch*.

Watercourses often flow down these valleys. The larger ones are *Rivers* or *Waters* but then there are terms like *Linn* (a waterfall), *Sike* (a small stream) and *Burn*. A *Slack* is a valley, usually with a marsh or a stream in it.

Side is a common suffix for a place-name based on trees and and shrubs. The terms *Dean* and *Shaw* apply to woodland as well, although this may now be long gone.

Animal names sometimes occur, so *Rae* is a deer, while *Kid* may mean goat. *Foul* and *Cock* sometimes refer to birds such as grouse, although the former can also mean muddy. *Drake* doesn't always mean a duck and may be derived from the Scots word *draik*, meaning soggy.

This is an example of how careful you have to be in ascribing origins to names, and how hard it can be to be certain of the result. For example, in the Coquet valley upstream from Alwinton there is a medieval site once called *Aldensheles*. Now the '*sheles*' part is clear; it's sometimes spelt '*shield*' or '*shiel*' and was a summer dwelling used when stock was taken to graze on the uplands. And at first sight '*Alden*' might mean alder trees. But investigation shows the place was also referred to as '*Aydonshields*'; maybe that means it was controlled by the owners of Aydon Castle, near Corbridge.

Place names can often provide useful information about the past, but extracting it can be a complex – and sometimes contentious – process.

The medieval wheel pit at the
Barrowburn fulling mill.

Chapter 3

The Marks People Left

Even when analysing the way natural events formed the Cheviot environment, it is impossible to ignore the human contribution. The clearance of trees and scrub for farming and the centuries of upland grazing that followed have helped make the hills what they are today.

But within the overall picture there are many smaller scale details. In this chapter we describe some of the structures and their remains that are the result of generations of human presence in the Cheviots and along the Border Roads. We look at where people lived and the effects that military presence and warfare have had on the landscape. We examine farming in more detail and explore how other crafts and occupations left their distinctive marks. And there's still the occasional mystery to be solved, things that make the passer-by wonder what their ancestors were doing and why they were doing it.

Where people lived

The most ancient, and most common, traces of human habitation in the Cheviots are the remains of roundhouses. People have been building circular dwellings since the Mesolithic, but the earliest known such structures along the Border Roads date from the Bronze Age. The design was still in use after the Romans arrived, although by then rectangular buildings were starting to appear, probably because they made it easier to build large roofed spaces.

Roundhouses were typically made of timber, although stone became more common later on. The biggest were about 40 feet across, with the average diameter being somewhere between 20 and 30 feet. Extending beyond the walls, conical roofs had a thatch covering of vegetation which in upland areas probably consisted of heather or bracken (Figure 3.1). Smoke from a central hearth escaped through this thatch making the interior quite snug, especially as it may have been shared with farm animals[1]. It's even been suggested that there could have been an upper floor in the larger houses, with the stock kept at ground level. A typical roundhouse would have provided accommodation for between 12 and 20 people.

Bracing the walls were timbers sunk vertically into the soil; these would have absorbed water and rotted, so the life of a roundhouse was limited. We have no specific knowledge of how long one lasted, but a fair estimate is that most survived for one or two generations before having to be abandoned or rebuilt.

Depending on local conditions, roundhouses may leave distinctive circular marks on the ground. These are typically in the form of a depression up to a foot wide marking the base of the original walls, although some houses are also revealed by the remains

---

[1] As late as the early nineteenth century, blackhouses in the Western Isles were built like this, with no chimneys or byre. The living space was shared with tethered stock, and it was believed that the cows should always have a view of the fire.

Figure 3.1 A stone-built roundhouse that once stood at the Brigantium Archaeological Reconstruction Centre at Rochester.

of ditches that were probably used for drainage, perhaps when stock was being kept inside the building. In well-preserved examples, you can often see the site of the doorway; these most commonly face east or south-east, avoiding the prevailing westerly winds and getting the best of the morning light. When on a slope, some roundhouses were built on terraces cut back into the hill to make a flat floor, groups of such houses forming scooped settlements. Even when excavated, roundhouses can be very hard to date. The people who lived in them had few material possessions and even fewer of them have survived. However, it's probably fair to say that the houses that can be most easily detected usually date from the Iron Age.

Roundhouse settlements were sometimes surrounded by a palisade – a timber wall that shows up in the form of another ditch or groove. A single wall would have protected the inhabitants from marauding animals, but a double palisade would have been of greater military value, allowing perhaps for structures like raised walkways from which the settlement could be defended. There are fine examples of two such palisaded enclosures on High Knowes, which are described in the chapter on the Salter's Road.

These enclosures are generally thought to date from the late Bronze or the early Iron Age, and to be the precursors of some of the best known sites in the Cheviots – the hillforts or camps. A number of these have been excavated, including some near The Street and Clennell Street; these date from the late Iron Age, sometimes with use extending into the Romano-British period.

A key topic to address is the name. The label 'fort' is often used and dates from a time when it was generally believed that aggressive behaviour dominated the Iron Age. There can be no doubt that some of these sites were indeed involved in warfare; excavations in the south of England have revealed the remains of people who definitely died fighting. No such evidence has been found in the Cheviots, mostly because soil conditions are bad for the preservation of bodies, but while some of the structures are in eminently defensible positions and clearly built with protection in mind, others are much more vulnerable, positioned on slopes or spurs below the tops of hills (Figure 3.2).

Figure 3.2 Looking down on Hayhope Knowe from Clennell Street; not an ideal defensive location.

Defence may have been only one of the issues considered when they were built, with other factors including access to water and farmland, as well as the need to show strength and status. Here there are parallels with some medieval castles like Tintagel and Orford, where a display of wealth and the incorporation of cultural and mythical references seem to have been just as important as military considerations.

In general, we will describe these structures as camps rather than forts. This terminology is given more weight by the fact that although the surviving examples are usually found on hills, the increasing quantity and quality of aerial photographs shows that circular structures with ramparts were not confined to the uplands; now ploughed out or destroyed by other human activity they were also common across the lowland plains.

The defining characteristics of the camps are the ramparts. Varying from one to three or more in number, it has been suggested that generations of builders progressively strengthened the defences by adding more of them. This may well have happened in some cases, but we shall see that in others the development pattern was probably more complicated. Although the ramparts now appear to be mostly earthen in nature, they usually have stone cores and examples show they sometimes had a masonry facing. At some camps traces of timber palisades have been found, which may have been part of wooden box ramparts built around the earth and stone core (Figure 3.3).

The interiors of these camps vary considerably, ranging from those that are full of roundhouses, with even the remains of simple streets being visible, to those that are almost devoid of features. Some camps show signs of overlying rectangular enclosures and platforms; these may well be the remains of later Romano-British settlements. It's not clear what all this variation means: were some camps residential, while others

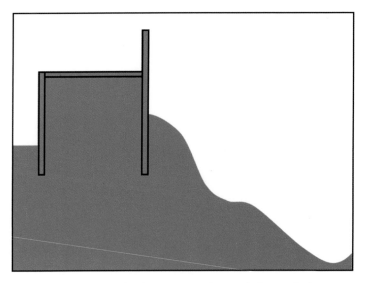

Figure 3.3 A wooden box rampart above a defensive ditch.

supported different types of activity? Were some camps built and then not heavily used? Were they lived in all year round, just used seasonally or only in times of trouble? All we know is that they represented a substantial investment in labour and organisation. They could, however, have been built fairly quickly if enough workers were available. An experiment in East Anglia in 1966 used inmates from Leicester prison to build a length of earth and turf rampart with tools that would have been available to the Romans; it showed that 100 men working in ten-hour shifts would take between nine and 12 days to build 100 yards of rampart.

After the Iron Age, the next structures to have left major marks on the landscape are the Roman forts and camps. These are described later in this chapter in the section on warfare, but it's interesting to note that there are few remains of more recent construction in the Cheviots that are remotely as impressive as those from the Iron Age or the Roman periods.

Among the exceptions are structures that date from the Dark Ages called nuclear forts – and there are very few of these. The term 'nuclear' is used to describe a central stronghold surrounded by defensive enclosures; ideally sited on the tops of long narrow hills they exploit natural features to bolster their strength. The most spectacular one in the Cheviots is that at Moat Knowe, described in detail in the chapter on Dere Street; the only other one in the area is probably the structure on top of Chatto Craig about two miles south of Hownam, just to the west of the road leading down to Towford and Pennymuir and about a mile east of Dere Street.

Equally, there are few remains along the Border Roads that definitely date from later medieval periods. This is partly because modern villages have almost always been built on the sites of earlier settlements, making it hard to identify the site of any medieval activity. This is the case at places like Hownam and Alwinton, where there are no signs of any early domestic buildings. The church at the former, however, is mentioned as early as the twelfth century among records of transactions showing the movement of land tenure from the native nobility to their Anglo-Norman equivalents. The process may have been facilitated by marriage or cultural integration, with successive generations of names like Eilaf and Orm in one family being transformed into John and then William. The church at Alwinton dates from a similar period, but there is really nothing to see of the then-adjacent village (see Chapter 4).

The one exception to this is Alnham. Here, large areas of rig and furrow can be seen that may well reflect the patterns of medieval fields. Although most of the early village has disappeared, one field still contains some remains of the seventeenth-century settlement, which was probably not that different from its medieval predecessor.

In the lowlands, the remains of medieval housing can sometimes be seen in the form of deserted medieval villages (DMVs); when well-preserved traces of streets, gardens and village greens are still discernible. There is little like this in the uplands. The only DMVs on the Border Roads are those on Dere Street at Chew Green (Kemylpeth) and at Leafield Edge, not far from the Salter's Road north of Alnham. In both cases, sets of low earthworks mark enclosures and rectangular outlines and platforms suggest the remains of buildings. Kemylpeth has old field systems nearby, but it's not clear if these are medieval or later, while at Leafield Edge there are large areas of well-preserved rig and furrow which are almost certainly medieval in origin.

Figure 3.4 The remains of a group of shielings at Partridgeside, above the Coquet south of Barrowburn. There is a large one in the foreground, and there are two more beyond it. This is probably the 'Parder Side' listed in the 1604 survey of the Manor of Harbottle.

There are the remains of other early housing along the Border Roads. Transhumance involved moving stock to the uplands for the summer months. This meant that home pastures could recover and be used for crops such as hay, while animals grazed on marginal land that would be unproductive at other times. People accompanied the stock and lived in structures known as shielings. These were little better than huts or bothies built from stone, wood and earth and their remains may show up as low, usually rectangular, earthworks, sometimes clustered together in small groups (Figure

3.4). Writing in the late eighteenth century, the Welsh naturalist Thomas Pennant described Scottish shielings:

> '...some were oblong, some conic, and so low that the entrance is forbidden without creeping through the opening, which has no other door than a faggot of birch twigs placed there occasionally; they are constructed of branches of trees covered with sods; the furniture a bed of heather, placed on a bank of sod, two blankets and a rug...'.

Without excavation, shielings are almost impossible to date; the centuries of cross-border conflict would have discouraged permanent settlement but the practice of transhumance started very much earlier. It probably continued sporadically through the troubles and only died out in the seventeenth and eighteenth centuries as increasing numbers of permanent upland farms were established.

As well as shielings, there are deserted farms along the Border Roads. Sometimes these are obvious – with remains ranging from standing walls and gables to what looks like no more than a large shieling. But sometimes there is almost nothing left; there are sites like Wholehope, for example, where a farmstead on Clennell Street that was in use well into the twentieth century has now been almost completely demolished. And in the same way that modern villages have been built on top of old ones, so old houses sometimes get incorporated into modern farms – perhaps as barns. There are also longhouses. These are rectangular structures, sometimes post-medieval and often with a dividing wall across them about a third of the way along. The larger section was used for stock, while people lived in the smaller one where there may be the remains of a hearth on a beaten-earth or crudely cobbled floor. Ideally, this section would have been higher than the one for stock to prevent waste draining into it. When animals spent the winter inside, a considerable amount of manure would accumulate. In the spring this could be cleared out by removing part of the end wall; sometimes a horse helped with this and the result was a 'horse hole'.

One reason so few medieval, or even later, houses survive is that many of them were poorly built. In the 1790s, the shepherds' cottages of Roxburghshire were described

Figure 3.5 Gilly's drawing of Northumberland farm workers' cottages.

as *'miserable temporary hovels'*, with walls of stone and turf and roofs of slender timber covered with turf and rushes. As late as 1841, when William Gilly was vicar of Norham, he wrote that the houses of farm labourers were *'built of rubble or of unhewn stone'* and that *'the thatch, yawning to admit the wind and wet ... looks more like the top of a dunghill than of a cottage'* (Figure 3.5). Such houses may not have been as sturdy as their Iron Age predecessors.

Warfare, and the military through the ages

Although we have said that there were many factors involved in the construction of hilltop camps or forts, and that military considerations were probably only one of them, there can be no doubt that prehistoric Britain was from time to time a violent place. However, there are no records of these early skirmishes and wars, and the Romans represent the earliest military presence we know of in the Cheviots.

Their first serious invasion of the British Isles was in AD 43, but it took some time for them to get established in the north of England. Having been appointed governor a year or so earlier, in AD 79 Agricola mounted a campaign with the objective of invading Scotland and subduing the Caledonian tribes. Probably advancing up both sides of the country, his troops were almost certainly responsible for building Dere Street and the earliest camps along it.

The next 60 years saw little activity in the border area, although slightly further south work on Hadrian's Wall started in AD 122. In AD 142, the emperor Antoninus Pius started the construction of a wall across Scotland between the Forth and the Clyde, an undertaking that lasted for twelve years and led to renewed activity north of Hadrian's Wall. There are few remaining records of this, but it is reasonable to assume that Dere Street and the Agricolan camps along it were heavily used; it is believed that the first permanent stone fort at Rochester (Bremenium) was built around this time.

The Antonine Wall was abandoned some eight years after completion, and the Roman army regrouped at Hadrian's Wall. But trouble with the local tribes continued and Septimius Severus commanded the next and last major campaign in the north between AD 208 and 211. With experience of frontier operations in Tunisia, Libya and Arabia, his army reoccupied the Antonine Wall, rebuilt camps and conducted punitive operations. But after just three years he fell ill, withdrew to York and died; his son discontinued the offensive and once again Hadrian's Wall became the frontier, although some northern forts along Dere Street such as those at Rochester and Risingham continued as outposts for at least 100 years and there are records of the occasional foray beyond them.

The main unit of organisation in the Roman army was the legion. Consisting of some 5,000 infantry soldiers, with any cavalry supplied by skilled provincial forces, it was divided into smaller groups such as cohorts (about 500 troops) and centuries. Accompanying auxiliaries were responsible for essential non-military functions such as the management of the baggage train; it's likely that the number of these at any one time depended on whether a legion was in post, on the move between secure locations or on active campaign.

The army on the move used marching camps, which were managed in different ways by different generals. When on campaign in Spain, for example, Scipio Africanus the

Younger was renowned for having his troops build camps for the night and destroy them the next morning, presumably to prevent use by the enemy. The camps along Dere Street seem to have been afforded a degree of permanence, if only because they were probably not under immediate threat and were in regular use when the army was active in the area.

Although occasionally in the shape of a parallelogram, camps were usually rectangles formed by sets of ditches and ramparts, sometimes topped with wooden palisades. In case of attack, their characteristic rounded corners gave the troops inside more space to manoeuvre and fight than in corners that came to a point. While contemporary authors described the standard layout of the buildings inside permanent forts in great detail, it's far from clear if such rules were followed in marching camps; no Roman buildings have been found in any Cheviot camp north of Rochester (Figure 8.3), and the majority of troops probably used leather tents.

Camps had at least four gates, usually with one in the middle of each side, although large camps might have two in the longer ones. Despite their name, these were just openings in the ramparts protected either by banks (*tituli*) built across them some yards outside the camp, or by extending the ramparts on one or both sides of the opening in a curve inwards or outwards. These were known as *claviculae* and they blocked direct access through the gate while leaving a gap at one side (Figure 3.6).

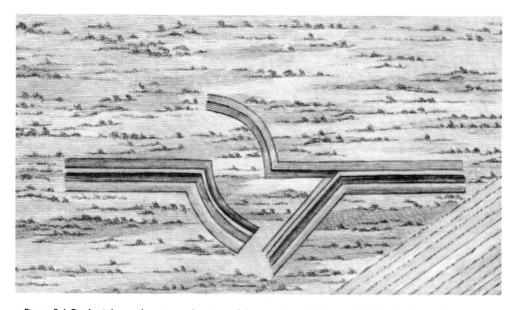

Figure 3.6 Roy's eighteenth-century drawing of the remains of defences (claviculae) around a gate at the Roman camp at Dalginross in Perthshire.

Streets ran from gate to gate inside the camp, and living quarters were set some way back from the ramparts to distance them from any attack and provide more room for defence.

Once the Romans were established in an area, they built roads. While the scale of these varied depending on the traffic, and while roads in high-status locations might be better finished, they all shared the same broad design. This consisted of a strip of land, perhaps 20 or 25 yards across, bounded by drainage ditches. In the centre of this

Figure 3.7 A cleared section across the Roman Road near Holystone. This road connected Dere Street near Rochester with the road between Corbridge and Berwick known as the Devil's Causeway'.

strip was the road itself, a well-drained set of layers of earth and hard-core ten or even 15 yards wide. Often slightly domed and bounded by a kerb, this was known as the *agger*; up to three feet high, in some cases it was paved and then covered with compacted finer material. Surviving paved roads are rare in this country and some roads that were once considered Roman have turned out to be post-medieval turnpikes, but Figure 3.7 shows an example of paving uncovered near Holystone, on the road that linked Dere Street with the main road running further east between Corbridge and Berwick.

After the Roman occupation there are few archaeological remains of military activity in the area for well over a thousand years. However, starting in the thirteenth century, there is good documentary evidence of burgeoning border disputes and more formal military incursions.

In Coquetdale, at Harbottle, there are records of the physical and financial damage these caused. The castle there was attacked by the Scots in 1296, and after their victory at Bannockburn in 1314 there were further raids into northern England. Finally captured by Robert the Bruce in 1318, the castle subsequently went through cycles of ownership and accompanying decay and repair. In 1387, on the death of the then owner Thomas Umfraville, his holding of the castle and two-thirds of the manor were described as 'worth only 100 shillings a year because of the war and the destruction and burning by the Scots'.

Organisations suffered in ways other than physical destruction. In 1297 the monks of Newminster Abbey, by then large landowners in the Cheviots, promised the Scots unspecified gifts to escape arson; unfortunately, they failed to deliver these and the Scots retaliated by abducting the prior.

The disruption caused by these campaigns opened up opportunities for less formal cross-border raids and internecine warfare. Known as reiving, a term that, like ruffian, has its roots in an Old English word for robbing, the actual attacks and cattle rustling have left little trace, but the protective measures taken by local inhabitants can still be seen. The most obvious of these are the bastles (Figure 3.8). Surviving examples date from around the sixteenth century; they are robust, two-storey stone buildings where stock could be protected at ground level with the first floor, accessed only by ladder, used for housing people. With thick walls and few windows and perhaps surrounded by a substantial stone wall (a barmkin), they offered a reasonably secure defence against raiding parties for whom speed was a priority and who did not have time for a lengthy siege.

The other type of defensive building, the pele, was a tower with two to four storeys and was usually built by someone of higher status than a bastle owner. Dating from

Figure 3.8 The bastle at The Raw, near Elsdon. The lower level survives intact but the upper part has been restored and the external steps are a more recent addition.
(Image © Mike Quinn under Creative Commons Attribution 2.0 licence).

the fifteenth and sixteenth centuries, peles were often associated with a village or a church and provided local people with shelter during raids. At times, they fulfilled a quasi-official function; in 1455 an English Act of Parliament required them to have an iron basket on their roof in which a fire could be lit to warn of an attack.

The English and Scottish governments took steps to control the area, although it's not clear that their hearts were always in it. The Borders were divided into three Marches – East, Middle and West – and these were managed by a hierarchy of Wardens. The Border Roads would have been the routes by which these local governors travelled and met with their counterparts. Records show that places along Dere Street and Clennell Street were used for such meetings, and we will describe these activities in the chapters about those roads.

But even if the authorities tried to control the area, they had little success. Records show that tax receipts in Alwinton, on Clennell Street, dropped by almost three-quarters between 1296 and 1336. Two hundred years later, when Henry VIII seized the monasteries, he sent surveyors to inspect Newminster Abbey's landholdings in the Cheviots. They reported that there were no buildings in the area, that the only business was summer pasturage, and that even that was a foolhardy undertaking because the Scots were in the habit of coming south, killing the people and taking the cattle.

The troubles died away in the early seventeenth century with the unification of the Crowns, when James VI of Scotland became James I of England. The military next moved through the area when English armies went north after the Jacobite rising of 1745. They left no trace of their passing on the ground, but an important by-product of these campaigns was the set of maps produced by William Roy and described in Chapter 2.

The twentieth century saw the largest and most recent military project in the area – the establishment of the Otterburn Training Area. Starting in 1911 the War Office, now the Ministry of Defence, purchased over 60 farms or parcels of land to form the largest firing range in the UK; it now covers nearly 100 square miles of the southern Cheviots.

Access to land in the Controlled Area south of the Coquet is restricted because there may be firing with live ammunition. The Open Area, mainly north of the river up to the border, is unrestricted, but you may still see troops there, often moving uphill alarmingly quickly. At times, however, access has been more limited. During the Second World War, for example, there was a control point on the valley road just west of Alwinton, and passage was prohibited unless you had business beyond.

Most major traces of the current military presence are well away from the Border Roads, but the remains of the landing strips, the gun emplacements and the Otterburn camp itself will undoubtedly be fruitful territory for future generations of archaeologists. However, even in the Open Area you may still see traces of military activity such as bivouacs, firing points and shelters. Some of the farmhouses along the road up the Coquet valley, such as those at Makendon and Carshope, are now used exclusively by soldiers on exercises and an archaeologist from the Ministry oversees the management of all the known archaeological sites on the ranges.

Figure 3.9 A typical old field boundary. This one is above the farm at Trows by the Rowhope Burn.

Farming

With the land in the Cheviots being used for livestock and arable production for 5,000 years or more, the farmhouses and shielings we described earlier are not the only traces left by past generations of farmers.

Arable Farming

Field boundaries are among the most common remains, especially at lower levels. These take the form of low banks often built from earth taken from an accompanying ditch (Figure 3.9). Sometimes eroded sections reveal the presence of a stone core.

Early fields, the earliest in the Cheviots dating from the Bronze Age, are usually smaller than later ones but without excavation or additional context – such as the remains of dwellings – it's very hard to date their boundaries accurately. Even if there is additional context, it may not be contemporary with the original boundary.

There is one type of field boundary, or something very like one, that is linear rather than encircling in nature, and that is the head dyke. Found on slopes above medieval field systems, they marked the boundary between the arable land below and the moorland above, protecting the crops on the former from the stock grazing on the latter. The ditch dug to form the dyke is always on its uphill side; this made the barrier more formidable and also protected the fields below by holding and deflecting water draining down the slope. Figure 5.9 shows the head dyke above the old fields at Alnham.

Perhaps the most obvious sign of arable land use is rig and furrow (or ridge and furrow). Common in many parts of the British Isles, this consists of sets of ridges and furrows that were created by ploughing a field in a particular way. Even in the Cheviot

Figure 3.10 The bottom end of an area of reverse 'S' rig and furrow on a slope near Alwinton.

uplands such structures can be very clear, with a difference in height of a foot or more between the top of a ridge and the bottom of the adjacent furrow. In lowland areas the difference can be even greater, and it's interesting to imagine how pronounced the ridges must have been when they were still in use. But in some cases erosion has made the rig and furrow much harder to see, although a low winter sun or a light dusting of snow will often make it more obvious. Sometimes it can hardly be seen with the naked eye at all, but can be sensed as you walk across it and feel the regular but small changes in the profile of the ground.

Rig and furrow is often old, and the methods that created it lasted for a long time. One of the earliest examples known in the British Isles is at Hen Domen in Wales, where a system has been shown to extend under the ramparts of a Norman castle dating from AD 1070. In some places it may have been maintained until the nineteenth century; in fact, twentieth-century steam ploughing produced patterns that look very like traditional rig and furrow. There can be considerable variation in its scale; the ridge to ridge width may vary from around ten to 12 feet to upwards of 50 feet, although that size is rarely seen in the Cheviots. It is sometimes said you can get an idea of the age of rig and furrow by measuring these widths, with wider patterns being older. There are certainly cases where this is true, but there are so many exceptions that it's an unreliable guideline. The Welsh example mentioned above is clearly very old, but has a width of only some 13 feet.

A good way to understand the provenance of an area of rig and furrow is to look at the shape of the ridges. They are sometimes not straight, but rather in the form of a gentle reverse 'S' (Figure 3.10), although in the uplands the lie of the land may dictate other patterns.

This curve shows that the ploughing was carried out by a fairly large team of animals, almost certainly oxen, which were less efficient at pulling than well-harnessed heavy horses (Figure 3.11).

The 'S' shape is due to the way the rig and furrow was created. In its simplest form, a plough consisted of a single blade called a share that cut through the soil and a plate

Figure 3.11 An eleventh-century ox team. A labour-intensive operation for both man and beast.

or board at an angle above it called a mouldboard. As the plough moved forward, so the share lifted a long strip of soil which was turned by the mouldboard and deposited to one side. Almost invariably, the mouldboard was positioned on the right.

Rig and furrow was created by ploughing a field in a set pattern for many successive seasons. This pattern consisted of taking a strip of land within a field, ploughing a single line down the centre and then turning clockwise and ploughing another line

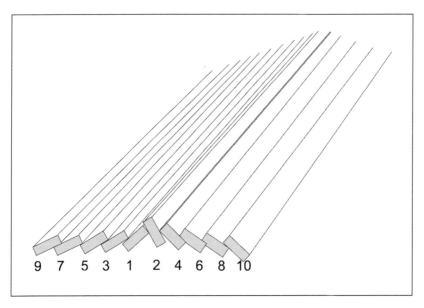

Figure 3.12 Soil migrating to the centre of a rig. Odd numbered sods were turned as the plough moved away from the viewer, and even numbers as it came back.

back, next to the first. On returning to the start point, the process was repeated with the plough creating lines next to the first two but just outside them – and always turning clockwise at the end of each line (Figure 3.12). The process stopped when the entire width of the strip, perhaps 20 feet or more, had been ploughed. The mouldboard always moved the soil to the right, and because that was always towards the centre of the strip, over several seasons the soil migrated away from the

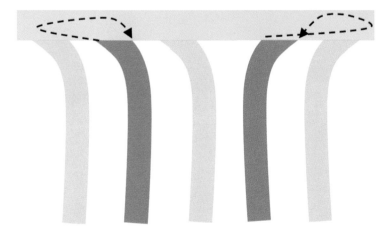

Figure 3.13 Paths of an ox team turning on a headland with reverse S (on left) and S-shaped rigs (on right).

edges, forming a ridge with a furrow on either side. If the ploughing pattern was repeated across the whole field on a strip by strip basis, the result was a field of rig and furrow.

There were headlands on the edges of the field which were not cultivated but used to turn the plough at the end of each pass. The 'S' shape resulted from the way the plough team carried out that turn.

With a large headland, the ploughman could have ploughed straight up it, turned the team around away from the ploughed area, and then ploughed back. The result would have been straight rig and furrow. In most cases, however, the width of a headland was restricted in order to maximise the cultivated area and there was no room to do this. This meant that as the ploughman approached the edge of the field he turned slightly, ploughing right up to the headland but meeting it at an angle so that his team ended up standing along its length. The result was 'S' shaped rig and furrow.

The shape is actually a reversed 'S' because of the way the turn was then made (Figure 3.13). After a pass across the field, the team was stopped on the headland, the plough detached and the animals, usually oxen, turned and brought back along the headland. The plough was turned clockwise and reattached to the team which had been moved on to the field to start pulling. If the 'S' shape was not reversed then the turning process became slightly more complicated. The difference on each turn was not big, but would have added up over a day's work.

Not all rig and furrow in the Cheviots is 'S'-shaped – sometimes because of natural topographical difficulties, but also because the size of the plough teams varied over time. The medieval draught animal of choice was usually the ox; it was cheaper to feed, being content with a diet of hay and straw while horses needed more expensive oats. Furthermore, oxen did not always need to be shod and an old one could have a spell at pasture and then be sold for meat, while an elderly horse had little value other than its hide.

However, the ox was more susceptible to disease and lacked versatility; one heavy horse could do the work of two or more of them, pulling better, working faster and

Figure 3.14 A combined ox and horse team pulling a cart in the eighteenth century.

having more stamina. Linked with other technologies, such as the wheeled plough, horses were increasingly used in the late and post-medieval period, sometimes harnessed in front of the oxen to make them move faster (Figure 3.14).

Horse-only plough teams were smaller – maybe consisting of just one animal – and so the need for the complex turning procedure at the edge of a field vanished, as did the 'S'. Oxen finally disappeared from common use in the nineteenth century.

In the large open fields of the English lowlands, rig and furrow marked possession of land, with individuals or families cultivating one or more strips. With the probable exception of fields around villages such as Alnham, it's not clear if this system of allocation was much used in the Cheviot uplands. But it had other benefits as well.

On hills, most rig and furrow runs up and down the slopes; this was partly because draught animals, particularly oxen, disliked working across a slope, but mostly because of the need for drainage, with the furrows shedding water rather than trapping it. Well-drained ridges could be used for crops like wheat that preferred drier conditions, while peas and beans were planted in the wetter furrows.

A small but real benefit was that rig and furrow slightly increased the surface area of a field. Imagine a piece of corrugated paper pulled out so it's flat; it covers a slightly larger area than the original. So it was with a field – it made a difference of only a few percent, but nevertheless that was a useful bonus for a marginal upland economy.

Other types of arable structures are found in the Cheviots. Over a thousand years before proper rig and furrow appeared, farmers had appreciated the benefits of such an approach. Cord rig, so called because on aerial photographs it resembles corduroy, is like rig and furrow in miniature. Typically, the ridge to ridge distance is less than four feet; created by farmers with spades, we know that it dates from the Iron Age or earlier because at places like Greenlee Lough near Hadrian's Wall it can be seen to underlie Roman structures. Along the Border Roads it may be found near hilltop camps and sometimes as part of field systems belonging to complete farms, such as that at Scowther Knowe near The Street (Figure 6.16). It's not known if it was mainly an upland phenomenon, simply because if it did exist in the lowlands it has been

Figure 3.15 Terracing above Alwinton to the west of Clennell Street.

destroyed by later agriculture. A version of cord rig persisted into more modern times in the form of lazy beds. These were small scale, hand-built rig and furrow systems; often close to a dwelling, they were probably used for horticulture rather than agriculture.

The other common arable features are cultivation terraces, otherwise known as lynchets (Figure 3.15). As the name implies, these take the form of long terraces that run across a slope or hillside; sometimes there may just be one of them, but there can be up to a dozen or more running parallel with each other.

Such terraces are hard to date, but around the country it's known that some were built in the Bronze Age while others are probably medieval in origin, created at a time when a growing population and the resulting land hunger encouraged the cultivation of ever more marginal land.

They were formed as a result of ploughing across the slope – either with draught animals or, if very old, by hand-ploughing with a primitive type of scratch plough, called an ard. The resulting disturbance caused erosion and the loose soil would gradually migrate down the hill. Although the process might have started by accident, it seems likely that on occasions deliberate attempts were made to control this movement by using regularly placed rows of stones or low wooden hurdles. The soil building up against these barriers formed terraces that were in turn easier to cultivate.

Arable Farming – the Crops
Where crops were grown was only part of the story; just as important was the nature of the crops themselves.

The sites of arable farming along the Border Roads played an important role in selecting the crops that could be grown there; some farmland was as high as 1,300 feet and exposed to more than its fair share of wind and rain. When we discussed the past climate of the Cheviots, we described a warm Bronze Age but a cooler and wetter Iron Age, with a continuing gradual deterioration interspersed with warmer spells. This probably meant that crop yields were in general low, a situation not helped by poor soil and a shorter northern growing season. What's more, the actual crops cultivated would have been low yielding anyway, the compensating factor being that they were hardy; it has been suggested that some farming communities traded productivity for predictability. It also seems likely that the higher sites were not in continuous use, but were farmed during warmer periods or when population pressures became extreme.

The first cereal crop cultivated in the British Isles was probably Einkorn wheat. Originating in the Middle East as long ago as 7500 BC, this was one of the earliest domesticated cereals and was commonly grown by Neolithic farmers. Its characteristics are very like those outlined above – it gives poor yields but is not fussy about soil quality. Its flour is not good for making bread, so it's often used in meals like porridge. Still grown in places, you can find suppliers on the web, but although its general use may have survived into the Middle Ages, in this country it's been abandoned as a commercial crop.

The other common ancient wheat was Emmer. Like Einkorn, it was hardy but made better bread. Again, it's still grown in some parts of the world, notably Italy, and is enjoying a resurgence as a health food.

Oats are believed to have arrived at some stage during the first millennium BC. They can grow in cool summers and tolerate rain, and so were good candidates for northern and upland cultivation. Domesticated barley is almost as old as some wheats and varieties of it probably appeared in Britain before oats; it has several uses, one of which is brewing beer. Although Tacitus describes this, it may be that he was referring to lowland crops because barley is generally less robust than oats. However, there is a strain called bigg or bere. Now only cultivated in a few places in Scotland, it gives lower yields than modern barley, but it grows quickly and tolerates poor climates. Derived from *bygg*, the Old Norse for barley, its name lives on in Newcastle's Bigg Market.

In the Iron Age, spelt wheat became more common in Britain and its remains have been found in the north-east; its use continued once the Romans arrived, together with that of barley, bread wheat, oats and some peas and beans. The charred remains of a third-century Roman military granary at Arbeia in South Shields showed that it predominantly held bread wheat and spelt with just a little barley. Towards the end of the first millennium, the traditional old wheats became much less common, with bread wheat and rye taking their place. Deep ploughing may have been introduced from mainland Europe at about this time, and with it the ability to create the rig and furrow structures we've described. The improved soil quality that resulted, together with the Medieval Warm Period, may have breathed new life into upland arable farming.

In summary, the most common crops grown at altitude were probably oats together with some strains of ancient wheat. On the lower slopes there would have been barley and rye, with more developed varieties of wheat in the valleys.

Figure 3.16 The entrance to a stell.

Pastoral farming – the structures

We turn now to animal husbandry and the visible remains it has left on the landscape of the Border Roads.

The most common structures in the Cheviots – and there are hundreds of them – are sheep stells, usually circular enclosures up to some 40 feet across with a single entrance (Figure 3.16). They are usually made of stone, although on occasions you will come across a ruined one built from turf. They are hardly used now, if at all, but when in operation they would have fulfilled a variety of functions. They often acted as shelters, although left to their own devices sheep usually prefer a straight wall, and they were places where a shepherd could manage sick stock or pen them for lambing and marking.

The origins of the stell are unknown, although William Roy's eighteenth-century maps sometimes show circular structures that may have been instances of them. Built of drystone – without mortar – the walls of a stell are battered, which means they are angled on both sides and are narrower at the top than the bottom. They are everyday objects, but even if abandoned a well-built stell can be a thing of beauty.

Until well into the nineteenth century, sheep milk was an important part of the Cheviot economy. Stells may have been used for milking, but folds or buildings called *buchts* were constructed specifically for this purpose. These took several forms, ranging from simple rectangular enclosures, perhaps with entrances at each end, to more complex structures with internal compartments. The term can still be seen in place names, such as Buchtrig, a farm to the east of Dere Street on the northern edge of the Cheviots.

Stock enclosures are the other common relic of earlier pastoral farming practices. Larger than stells, and probably handling both sheep and cattle, they may be circular or rectangular with walls of earth and turf, and perhaps stone as well. Some of these walls may have had a fence on top, but only excavation can determine that. Such enclosures are usually near farms or settlements rather than out on the open hills but, as always, there are exceptions to this rule.

Finally, there are stack stands. These are usually circular platforms on which stock feed, or fodder, was placed. Out on the open hillside, they were usually protected by a bank, built to discourage greedy livestock from getting an early meal. Farmers sometimes put branches on the ground inside a stand to stop the feed getting wet, but that may not have been possible in upland areas. Circular, turf-built, stack stands can be hard to distinguish from turf stells; the difference is that the stells have an entrance and the stands usually don't. Figure 7.2 shows a stell and a stack stand next to each other.

Pastoral farming – the stock

Although the names we use for ancient livestock are familiar ones – bulls and cows, sheep and goats – the animals attached to those labels often looked rather different from those in the Cheviots today. Across the board, for example, they were smaller.

The modern cattle that probably look most like their predecessors are Dexters, which were actually developed in the eighteenth century by breeding from Irish mountain stock (Figure 3.17). Usually less than four feet high at the shoulder, a Dexter cow weighs between 600 and 700 pounds and is good for both beef and milk; castrated bulls make good oxen, so they are all-purpose animals.

As a contrast to the Dexter there is the rather larger White Park breed, a type which is associated with the Northumbrian Chillingham herd. There are references to white cattle dating back to Roman times, and it is known that herds like the one at Chillingham survived because of a medieval process known as emparking, which involved enclosing an area of land to be used primarily for hunting deer.

There are surviving counterparts of prehistoric sheep as well, animals that can be raised in poor or upland conditions. Examples of such breeds include Soays

Figure 3.17 A Dexter cow with a passing goat to provide scale.

Figure 3.18 A Soay ewe.

(Figure 3.18); these provide both milk and wool, shedding their wool naturally every year in such a way that it can even be removed by hand, a process known as rooing. Soays are small; a fleece weighs no more than about two pounds and they do not provide much meat, but that used not to be high on the list of requirements for early farmers, with wool, milk and cheese being a flock's main products.

The Romans introduced larger sheep. Initially, these appear to have been used in lowland flocks, but by the fourteenth century there are records that describe the ancestors of the modern Cheviot breed.

It has been suggested that the few hundred modern feral goats in the Cheviots are descended from medieval flocks that were turned loose when sheep became the animals of choice.

They both provide milk and meat, but there the similarities end. While sheep like to graze, goats prefer to browse higher up, focusing on leaves, shrubs and weeds. This means they have less regular contact with ground-based parasites and so are more prone to infection if conditions force them to graze. They are harder to herd than sheep, and their coat is not of wool, but of hair. This can be used for clothing, but it's unlikely that there was much demand in medieval Britain for cashmere scarves and mohair socks. And goats have one final problem; get downwind from a billy in the Cheviots and you'll find out what it is. On almost every count, therefore, the sheep would have beaten the goat as a viable proposition on an upland farm. Two feral Cheviot goats can be seen in Figure 8.13.

The quad-bike and other developments have transformed the way upland stock is managed, but in the past animal care was very labour intensive. A monk called Ælfric of Eynsham, writing in the south of England at the end of the first millennium, described the work of a shepherd thus: '*In the early morning I drive my sheep to the pasture and in the heat and in cold I stand over them with dogs, lest wolves devour them, and I lead them back to their folds and milk them twice a day, and move their folds; and in addition I make cheese and butter, and I am loyal to my lord.*'

Other businesses and activities

Mills

From the medieval period onwards, rural economies often depended on a local corn mill to produce flour for bread. On a small scale, of course, individuals could always grind grain in hand-operated querns, although there is evidence that in some places landowners prohibited these in order to increase usage of their mills and the fees associated with them. In 1284 a Scottish edict attempted to ban them, imposing penalties for their use in other than extreme circumstances.

The relatively fast-flowing Cheviot streams and rivers offered good sites for watermills, and there is evidence of their construction on both sides of the border. A good place for a mill was often re-used, and those operating on medieval sites are known to have lasted into the nineteenth century, although by that stage they would have borne little resemblance to their predecessors. Their remains, if any, consist of building platforms by a river, and channels and streams that diverted water to a mill pond or the wheel. Sometimes the mills were small – just farm mills that serviced a local community. These would often have been powered by water from a pond filled by a nearby stream, with operations stopping when the pond was empty. In such cases, there may be no surviving remains at all, even the pond having been filled in.

A miller would have dried grain in a kiln; this consisted of either a stone-lined bowl dug into a nearby slope or a freestanding, usually circular, structure. A fire was maintained through a stoke hole at the base, and the resulting hot air dried the product. Some small settlements had communal kilns as well, usually to prepare grain for hand-milling.

Although mills were used for many purposes other than grinding grain, there are few instances of this along the Border Roads – the medieval fulling mill near Barrowburn on the Coquet being one. This is described in more detail in Chapter 6.

Coal Mining

We tend to think of coal mining taking place on a large scale in an industrial environment and surrounded by dense housing. While this image is largely true from the nineteenth century onwards, before that a lot of coal was extracted in rural settings, often using systems based around bell pits.

A bell pit gets its name because in cross-section it can look a bit like a bell, but it may be easier to imagine it as an inverted 'T' (or a long-necked decanter – see Figure 3.19). A vertical shaft was dug down to a coal seam, and then the miners would dig out into the seam in all directions for as far as they dared. The coal they dug was put into baskets and hauled to the surface by ponies, or sometimes women and children. Ladders provided access to the base of the shaft.

When the miners felt they had dug as far as they could, the pit was abandoned and another opened nearby, with the spoil from the second being used to fill the first. With the diameter of the chamber at the base of the first pit being up to 30 or 40 feet, the location of the second pit would have to be far enough away to ensure its chamber did not break through into the original one.

Bell pits were rarely more than 50 feet deep; the deeper the shaft, the more attractive it became to access the coal by driving linear supported galleries out into it. This was

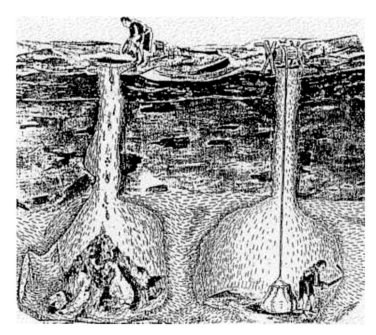

Figure 3.19 A simple bell pit in operation, with digging, lifting and refilling all done by hand.

more efficient, since it avoided the repeated sinking of new deep shafts to get to the seam. On the surface, however, it is now impossible to tell the difference between the remains of the two types of structure. All that is usually left is a shallow depression of varying diameter, sometimes with a low ridge around the edge. The depression may hold water but can also look like solid ground. It's worthwhile being careful on entering these; on occasions the shaft was blocked with the stump of a dead tree which is liable to collapse when rotten.

Droving

At some stage all the Border Roads would have been used for the movement of livestock, ranging from long distance droving from Scotland to the movement of sheep and cattle either to nearby markets or just between pastures for better grazing.

Although no records exist, moving stock for seasonal grazing must have started in prehistory; documents from establishments such as Newminster Abbey tell us it happened in medieval times. There are indications of some commercial droving in the late medieval period, with records of the cattle fair at Stagshaw Bank, above Corbridge, dating from 1204. However, during the 300 years of border troubles before the Union of the Crowns in 1603 a common type of stock movement was theft, as warring factions appropriated each others' cattle, often for them to be appropriated straight back again.

Although more orthodox droving restarted in the seventeenth century, there were still hurdles to surmount; in the 1660s, for example, England temporarily banned imports of cattle from both Scotland and Ireland. But after political union in 1707, cattle became Scotland's major export to England and by the end of the eighteenth century some 100,000 head were being moved south each year (Figure 3.20). These would have been collected from all over the country and brought to markets at places

Figure 3.20 Cattle leaving Skye, probably for market in the south.

like Falkirk. From there many would have crossed the Cheviots to English markets such as those at Newcastle and Stagshaw Bank; some, of course, would have then been taken even further.

The logistics of moving large numbers of cattle meant that progress was slow; equally, a gentle pace was desirable because it meant that the animals did not lose condition before being sold. It seems likely that a daily leg of 12-15 miles was the most achieved, with overnight stops being governed by the availability of grazing, and ideally the presence of an inn. Progress over the hills may have been even slower, although routes such as Dere Street, Clennell Street and the Salter's Road dip into valleys (the Coquet, the Usway and the Breamish), providing sheltered places to stop overnight.

The work was hard. In the late nineteenth century an old drover, George Robson, then aged 80, reminisced abut his youth and talked to a newspaper reporter about how large quantities of both sheep and cattle were taken over the Cheviots to the market at Morpeth.

> *'A good deal of rough and ready work was also performed in the summer months when our way from Yetholm was by Cocklawfoot over the Cocklaw or west end of Cheviot by Uswayford, Wholehope and Alwinton and thence by Rothbury or Tosson over the east end of dark Simonside to Longhorsley. This route was chosen because there were no turnpike gates that way between Morpeth and Kelso.*

> *In a storm when the mountain streams came down in torrents, it was a very trying and difficult time for us. We had often to wait half a day until the small rivers subsided sufficiently to enable us to pass through sometimes fifteen hundred sheep and lambs and a hundred or two head of cattle. In order to get on we did not always wait till it was quite safe to pass them, and I have stood nearly up to my waist in the streams keeping the sheep and lambs from being carried down by the current. After being in the water this*

way for a day or two together we were of course as wet as water could make us, but we could get no change of clothes until we reached home four or five days afterwards.'

This is a description of animals being moved along Clennell Street. As we shall see in Chapter 4, they would have had to cross the Usway Burn next to the old farm at Uswayford, and this may well be one of the streams he described.

Many of the enclosures and stack stands in the Cheviots will be relics of this droving, although they would have been used for local stock as well. There are other clues too; the presence of sunken tracks or hollow-ways on slopes and places where several parallel routes cross a short area are indications of heavy usage. At least two of the Border Roads have at some stage had droving in their names; an eighteenth-century estate map of the land above Alnham calls the Salter's Road *'The Drift Road to Scotland'* – *drift* being a synonym for drove – while in the west, a track branching off Dere Street at Featherwood that led down to Elsdon became part of a route known as the *Great Drift Road*. There are names in the landscape too; a hill to the north of The Street at Barrowburn is called Kyloe Shin; *kyloe* is a Scots term for a type of Highland cattle, especially those from the west and the Hebrides.

The Industrial Revolution and the increasingly urban nature of English society developed the demand for imported meat; drovers responded by bringing ever more cattle to southern markets and by adding larger numbers of sheep to the mix. However, industrial development was also droving's downfall. From the middle of the nineteenth century the expanding railway network handled ever larger numbers of cattle, moving them more quickly and delivering them in better condition. By the twentieth century only a few farms north of the border were bringing stock south to small markets like that at Rothbury, taking three or four days on the journey. The sound of hooves on the Border Roads had almost disappeared.

Smuggling and Distilling

Usually driven by customs duties or differential taxation, smuggling has been as common throughout history as it is now. In the Middle Ages illicit trade in commodities such as coal and wool was rife in the north-east of England, but such goods were bulky and would usually have travelled by sea.

However, the Border Roads played their part in the transport of more portable goods. In the chapter on the Salter's Road we will discuss salt smuggling, but here we will focus on the best-known type of unlawful trade in the Cheviots – that of whisky.

A description by Eneas McKenzie of an eighteenth-century drinking house at Slymefoot, on the Coquet some five miles upstream from Alwinton, is one of the earliest references to alcohol in the Cheviots. However, there are many more records that provide details about activities in the early nineteenth century; although this was a time when gin was more popular than whisky in most of England, Scottish preferences had made their way into Northumberland[2].

Between 1802 and 1830 the duty on whisky in Scotland was always lower than in England, usually by about four shillings a gallon. If legal Scottish whisky was purchased just north of the border and quietly taken south for sale, this four shillings was pure profit. Writing in 1835, Stephen Oliver described how dealers with light carts would head north by *'unfrequented roads',* spend a day in a Scottish village and return south

---

[2] In the eighteenth century, English gin consumption was estimated at between eight and ten million gallons a year. Even then, this was felt to exceed government guidelines.

the next night. He wrote that *'an angler who happens to be near the head of the Coquet in the grey of the morning may sometimes observe a man driving a cart … who by suddenly halting or altering his course shows that he is anxious to avoid a meeting'*. Even though this traffic meant additional business in Scotland, not everyone there welcomed it; the minister at Hownam complained that *'lawless gangs of smugglers from the English borders have long infested this neighbourhood'*.

The whisky trade, however, did not go unchallenged. Government figures show that over 50 excise officers (known as *gaugers*) were employed along the border, all of whom were on a bonus scheme linked to the amount of distilling equipment, whisky or raw material they seized. Despite this, it's not clear that they always tried that hard to catch offenders. There were no bridges over the upper stretches of the Coquet and one of them often made the excuse that he was *'stopp'd wi' witters'*. This caution may have been understandable. In 1830 three unarmed excise men tried to apprehend two smugglers near Kirkwhelpington. They were badly beaten up, with stab wounds and blows to the head from cudgels that exposed bone. The smugglers were eventually caught by an armed party from Wallington, but not before they had been cared for at a sympathetic local farm.

However, policing, fines and changes in duty meant that eventually smuggling died away. Whereas up to a fifth of the people of Yetholm had once been engaged in the activity, by the 1840s the amount of illegal whisky going to England was *'scarcely worth calculating'*.

The other form of illegal activity involved illicit distillation to avoid paying tax altogether. Initially explored by the archaeologist John Philipson some 60 years ago, remains of stills can still be found along the Border Roads. Following a list of six sites provided by David Dippie Dixon in his book on Upper Coquetdale, Philipson succeeded in identifying three of these while adding a possible fourth. One or more of them were operated by the well-known Black Rory; there is no hard evidence that such a person actually existed and it may be that he was a figure invented by the real distillers as a cover for their own activities, especially as he had a name – *Ruairidh* – that sounded as if he came from north of the border. But it was a good story.

Of these stills, three are near Clennell Street or the Salter's Road, while the fourth is on the Blind Burn, in the Buckham's Walls area. We will describe these in more detail in the relevant chapters, but in general they consist of remote buildings near a water supply with a kiln at one end and a floor for malting. This process involved soaking grain, and then laying it out on the floor and turning it regularly for a number of days to dry it. This green malt, as it was known, was then further dried in the kiln to develop the desired colour.

It is not exactly clear when or for how long these stills were used. Philipson excavated one on the Wholehope Burn and found pottery with dates ranging from the eighteenth century to about 1830. On an 1862 plan of Alwinton Common this location is marked as an *'Old Distillery'*, but tradition has it that some distillation was being carried out at remote sites as late as 1870. Given that the practice still continues elsewhere in the British Isles this seems entirely plausible; in 2013 revenue officials in Ireland discovered a *poitín* distillery in County Cavan with 900 empty bottles, 2,000 litres of alcohol wash, seven 200-litre barrels, one pump and two copper cylinder tanks. Black Rory would have been jealous.

Pubs and Drinking

Having a place to meet, eat and drink has always been important for communities, and those along the Border Roads were no exception. There is still the occasional pub, but less than 100 years ago almost every village had at least one inn. In Alwinton, for example, on Clennell Street, the Rose and Thistle is still in business but nineteenth-century OS maps show a Red Lion as well. In Hownam, on The Street, an 1859 OS map shows two inns on the road through the village, the Shepherd's Arms and the Dickson's Arms (Figure 6.20). The former had closed by 1892 but the latter was apparently still operating in 1917; both buildings are now private houses.

Looking at early census records for these two inns helps us understand their different commercial natures. In 1851 the Shepherd's Arms was operated by William Patton, described as a merchant inn-keeper. The Dickson's Arms, however, was occupied by Samuel Hall and his wife. Samuel was a blacksmith (the smithy was about 100 yards away) and his wife had no listed occupation, so the inn may have been more of a part-time venture. Other drinking houses in the Cheviots almost certainly followed this model. Examples are the one at Slymefoot on The Street and that at Chew Green, whose existence is based on reports of old glassware being found near the remains of the farmhouse. If places like this operated commercially, they were probably farms or smallholdings that made extra money by catering to the needs of locals and travellers along the Border Roads.

Pedlars and tinkers

The Border Roads themselves, and the lowland tracks they linked to, would have been extensively used by itinerants making a living by selling what they could carry or working for the communities they passed through. These people have left little trace,

Figure 3.21 Census enumerators were assiduous in visiting everyone, householders or otherwise.

but occasionally they surface – either in the form of the goods they left behind them or in records such as censuses or quarter sessions (Figure 3.21).

In Chapter 2 we described how tobacco pipes could be used to help date archaeological sites. On both sides of the border their presence reveals the remains of trading networks that transported goods from Edinburgh or Newcastle for 50 miles or more, carried by pedlars doing business at farms and settlements as they travelled the area. Craftsmen travelled for work as well, with the 1841 census in Alnham listing an extended Scottish family of travelling tinplate workers en route to their next destination.

Of course, the Salter's Road was itself named after a trade – the travellers that carried salt to Scotland and sold it to the communities on both sides of the border. The background to this trade is explored in Chapter 5.

Figure 3.22 The Woden Law quarry.

Quarrying

Although the Cheviots are mostly rolling, grass-covered hills, rock is rarely far below the surface – and is sometimes actually on it. This means the hills are littered with quarries.

Sometimes the extracted stone was put to obvious use, like the construction of a nearby house or an adjacent wall. Quarries were dug by the Romans to extract material for their roads and examples of these can be seen all along Dere Street. This type of work lasted for almost two thousand years: stone-breaking was a common occupation recorded in nineteenth-century censuses and as late as the 1920s there were gangs on the Otterburn ranges, extracting stone for the roads on the War Office's new land.

Elsewhere the use of stone may be less obvious; old field boundaries, for example, usually look as if they consist of earthen banks, but investigation often reveals a stone core put there for strength or as the footings for an ancient wall. Similarly, in many cases the ramparts of Iron Age camps, now grass-covered, would originally have had a stone facing. At the north-east end of Woden Law a substantial quarry is obviously the source of such stone for the neighbouring camp (Figure 3.22).

Figure 3.23 **Cross Dyke near Green Knowe on The Street.**
(Image © Andrew Curtis under Creative Commons Attribution 2.0 licence).

Other structures

Linear earthworks

A walker in the Cheviots will frequently come across long earthen banks, sometimes containing pieces of stone or rock. Some of these banks are boundary dykes, marking the edges of ancient estates; some may even be the result of medieval emparking. Others are just field boundaries protecting a cultivated area; we discussed some of these in the section on farming. But then there are structures called cross dykes.

The archetypal cross dyke is a bank of earth with an accompanying ditch built across a ridge at right angles to any path running along it. Usually the bank peters out some way down on either side of the ridge, often when the slope becomes quite steep. Some cross dykes are very obvious, being up to four feet high in places, ten feet wide and up to 300 yards long (Figure 3.23). Erosion and human activity have damaged some of them and completely destroyed others.

No-one knows precisely what they were for. It's been suggested that they marked boundaries, protected nearby settlements from stray cattle, acted as control posts for passing travellers or discouraged reivers. Those few that have been examined in detail turn out to be pre-Roman in origin, but that doesn't mean they all are. Nor should we accept that they were all built with a single purpose; things are rarely that simple.

Cairns

The Cheviots are also littered with cairns, ranging from small piles of stones to massive structures over 100 yards long. Some are modern, often built by walkers to mark paths or a summit, while others date back to the Neolithic.

Large cairns are usually funerary in nature although, confusingly, small ones can be too. Long cairns are rare but not unknown in the Cheviots, and like their counterparts, the round cairns, may contain burial chambers; sometimes the burials took place in

Figure 3.24 ***Clearance cairn.***
(Image © Andrew Curtis under Creative Commons Attribution 2.0 licence).

small, slab-sided structures known as cists with human remains accompanied by a few personal possessions. Other burials were in pots that held the ashes of a cremated individual. Inhumation practices changed in the late Bronze Age, and in general after about 1000 BC funerary cairns are rare, although there are regional exceptions. Cairns are very often damaged – almost certainly because at some stage they have been robbed.

Figure 3.25 ***A single standing stone near Hownam.***

Figure 3.26 Hollow-ways on the slopes just to the west of Alnham.

Then there are smaller piles of stones, sometimes organised in cairn fields. These are often clearance cairns; dating from the Bronze Age or later, they are the result of early farmers gathering stones in order to release as much cultivatable ground as possible (Figure 3.24). Sometimes stones in clearance cairns display distinct scratches; these were made by a plough and show that the stones in question were still out in the field when cultivation started.

Standing stones
These can range in size from slabs a foot or so high to more impressive objects as tall as the passer-by. While there are places in Northumberland and Roxburghshire where such stones are grouped together – presumably marking a place of social, religious or astronomical significance – only one of these, the Five Stanes near Dere Street, is on a Border Road; most other instances are just solitary stones (Figure 3.25). Where these stones are believed to be prehistoric, their purpose is usually unknown; it may be that they marked a burial, acted as a boundary marker or were part of a larger structure that has now disappeared. However, there are instances of more modern stones whose purpose is clear, and it is usually to mark the boundary between estates or parishes. On occasions there are inscribed letters on opposing faces identifying the landowners, the farms or the parishes on either side.

Hollow-ways
On many of the Border Roads there are slopes covered with hollow-ways. These are indentations on a hillside that range from gentle depressions to deep trenches of varying widths; they are signs that stock, or even horses and carts, have passed that way and eroded the ground underneath. An initial depression attracts water after a rainfall; this flows down the slope causing further erosion and a vicious circle starts, which ends when the going becomes too difficult and the traffic finds another route, perhaps only a few yards away. When this happens, you end up with a braided set of paths up and down the slope (Figure 3.26).

Sheep stell near the Usway Burn.

Chapter 4

Clennell Street

As with all the Border Roads, Clennell Street has always been part of a larger network of routes and tracks that extended for many miles outside the Cheviot uplands. On William Roy's map of the 1740s it is identified as the *'Road from Morpeth to Kelso'*.

Its origins are ancient, with evidence of Iron Age and Bronze Age activity along the route. In 1181 the monks from Newminster Abbey started to develop substantial landholdings in the area, and records of their business arrangements and land ownership appear in their chartulary. This refers to the *'magnam viam de Ernespeth'*, which from the context appears to be a reference to Clennell Street. It's likely that this name derives from the Old English phrase *'earnes pæð'*, meaning eagle's path – an interesting observation about the area's wildlife in the Middle Ages, and a label that may have been in use a thousand years ago.

The name 'Clennell Street' appears to be comparatively recent; based on that of a major local family it's shared with a hill, a hall and a lost settlement near Alwinton. For the purposes of this book, our start point will be just south of there. The route then heads north and west past Wholehope and Uswayford and up to the border, before dropping down to the farm at Cocklawfoot. It then follows the line of a small metalled road towards Town Yetholm.

Alwinton to Wholehope (Map 4.1)

The earliest building in Alwinton is the church. Although heavily modified in the nineteenth century, parts of the fabric are much older, with some elements probably dating from the twelfth century. The Newminster chartulary notes that early in the thirteenth century Master Thomas was the parson and records that a pound of pepper and a pound of incense should be handed over as gifts on the feast of St. Michael – presumably then, as now, the church's dedicatee. Away from the church, in 1296 the Lay Subsidy Roll recorded 40 taxpayers in the parish paying a total of £6 12s. 3¼d. The border raids that ensued clearly damaged the local economy, because in 1336 the same system showed just eight taxpayers, with a total take of £1 7s. 4d. From the middle of the fourteenth century, North Northumberland was excused payment of Lay Subsidies in an effort to offset the destruction caused by Scottish attacks.

The church is nearly half a mile from the current village, which reflects changing patterns of settlement. There are no surviving early maps of the parish, but from the sixteenth and seventeenth centuries there are references to two Alwintons – initially *Over* and *Nether* and then *High* and *Low*, the latter name still being in use for the area near the church. In 1580 a Muster Roll for the Middle Marches shows *Over Allenton* raising just one man while *Nether Allenton* contributed three, but the Armstrongs' map of 1769 shows only two buildings next to the church, so the depopulation must have

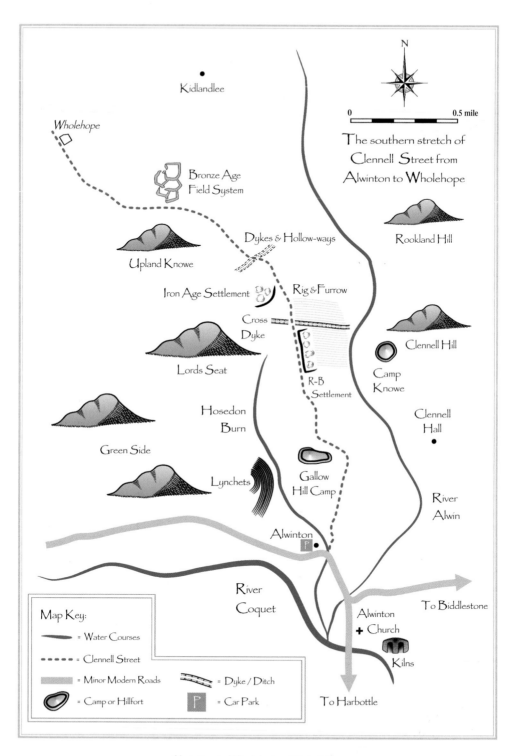

N

0   0.5 mile

The southern stretch of
Clennell Street from
Alwinton to Wholehope

Kidlandlee

Wholehope

Bronze Age
Field System

Rookland Hill

Dykes & Hollow-ways

Upland Knowe

Iron Age Settlement   Rig & Furrow

Cross
Dyke   Clennell Hill

Lords Seat   Camp
                                            Knowe

R-B
Settlement   Clennell
                                            Hall

Hosedon
Burn

Green Side

Lynchets   Gallow
                        Hill Camp   River
                                            Alwin

Alwinton

Map Key:
        = Water Courses
- - - - = Clennell Street
        = Minor Modern Roads   = Dyke / Ditch
        = Camp or Hillfort   P = Car Park

River
Coquet

Alwinton
+ Church

Kilns

To Biddlestone

To Harbottle

Alwinton to Wholehope. (Map 4.1)

happened by then. In fact, this map showed pairs of buildings almost everywhere, and so these two might just represent a single house. It is believed that in the sixteenth and seventeenth centuries the parish priest lived in a pele tower or a *'little bastle'* that later fell into disrepair. It's not known where it was; the fields around the church show no sign of it, and it may be that it lies underneath the current vicarage.

About 200 yards south-east of the churchyard, close to a track along the north bank of the Coquet, is a set of lime kilns, a relic of a more industrial past (Figure 4.1). These are easy to access, well-preserved and, as a bonus, host colonies of bats.

Burning limestone to produce quicklime is a long-established process, but until the post-medieval period the lime was generally used for mortar. But with the advent of cheap coal its use in agriculture grew, with its addition to acid soil improving both rough pasture and arable land.

The Alwinton kilns were built by the Selby family in 1827 to produce lime for their land a mile or two away at Biddlestone. Abandoned in 1866, they are fairly typical of their type, having large chambers in which limestone was burnt. Sometimes this was done as a single operation in a process known as flaring, with burning lasting several days before the whole kiln was emptied and the lime extracted. A different approach, called drawing, saw the kiln filled with alternate layers of fuel and limestone. This was burnt continuously, with the finished lime being extracted from the base while fresh material was added at the top. Neither was a very efficient process, as about half a ton of coal was needed for every ton of lime produced. It may be significant that these kilns were near the end of the Coal Road, a track that led to the East Wilkwood coal

Figure 4.1 The Alwinton lime kilns.

workings about two miles to the south-west. Opened in the middle of the eighteenth century, these had shut by 1850.

As it heads north from the east end of Alwinton, Clennell Street passes a reminder of a busier village. This is a two-storey, double-fronted house that until the end of the nineteenth century was an inn called the Red Lion, and from the 1870s doubled as a *'Provision Shop'*. By 1911 it had become a Temperance Hotel, and subsequently acted as the post office. In fact, there had been a post office in the village as early as 1881; it was initially next door and run by the local bootmaker.

Although we know something of medieval Alwinton, people were living in the area long before that. A few hundred yards north of the village, Clennell Street passes below Gallow Hill (or Castle Hill), on top of which is an Iron Age camp (Figure 4.2). In a good defensive position, this is oval in shape, enclosing an area about 150 yards from east to west and 50 yards north to south. The slopes to the north and south are steep and have just a single earth and stone rampart at the top, while those to the east are slightly more gentle. What look like additional ramparts on this side may be the result of the slope being artificially cut away, in some places resulting in a very steep face.

Figure 4.2 The camp on Gallow Hill from the north. The dyke protecting the plateau is the long line on the right.

There is an additional defensive rampart at the west end, probably because there is a small plateau outside and below the main ramparts. The plateau itself, most easily accessed from the north, is protected from an approach in that direction by a linear dyke. This is attached to the camp's main ramparts, is about 80 yards long and runs from east to west. Few other camps in the Cheviots have this sort of external feature; it has an entrance midway along it, and the camp itself has entrances at both the east and west ends, although the latter is badly damaged.

Further west, the slopes above Hosedon Burn are covered with agricultural terracing or lynchets that may also date from the Iron Age (Figure 3.15). When the bracken is low, similar structures can just be made out on the hillside north of the camp.

The only signs of occupation inside the camp are low banks that pick out a roughly rectangular building in the centre; orientated north-south, it's about 20 feet long and 12 feet wide. Like the rest of the camp, this has never been excavated, and may be a later addition. One possibility is that it is contemporary with building remains outside. These are particularly obvious at the foot of the north slope, where banks and enclosures reveal activity that may postdate the camp itself.

As it passes Gallow Hill, Clennell Street heads north up a ridge with the Hoseden Burn to the west and the River Alwin to the east. On the far bank of the Alwin is Clennell Hall.

The Clennells lived in Coquetdale for hundreds of years. A settlement called Clennell was listed as one of the 'Ten Towns of Coquetdale'; there are records of a mill there in the early eighteenth century but no sign of the village remains, although nine men from it were listed in the Muster Rolls of 1538, over half the contribution of both Alwintons combined. There is, however, a surviving hall based on a pele tower which was probably built between 1509 and 1541. There were some additions later in the sixteenth century, but in 1895 a substantial programme of renovation and extension resulted in the large house that can be seen today. Areas of rig and furrow to the north of it may be linked with the old village.

On the south-eastern spur of Clennell Hill, about half a mile to the north of the Hall, is another Iron Age structure, Camp Knowes. Clearly visible from Clennell Street, it occupies a commanding position over the Alwin valley and encloses an area of about two acres.

Apart from the section to the north-west, below which there are very steep slopes, much of the original camp was probably protected by a double rampart. At some places, especially to the south-east, the outer bank has been destroyed by the ploughing that created the extensive rig and furrow on the slopes below. It also may be that some of the stone in the ramparts was robbed to build dykes and field walls. The camp is most easily approached from the north-east, down the slope and across the saddle from the main part of Clennell Hill. At this point the double rampart is most obvious, being about five feet high in places.

The main entrance is on the south-east side. The interior contains a few low banks which are probably the remains of small enclosures, and there are at least two hut circles – one about ten feet across and the other twice that size. Some reports have identified more, but these are very hard to make out.

Back on the Clennell Street ridge opposite Camp Knowes there are two interesting structures.

One is a cross-dyke running at right angles across the path (Figure 4.3). Up to four feet high in places it's well preserved and is one of the best examples of its kind in the Cheviots. Cut through by twin tracks, to the west of the ridge it's quite short, terminating after about 60 yards as the slope drops steeply down towards a burn. To the east, the gentler gradient means the dyke is longer; for the first 200 yards it is very obvious, but after that it can be traced in a diminished and sinuous form for another 100 yards before stopping just short of a small, sharp drop above the floor of the Alwin valley. As with most cross dykes, its original function must be a matter of

Figure 4.3 The Clennell Sreet cross-dyke, looking east.

speculation, but at first sight this looks very much like a structure built to block the ridge – impeding or controlling access by stock, people, or both.

Immediately to the south of the dyke and to the east of the main path, is a large patch of disturbed ground full of ridges, banks and hollows, covering about 120 yards from north to south and 80 yards west to east.

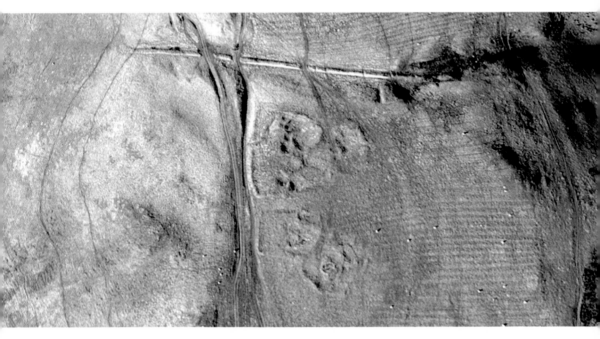

Figure 4.4 Clennell Street runs up the centre of the picture The R-B settlement is to its right with the cross dyke to the north. There is rig and furrow on the eastern slopes.
(Image © 2016 Google, Infoterra Ltd. & Bluesky).

Better seen from above (Figure 4.4), these disturbances are the damaged remains of two adjacent Romano-British (R-B) settlements, one to the north of the other. Each is surrounded by an enclosing dyke, while inside there are irregular, smaller enclosures and courtyards – some quite deeply scooped – and hut circles. Archaeologists have counted as many as 20 of these, with diameters ranging from ten to 23 feet. The main enclosure walls around the settlements are more obvious on the side next to Clennell Street; this could be because they were bigger on that side in the first place, with more protection being needed, or because the other side has been damaged by subsequent farming activity.

This activity took the form of ploughing that created an area of rig and furrow extending about 180 yards north of the cross dyke and 350 yards to the south. The work was concentrated on the upper levels of the ridge and it peters out about 200 yards to the east of Clennell Street. In all, the ploughing covers about 20 acres.

At ten or 12 feet wide, it's too broad for cord rig, and it postdates the settlements because it encroaches on their eastern boundaries. It's hard to tell how much damage it has done to them; almost by definition, the surviving structures have not been destroyed and others may have disappeared completely. But now, the rig and furrow itself can be hard to see unless the conditions are right; one way of detecting it is to crouch down and look to the east so that its profile is silhouetted against the near horizon.

It isn't possible to establish any real chronological relationship between the settlements and the cross-dyke. That they are so close to each other can hardly be coincidence, but whether the dyke was built to protect the settlements, or the settlements exploited an existing dyke – or if there was a more complicated connection – must be a matter of speculation.

However, there is evidence that there was activity in the general area before Romano-British times. About 400 yards north of the cross-dyke and just past the point where Clennell Street swings to the north-west, are the remains of a settlement thought to date from the early Iron Age. It's roughly circular, about 150 feet across and in a location with poor natural defences. To the east and south it is bounded by a groove that may mark a palisade that once encircled the whole settlement. Inside, there are traces of eight or nine roundhouses between 23 and 36 feet in diameter; they are quite tightly packed but do not seem to overlap, so they may have been in use concurrently.

The site was surveyed but not excavated in the 1970s by George Jobey, an archaeologist who worked extensively in the north-east and the Borders. Starting as an extra-mural tutor for Newcastle University, he was eventually appointed Professor in 1981. He believed that this settlement might date from the sixth or seventh century BC.

About half a mile further on, and about 200 yards north of Clennell Street (which is now running from east to west) is an even earlier site. This dates from the Bronze Age and was excavated over several seasons starting in 2006, as part of a project led by Rachel Pope of Liverpool University, with students helped by local volunteers. In all, about seven acres were surveyed, identifying cairns and house platforms inside both open and enclosed settlements, together with complex sets of field systems and some cord rig. One roundhouse was excavated, and a metal cloak fastener found in one of the walls suggested it dated from the Early to Middle Bronze Age, making it up to 4,000 years old. With a clay-lined hearth pit, the house had been built with walls made of stakes, possibly strengthened by either turf or wattle and daub. It appeared to have been occupied in three distinct stages, while investigation of the adjacent field system showed that it too had developed in multiple phases. This suggests use over a considerable period of time, but at a height of over 1,100 feet, whether occupation was permanent or seasonal is a matter of debate.

Between these Iron Age and Bronze Age settlements, Clennell Street drops into a saddle that is full of archaeology – but archaeology that is very hard to decipher, with a confusion of hollow-ways, ditches and dykes, not to mention forestry that encroaches from both sides. It's been suggested that one or two of the dykes may have been cross-dykes, but if they were, and if their purpose was to obstruct passage along Clennell Street, then it was not an ideal place to build them. Most such cross-dykes are draped across a steep-sided ridge, but here the gentler contours mean that if such a structure were to be effective it would have to be about twice as long as the cross-dyke we've described to the south. Indeed, it's possible that one of the sets of banks and ditches may be recent. The ditch is unusual, essentially being a line of shallow pits separated by narrow baulks. It's been pointed out that this looks like an interrupted piece of modern military construction, with each pit dug by a single soldier as the first step in making a continuous trench. If this is so, then it's a salutary reminder that the story of a twentieth-century structure can be lost completely and quickly.

Wholehope and Kidland *(Map 4.2)*

Past the Bronze Age settlement, Clennell Street climbs the shoulder of Wholehope Knowe and enters an area redolent with history.

People may have lived here for hundreds of years, although early references are not definitive, with potential for confusion with a Wholehope Hill that's between two and three miles away to the north-east. In 1233 *Holehope* was listed as paying tithes to the vicar of Alwinton. The 1296 Lay Subsidy Roll for the parish lists a *Roger de Holhop*, whose worth was assessed as £1 14s. 2d (Figure 4.5). This was about average, and Roger may have been a tenant of the Newminster monks, who by this stage owned most of Kidland.

This was a large estate consisting of the north-east part of the parish of Alwinton, bounded by the Rowhope Burn to the west and Cushat Law to the east. In all, it

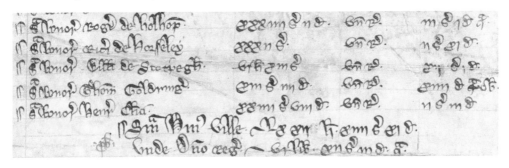

Figure 4.5 Roger's entry is at the top of this extract from the list of Alwinton taxpayers.
(Image courtesy National Archives)

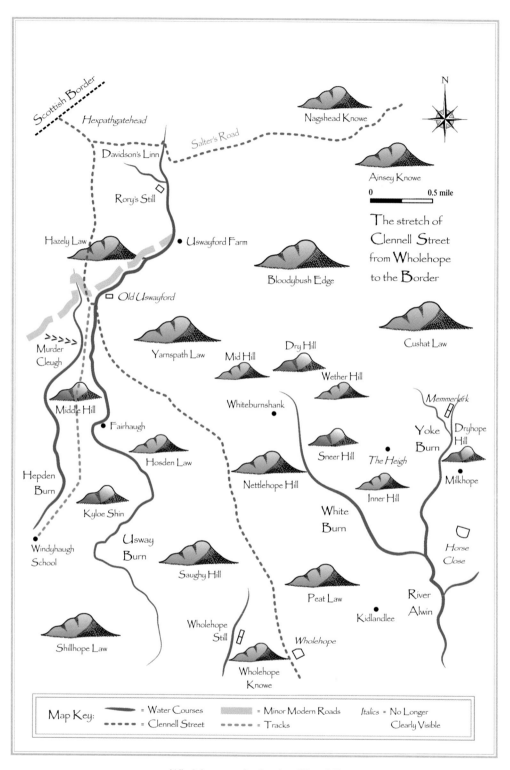

Wholehope to the Border. (Map 4.2)

covered some 17,000 acres, and became Crown property when Newminster Abbey was dissolved in 1536, staying that way until James I granted it to James Maxwell, Earl of Dirleton, in 1623 for the annual sum of £80.

The area had fallen into disuse during the border conflicts, but the Armstrongs' map of 1769 shows a building called *Wheelhope*, with *'Sir Digby Legard B*' written next to it. This doesn't mean that Sir Digby lived here, but rather that he owned it. In fact, by this time the Yorkshire-based Legard family owned large chunks of Kidland, having acquired them piecemeal in earlier years as the estate was broken up into discrete tenanted farms to make it more profitable.

We can trace some of the later story of Wholehope farm through census returns. Lived in by shepherding families, in 1841 the occupants were the Elliotts: Andrew who was over 70 years old, his wife Jane who was 55 and their three children aged between ten and 25. In 1851 there was the five-strong Hornsby family – with a servant – but ten years later nine Mordies were packed into the property, as well as a boarder. The family stayed there until the 1880s, although in later censuses their name is recorded (correctly) as Murdie. In fact, examination of the 1861 census shows that spelling was not always the enumerator's strong point: 'shepherd', for example, being invariably spelt with two 'p's.

Figure 4.6 The Wholehope Youth Hostel in 1957. (Image courtesy Mick Robson).

In the Alwinton parish records there is also an unpleasant reminder of how hostile and unseasonal Cheviot weather can be. On 25th April, 1808, the burial is recorded of George Hay of Jedburgh: *'Carrier. 80 yrs. Perished in a storm about a mile from Wholhope'*.

Acquired by the War Office in 1941, the farm was abandoned in 1942, although we don't know if this was deliberate policy or because military activity made it too hard to work there. After the war, it was restored by the Youth Hostel Association at a cost of some £50 and opened for business in 1949 (Figure 4.6). Although remote, with sanitation initially heavily dependent on the nearby stream and a spade, users

Figure 4.7 Wholehope 50 years on.

made light of the three-mile trek from the Rose and Thistle in Alwinton, the weather and the cramped conditions.

It was well-used in the summer, but the building became increasingly hard to maintain and the YHA closed it in 1964. It was finally demolished in the 1970s; only some ruined walls remain to remind the passer-by of its history (Figure 4.7).

However, the farm turned youth hostel, and the adjacent enclosures probably associated with it, are not the only items of interest in the area. Less than half a mile to the north-west, on the other side of Wholehope Knowe and on the east bank of the Wholehope Burn, are the remains of an illicit whisky still. It was excavated between 1951 and 1954 by the Coquetdale businessman and antiquarian John Philipson, assisted by a Colonel Chipper and a Captain Walton. They identified three buildings including a kiln house set into the hillside, a malting house with a cobbled floor and a building for working in or living. Unsurprisingly, it is not now easy to find, especially when the bracken is high, and once located what can be seen is not as distinct as in Figure 4.8. The remains of the kiln, however, are still visible on the ground.

The still was located on a small haugh in a crook of the burn; two of the buildings, aligned north and south, were parallel with the stream while the third, the kiln-house, was set at right angles to it. A track to the east ran up the slope behind them, and its depth led Philipson to suggest that it had been heavily used.

From left to right in Figure 4.8, Philipson thought that the two room building had been used for working and maybe living, because most of the finds were made there. These included pieces of glass and domestic pottery produced at various times between 1760 and 1830. Even if not new when used at the still, they gave an indication of the period over which it was in operation.

This building was the only place on the site where coal was found, suggesting that the still might have been in here as well, with coal providing a steadier and more

Figure 4.8 The Wholehope still in the 1950s. The total length of the two buildings in the foreground is 55 feet. (Image courtesy of Society of Antiquaries, Newcastle upon Tyne and Julian Philipson).

predictable heat than peat. Even more interesting was the identification of an apothecary's phial. This had probably been used to test the product during distillation, being tied to a string, weighted and then lowered into the keg to retrieve a sample or two.

The middle building measured 25 by 17 feet and was the only one with a stone floor, which would have been used for malting. When examined, it was completely covered with a thin layer of ash. Philipson's explanation was that it had probably had a turf roof which had been burnt around the time the still was abandoned.

The final building contained a circular kiln with an external diameter of about eight feet, the remains of which can be seen in the picture. This was where the malt was finally dried; a careful examination of its contents revealed that it had been fired with peat. There was also a black, tarry internal residue containing caramel. This must have been a by-product of the drying process; when grain is dried the starch in it turns to sugar, which burns if the drying is too intense.

Returning to Wholehope itself, it is not the only deserted farm in the area. Economic pressure led to forestry planting that started in the 1950s, covering the area that was once the province of farms further to the east such as Whiteburnshank, Milkhope, Dryhope, The Heigh and Kidlandlee. The first two survived as farms into the 1970s and some of their buildings were restored as outdoor activity centres.

Whiteboreshank is mentioned in a survey of 1536 and the death of a Persivell Davison who lived there was recorded in 1637 with his estate being valued at £239 3s. 11d; this meant he was reasonably well off, but other farmers in the area had similar assets. An Alnham estate map of 1776 shows a track heading west labelled '*To Milkhope and Dryhope*', but 50 years later another map marks Dryhope as '*in ruins*' and the Ordnance Survey map of the 1860s shows nothing. Its land was absorbed by Milkhope. The precise site of the farmstead is unknown, but it may have been in a now-forested area on the northern slopes of Dryhope Hill above the Rigg Burn.

The earliest reference we have to The Heigh is in a will of 1715; still operating in the 1930s and maybe later, its ruins are in a clearing about a mile north of Kidlandlee.

They consist of a fenced-off rectangular flat-topped mound of rubble blocks about 100 feet long and 20 wide. This is probably the result of the farm buildings being demolished, with the walls pushed over and consolidated on the structure's original footprint – perhaps because the ruins were considered dangerous. A hollow at the eastern end may be the remains of a room, but it's very hard to tell because a more recent pile of stones has been dumped immediately next to it. Parts of a drystone-walled enclosure to the north of the farm can still be made out, as can further lengths of wall deeper in the trees.

Kidlandlee was at the heart of the estate. Its associated landholdings were quite extensive; by the 1750s the owner, James Burne, was also landlord of Windyhaugh, a farm on The Street about three miles to the west, and titleholder of the Featherwood estate on Dere Street, over on the western side of the Otterburn ranges. Kidlandlee was later notable for a shooting lodge built there by a retired naval officer, Christopher Leyland. He helped his brother develop the *leylandii* cypress, and inherited Haggerston Castle near Berwick. Fond of follies, he built a water tower there with an integrated astronomical observatory, and a zoo complete with a herd of bison, some kangaroos and a bear. The shooting lodge at Kidlandlee was a similarly eccentric project (Figure 4.9).

Figure 4.9 A contemporary photograph of the Kidlandlee shooting lodge. The stables are on the left.

With building starting around 1896, the lodge had a luxurious interior and its 13 bedrooms could clearly accommodate enough guests to do serious damage to the local wildlife. Steam turbines[1] generated electricity and supplied central heating, but despite this the lodge was only used in summer. For the rest of the year only a married couple lived there as caretakers, but it still brought employment and people to an area that had seen 50 years of population decline. In response to this, in 1914 the council opened a school at Kidlandlee.

Good things seldom last. Leyland died in 1926 and the estate was sold in 1931 to cover debts and death duties. After that the lodge was used even less and explosive charges were eventually used to demolish it in 1956. Before the final destruction, the parquet flooring was rescued and local people report that that it burnt beautifully in their hearths that winter. The main building is survived by a once elegant stable block

---

[1] Built by Parsons of Wallsend. For a time, Leyland both funded and captained the Parsons-designed Turbinia, the world's first steam-turbine driven ship. It is now in the Discovery Museum in Newcastle.

situated to the north of the house, and the old kennels and a croquet lawn can still be seen. With only five pupils left, the school shut in 1957, bringing an era to an end. The schoolhouse is now a private dwelling and the estate cottages are used as holiday lets.

Figure 4.10 The overgrown rectangular ruin of Memmerkirk.

Finally, there is Memmerkirk. This is a set of ruins less than two miles north of Kidlandlee, where indistinct grass mounds next to a forestry track form a rectangle about 50 feet long and 15 across (Figure 4.10). Although not mentioned in the Newminster chartulary, in the eighteenth century a belief developed that this was the site of a medieval chapel built by the monks, but it was not properly excavated until 1962 when Barbara Harbottle led the investigation. She was a medieval specialist who worked in adult education, later becoming the first Tyne and Wear county archaeologist. The dig showed that the building had no discernible religious origins, being orientated in the wrong direction and having the wrong configuration. With three rooms, a hearth suggested domestic use; in Harbottle's opinion it had originally been a crudely-built medieval longhouse, but the presence of post-medieval pottery and smoking pipes implied some seventeenth-century activity. This may have been simple re-use of the site, perhaps as a shieling, but Harbottle suggested that the stories about a chapel might have started if dissenting Presbyterians had used it as a safe place of worship.

There is some slight evidence to support this. In 1762 James Burne of Kidlandlee left money in his will to 'the Congregation of Protestant Dissenters' of Harbottle. Although we don't know exactly when he or his forebears took over the estate, a list of dissenter burials in Alwinton shows that the family was already there by 1719. The Harbottle congregation had started to meet in a private house in 1713, so the Burnes may have encouraged meetings at Memmerkirk before that.

Wholehope to the Border *(Map 4.2)*

After Wholehope, as Clennell Street heads into an area of forestry, there are several dykes and ditches near the track. The function of these is mostly a matter of speculation. Some may be the result of modern improvement, while others may be much older. It's been suggested that at least one of them acted as a medieval boundary for the Newminster estate because their chartulary mentions ditches that marked landholdings in the area. The forestry itself, although now being felled, has almost certainly destroyed or concealed more structures. Just south of the trees on Hosden Law, for example, about 400 yards west of the track, are the poorly preserved remains of two or three roundhouses. It's entirely possible that more are – or were – inside the planted area.

Early OS maps rather enigmatically show 'Stones' along this section of the route and a site called Drummers Well. This is now lost, as are at least two cross dykes that were recorded before the forestry was planted.

After two miles or so, Clennell Street leaves the forested area and drops into the upper reaches of the Usway valley, skirting round Yarnspath Law, a name clearly derived from the old name for the road. To the west, on the other side of the Usway Burn, is another area of woodland that cloaks a deep sided valley: this is Murder Cleugh.

It's not the only place with this name. On The Street, for example, there is a Murder Cleuch near the triple cross dykes we describe in Chapter 6, and there's another north of Galashiels, but the one near

Figure 4.11 The memorial stone at Murder Cleugh.

Clennell Street is linked with a known crime. In fact, a small memorial to the victim has fairly recently been erected near the head of the cleugh (Figure 4.11).

The Northumberland quarter sessions for July 1610 record that 'Robert Lumsden of Horsholes, "Scotchman"; at Oswaiford, murdered Isabella Sudden f. of Oswayford, with stones worth Id, struck against her stomach so that she languished and died on 28 July'. You do wonder why the value of the stones was considered important in such a context.

An entry the next year gives slightly different information. It identifies Isabella as the wife of Andrew Sudden of *Halliston* and says that 'she languished from 20 July until 4 August next when she died'.

This was not only a violent crime, but a particularly nasty one. Speculation is always dangerous, but had the married Isabella been having an affair with Lumsden? Was she killed like this because she was pregnant?

Lumsden may have had other affairs. We don't know what happened to him as a result of the Uswayford murder, but he escaped with his life. In 1630 a report of events surrounding an attempt to take him before the High Commission Court of Durham says 'It was vehemently suspected that John Galland his wife and Lumsden tied together in adulterie'. When the Court's agent went to apprehend him he was accompanied by a John Pottes, the man who had made the accusation. On arriving at Lumsden's house, they tried to arrest him but Lumsden's followers robbed them and beat them up so badly that John Pottes 'did keepe his bedd one moneth after, and was hopeless of recovery'.

The Durham Court made several more attempts to capture Lumsden. He was finally caught in 1634 but continued to defend himself, producing witnesses who claimed he was a model citizen and a pillar of the community. Eventually he was convicted and sentenced to serve a month in gaol, acknowledge his offence at the Market Cross in Alnwick and pay a fine of 100 marks (£66). He seems to have been dilatory about this, but the Court eventually accepted a token payment from his son George and the case was finally closed in 1639.

Where was Horsholes, where Lumsden lived? A paper by a James Hardy in the History of the Berwickshire Naturalists' Club written in 1885, says that 'Fairy-pipes had been picked out of old ash-middens at the "Horse-Holes", a recess in the green braes at Milkhope where half-wild horses might retire to at night for shelter'. Sure enough, near the old Kidland farm of Milkhope east of the River Alwin, just over three miles from Uswayford, there's an enclosure on the modern OS map called Horse Close. Hardy said there were remains of old buildings close by; if the 'Fairy-pipes' were old smoking pipes then that might be a sign that people were living there in the seventeenth century.

As it leaves Yarnspath Law, Clennell Street drops down the slope to a footbridge over the Usway by the site of an old ford. This stretch of the valley is home to Uswayford farm.

There do not appear to be any reliable references to a medieval farm here, but that is not to say that the area was not used. Certainly the Usway Burn acted as a marker for boundaries defined by the Newminster monks, with spellings such as Osweiburne.

In the middle of the seventeenth century Sir Thomas Widdrington of Cheeseburn Grange, near Stamfordham, became a landowner in Kidland. However, the family had interests in the area before that, because the will of Henry Widdrington[2] of Nethertrewghitt (Nether Trewhitt or Low Trewhitt, near Rothbury) who died in 1625 lists possessions at Oswayford. Henry clearly lived at Trewhitt, because all his household goods were there, and he must have farmed there too because he kept 300 oxen. But he had many more livestock up at Uswayford, with cattle, sheep, horses and pigs worth a total of £194 14s.

The current Uswayford farm is about a mile up the valley to the north-east from the footbridge, but this was not its original location. Until some stage in the nineteenth century it was situated on the haugh on the south-east side of the burn, about 150 yards upstream from the bridge or ford.

It's not clear when the farm was moved; early maps always show it close to the burn. The Greenwood brothers surveyed the county in 1827 and 1828 and their map marks it there, but the first Ordnance Survey of 1861-3 shows it in its current position, with the original farm labelled 'Old Sheepfold'.

---

[2] The nephew of Sir Henry Widdrington of Swinburne Castle, the parliamentarian and Sheriff of Northumberland.

*Figure 4.12 **Old Uswayford farm with the enclosure bank in the foreground.***

The ruins of the old farm are still clearly visible when bracken isn't growing. Built roughly parallel with the burn, examination of the site shows several distinct structures; working downstream (from right to left in Figure 4.12) the first building has two rooms, each about 20 feet long and ten feet wide. Then there is a small gap, followed by a second building, also divided into two sections each ten feet square. There are some entrances, but it's not clear if these are all original; the second room in the first building may have the remains of a hearth.

A low bank surrounds the farmstead, forming an oval-shaped enclosure about 60 yards long and 20 wide. This was probably built to keep animals out, because there are old stock enclosures within a few hundred yards of the farm on both sides of the burn. Some of these might also have been used for animals being taken along Clennell Street.

A well-defined track leads diagonally up the slopes of Yarnspath Law above the ruin. It's not entirely clear where this went to, but before it peters out it turns away from Clennell Street, suggesting that it may have originally headed east, perhaps connecting with paths going to the Breamish valley. Uswayford lands extended that far quite early; a 1726 map of the Alnham estate shows *'Useyford Ground Bounders'* on the west side of the river Breamish.

It's worth considering why the farm would be sited at the edge of an estate of that size, and on haugh land that periodically floods. It may be that these disadvantages were outweighed by being close to Clennell Street. This would have had practical benefits; the farm would have had better access to markets both north and south and could have done business with passing travellers, perhaps selling them produce from the whisky still further up the valley that's described in the next chapter. There might also have been some element of self-protection. With a heavily-used route running through your property, it probably made sense to live close to it and watch out for any mischief (Figure 4.13).

There is an interesting area to the west of the old Uswayford farm. As well as some of the stock enclosures mentioned above, in the nineteenth century a burial cist was

Figure 4.13 An artist's impression of Old Uswayford. (courtesy John Tribe)

found on top of the ridge that separates the Usway Burn from the Hepden Burn; the small mound it came from can still be seen. The human remains in the cist are now lost, but were apparently sent to Frank Richardson[3], who was the Harbottle doctor from about 1850 to the 1880s. Close by, there is a circular depression that is rumoured to be the site of a cockfighting pit, presumably built for the entertainment of the drovers and other users of Clennell Street. While this may be so, and while cockfighting was a popular rural activity until well into the nineteenth century[4], the structure of this hollow is unlike the remains of many other known pits. Although these varied in style, those in the open air tended to be larger, with a circular ditch surrounding a flat area on which two men, known as *setters* or *pitters*, would stand and introduce the birds to the fray. But perhaps procedures in the hills were more informal.

Nearby is a good example of something that looks ancient actually being used in living memory. We tend to think of hollow-ways as the result of wear and tear on old routes, and there is apparently one such structure on the west side of the ridge in question, which is known as the Dipper Bank. And although it may have ancient origins, it was in use up to the 1960s.

The deep scar in the hillside was the route of the road from Rowhope up to Uswayford until the Forestry Commission built the current loop round to the north. Cart-horses had to negotiate the ascent, towing only half-loads. They would pause at the bottom to prepare themselves, set off at pace and get to the hairpin bend halfway up, where the carter would apply the brakes and let the horse recover for the final stretch. When lorries were first used they didn't find it easy either, summoning up full revs and holding the engine valves open with pennies to make the climb.

---

[3] Not be to confused with Bernard Richardson, the Harbottle doctor from 1947. Frank had a greyhound, King Death, that won the Waterloo Cup in 1864 – and 500 guineas to go with it. Waterloo House in Harbottle commemorates this.

[4] There were pubs called the Fighting Cocks in both Rothbury, now the Turk's Head, and Netherton.

There was easier access to the farm along a path that continues south along the top of this ridge, crossing Middle Hill and descending to Barrowburn. Negotiable on foot and by pony, this was the way Uswayford children walked to Windyhaugh School, a seven-mile round trip every day. On the way they would pass Fairhaugh, down below them by the burn in the Usway valley. Now a holiday home, this was a farm as early as the mid-seventeenth century but lost its land to forestry like many others described in this chapter.

The ridge above old Uswayford was also the site of a guide-post. With a modern one now a little to the north of the original, this pointed the way to the many paths that converge on this point. Not only was there Clennell Street, connecting Morpeth with Kelso, but the tracks we've described down to Rowhope and Barrowburn in the Coquet valley. Other paths went east to the Breamish valley and north-west towards Windy Gyle, opening up other routes into Scotland.

Although the activity has left no archaeological trace, these links meant the area was frequently visited. A survey of the border in 1541 describes part of it thus:

> 'Fyrst begynynge at the hangyng stone, whiche ys the very uttermost p'te of the said mydle m'ches towarde the Este, the said border stretcheth & goeth eastwarde to the butte rodde, And from thence to hexpathgate head, and so styll west to the wyndy gole … '

Some of the names mentioned are in use today. With *hexpathgate head* positioned between the *butte rode* (Butt Roads) and *wyndy gole* (Windy Gyle), it must have been at or near the place where Clennell Street crosses the border. This seems to be confirmed by the fact that a few hundred yards into Scotland, the modern track passes to the west of Hexmoor Cleuch and Hexmoor Sike.

Another sixteenth-century survey of the Middle Marches mentions a second place – plain *Hexpathgate* (without the 'head'). It is described as two miles from the Hanging Stone on the way to Harbottle, which implies it was not on the border, but rather to the south of it. It may be that Hexpathgate was near the junction of the routes in the Usway valley, while Hexpathgatehead was, as the name suggests, on the border above it[5].

Hexpathgatehead was where the Scottish and English Wardens of the Middle Marches would meet to try to resolve differences and keep the peace during the troubles. This did not always work, because in July 1585 Lord Francis Russell, Earl of Bedford and a member of a group of gentlemen sent to '*keep a truce with the opposite warden*', was killed.

A manuscript in the Cotton collection at the British Museum recounts both sides of the story. The English claimed that their party was ambushed at the border and that the whole incident was premeditated. They went as far as naming the people they thought were guilty of the crime. The Scots said that the English party had encouraged aggression by coming threateningly close and that the Scots had thought themselves in danger. '*The whole disorder*' had been started by the English and matters had then got out of hand.

Leaving aside who was wrong, and it may have been both sides or even just an accident, Francis Russell is remembered by a cairn on the summit of Windy Gyle, about a mile

---

[5] The origin of the 'Hex' element in these names is not entirely clear. Some researchers have suggested there is a connection with the Old English *hægstald* or *hagustald* meaning 'warrior'. If true, this hints at early medieval military movement in the area.

Figure 4.14 Russell's Cairn, with the later trig point.

to the west of where Clennell Street crosses the border (Figure 4.14). This was not built for him and it's probably not where he was killed; the name first appears on the Armstrongs' map of 1769, while some 20 years earlier Roy apparently labels it *Slays Carn*; this is probably a Scottish name and could conceivably refer to to a death. Of Bronze Age origin and large, about 55 feet across and eight feet high, it's in fairly good condition, although the Ordnance Survey has inserted a now-defunct triangulation point into it. These can have very deep foundations and it's not clear how much of the cairn was disturbed during its construction.

There are other cairns of varying sizes all along the border ridge. Some are modern, while others are older but probably with modern additions. It's possible that some, at least, are also from the Bronze Age. If they were burial cairns, then the anticipation that you would be laid to rest in a place with such views might have consoled you in your final days.

Just short of the border ridge, Clennell Street is joined from the east by the Salter's Road. Once over the border, the track continues north, passing through an area where there has been some peat-cutting to a spur jutting out from the border ridge called Outer Cock Law.

The Border to Cocklawfoot *(Map 4.3)*

At this point the track drops some 300 feet down fairly steep slopes. Negotiating Outer Cock Law has clearly always been difficult. The current track curves round the hill to the east, but there is another path that does the same to the west. Now disused, this is best seen from the north once more level ground has been reached. Between the two paths some maps mark a whole series of earthworks, mostly orientated with the general line of Clennell Street. These are actually hollow-ways, the remains of abandoned routes that went more directly down the slope (Figure 4.15). At least half a dozen of these can be made out, although there is just one earthwork that may have been built for another purpose; even that is far from clear.

After leaving Outer Cock Law, Clennell Street heads across a plateau. After about half a mile, it passes to the west of Fundhope Rig. As the 'Rig' part of the name implies,

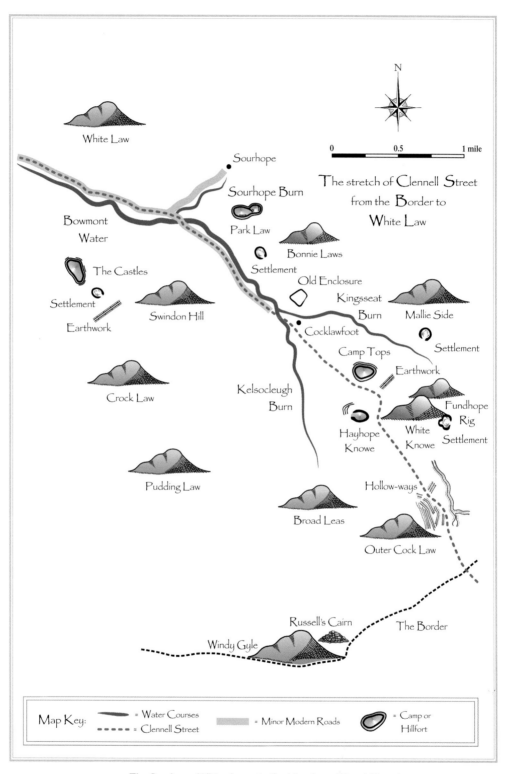

White Law

N

Sourhope

0   0.5   1 mile

The stretch of Clennell Street
from the Border to
White Law

Sourhope Burn

Bowmont
Water

Park Law

Bonnie Laws

The Castles

Settlement

Settlement

Old Enclosure

Kingsseat
Burn

Mallie Side

Earthwork

Swindon Hill

Cocklawfoot

Settlement

Camp Tops

Crock Law

Kelsocleugh
Burn

Earthwork

Fundhope
Rig

Hayhope
Knowe

White
Knowe

Settlement

Pudding Law

Hollow-ways

Broad Leas

Outer Cock Law

Russell's Cairn

The Border

Windy Gyle

Map Key: ——— = Water Courses   ▓▓▓ = Minor Modern Roads   ⬭ = Camp or
            - - - - = Clennell Street   Hillfort

The Border to White Law via Cocklawfoot. (Map 4.3)

Figure 4.15 The hollow-ways on the east side of Cock Law. The old track round the west of the hill can be seen at centre right.

this is a ridge-shaped hill with a long narrow top running roughly north-south, and at its southern end are the remains of an Iron Age settlement. There is an enclosure about 150 feet across consisting of low earth walls with an additional bank on the north side. If the purpose of the enclosure was defensive, then this may have provided additional protection from the line of easiest approach along the top of the ridge (Figure 4.16).

Inside the enclosure, careful examination reveals the presence of six hut circles with diameters of between 20 and 40 feet. None of them overlap, so they may have all been in use at the same time.

About 20 yards south-west of the settlement is a partly-curved linear earthwork that eventually peters out on the slopes of a hill next to Clennell Street called White Knowe. It's about 100 yards long, nearly three feet high in places, and built with a ditch on its northern (uphill) side. Cut through by a hollow-way, its age and purpose is unknown. If contemporary with the settlement, its function may have been to separate cattle from crops. Some aerial photographs have suggested the presence of cord rig in the area, but nothing can be seen either on the ground or with Google Earth.

A short distance further along Clennell Street and about 200 yards to the west of the path is another Iron Age structure, the camp at Hayhope Knowe. First identified by archaeologists soon after the war, it was excavated by Margaret Piggott in 1949. She had studied at Verulamium with Mortimer Wheeler and later worked at Sutton Hoo.

In 1948 she had excavated the Iron Age camp at Hownam Rings (see Chapter 6). It had a complex set of earthworks but she found the remains of an early palisade that later developments made impossible to date. Hayhope Knowe has a well-defined

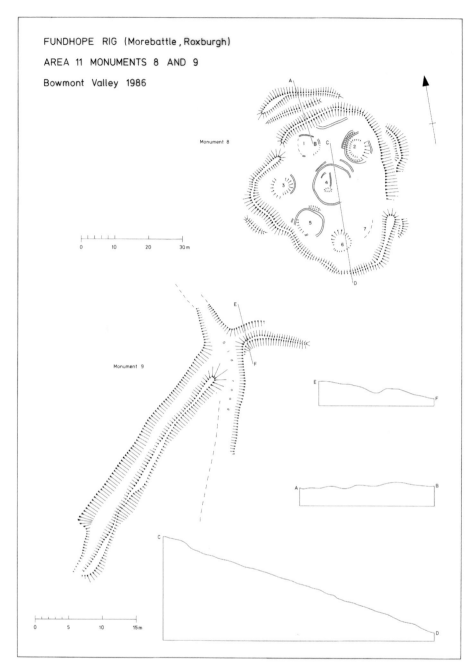

FUNDHOPE RIG (Morebattle, Roxburgh)

AREA 11 MONUMENTS 8 AND 9

Bowmont Valley 1986

Monument 8

Monument 9

0   10   20   30m

0   5   10   15m

Figure 4.16 **The settlement and earthwork at Fundhope Rig. (Image © RCAHMS).**

section of palisade that has apparently not been altered and it was felt that this was a good opportunity to learn more about such structures.

The camp is positioned towards the end of a spur that juts out to the west from the hill of White Knowe. There are slopes of varying steepness on three sides, but to the east there is an easy approach downhill from Clennell Street. This means that any attack from that direction would be quite simple. Possibly as an effort to counter this, an earthwork with an external ditch was built on three sides of the spur – to the east,

Figure 4.17 Hayhope Knowe from the south-west showing the outer earthwork, some hut circles and the palisade (highlighted). (Image © RCAHMS).

north and south – with an entrance at the east end (Figure 4.17). At first sight this looks like the rampart of the camp itself, but it's actually outside it; on the south side of the spur the bank is sporadic and it's not present on the west at all – perhaps because the slope there offered adequate protection, but perhaps because the project was never completed.

Within the area partly enclosed by the rampart are the remains of a double palisade surrounding a settlement measuring about 100 yards by 50 yards and aligned along the east-west axis of the spur. The palisades are visible in places as two shallow trenches between five and six feet apart with entrances on both the east and the west.

Figure 4.18 The western entrance at Hayhope Knowe showing the post holes. (We are grateful to the Society of Antiquaries of Scotland for permission to reproduce this photograph)[6].

Piggott excavated both of these, finding well-defined ends at each as the outer palisade looped round to return as the inner one (Figure 4.18). There were suggestions of a gate at the eastern entrance.

---

[6] The Iron Age Settlement at Hayhope Knowe, C. M. Piggott, PSAS LXXXIII, 1950, Plate XV

Figure 4.19 Piggott's impression of a Hayhope house. (We are grateful to the Society of Antiquaries of Scotland for permission to reproduce this image)[7].

In general, the posts forming the palisade were set about a foot apart, and Piggott calculated that about 1,600 would have been needed to make the whole structure. We don't know how high the posts were, or whether, for example, there was a raised walkway between them, but it is clear that construction would have been a considerable exercise.

Inside the palisaded area, Piggott identified 12 hut circles, with some of them being almost 40 feet across. Another six have since been located and most of them seem to be aligned on either side of a street that runs from east to west along the spur. Piggott excavated three of the huts she found, identifying features such as central hearths and concentric trenches for posts, while finding fragments of pottery, a clay spindle whorl and a spearhead. She proposed that Hayhope Knowe was a defended village dating from the first century BC and produced a suggestion for what one of the huts or houses might have looked like (Figure 4.19).

The external rampart was thought to have been built later, probably in response to local unrest. A remnant of a single palisade was found immediately inside its eastern end. This was not visible before excavation and seemed to have been built at much the same time, but there were no finds that could help date it. Nor does the cord rig in the area help. Visible in some aerial photographs on the north and south-east slopes below the ramparts but barely detectable on the ground, it seems to overlie parts of the camp's structure. It may represent a shift to a more agrarian economy, but it isn't known when this might have happened.

Back on Clennell Street and about 200 yards to the north of Hayhope Knowe, there's a short linear earthwork across a ridge that runs north from White Knowe. Only about 60 yards long, a gap in the middle marks where it has been cut through by a path running along the crest. There are now quad bike tracks here, but the alignment of an old hollow-way further to the north hints at an earlier route that skirted round the next structure to be described and then headed in this direction.

This next structure is Camp Tops. Another Iron Age camp, it's at the same height as Hayhope Knowe (about 1,100 feet) and is situated on a knoll at the northern end of that long ridge jutting out from White Knowe, with Clennell Street passing it on the

---

[7] The Iron Age Settlement at Hayhope Knowe, C. M. Piggott, PSAS LXXXIII, 1950, p60

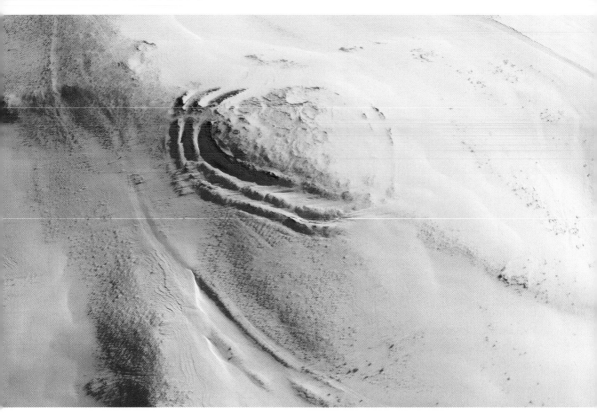

Figure 4.20 Camp Tops from the north-east. The earthwork in the foreground is the old hollow-way mentioned in the text; Clennell Street is to the top and right. (Image © RCAHMS).

west. Its position on the ridge overlooking the head of the Bowmont Water valley at Cocklawfoot about half a mile to the north means that it was well positioned to monitor traffic moving along the routes entering or leaving the hills.

Oval in shape, about 200 feet long by 150 feet wide, the camp has a triple rampart on its north and east sides, but elsewhere there is just a double one. To the south the ramparts have been badly worn away, possibly by ploughing (Figure 4.20).

It was probably built in at least two phases. The first consisted of a stone wall that once formed a complete circle but now is most visible as the innermost defence on the north and east sides. In places it exploits a natural shelf in the hillside, making it three or four feet high on the outside but very much less on the inside.

Subsequently, a double rampart was built around this inner wall, with an obvious entrance on the east side about 25 feet wide, and a narrower one on the west. Ten hut circles have been identified inside the camp, all between 30 and 40 feet across. Like those at Hayhope Knowe, some of these seem to be aligned along a street.

The similarity with Hayhope Knowe, which is only about 400 yards away, led investigators to suggest that there might be an earlier palisade surrounding these huts, especially as the street does not line up with the entrances through the ramparts. The site has never been properly excavated, but a trial trench was dug in the 1980s to look for any such structure. Nothing was found, but a small scale exercise like that is not conclusive.

A set of what looks like earthworks loops round the camp on the slopes to the north. These are not actually further defensive structures but rather the remains of the old hollow-way referred to above; this held a track running past the camp and heading towards the top of the ridge. It might be an earlier manifestation of Clennell Street heading up the hill.

As the modern track drops towards the valley and the farm of Cocklawfoot, built where the Kelsocleugh and Kingsseat Burns meet to form Bowmont Water, it's clear that this has once been an area of considerable activity. There are abandoned stock enclosures, old field boundaries – some very substantial – and ancient cultivation terraces. All these are situated around a working farm and are signs of a complex pattern of land use and re-use.

The farm is shown on Roy's map of the mid-eighteenth century, but people must have lived in the area long before that. For example, on the slopes of Bonnie Laws, a few hundred yards north of Cocklawfoot, there is an old enclosure measuring up to 180 feet across. This was originally bounded by a thick drystone wall whose foundations can still be seen in places. Outside the enclosure but immediately next to its eastern edge are traces of four roughly rectangular buildings, the largest of which is about 50 feet long. Judging by their relationship with the enclosure wall, they were built later. The site has never been excavated but with rig and furrow and old boundary dykes all around, it may represent the remains of an early farmstead.

The Kingsseat Burn joins the head of Bowmont Water from the east, and following its curving valley round to the south reveals even more activity, with old homesteads, cultivation terraces, the remains of what may be another medieval farmstead and an unenclosed settlement. This last, on Mallie Side overlooking the Cheviot Burn, has never been excavated either but is undoubtedly prehistoric in origin. It consists of 16 platforms cut into the hillside for round houses, but three of the platforms contain traces of rectangular buildings, suggesting that at some stage the site was re-used.

The Borders historian, Alexander Jeffrey, noted in the nineteenth century that Cocklawfoot was once the site of a pele or a castle that was besieged by Henry Percy after the Battle of Homildon Hill in 1402. Still in occasional circulation today, this theory is unfortunately not true, but results from confusion with a real castle at another Cocklaw, just to the east of Hawick.

However, there is a reference to farming in this area in a Tax Roll of 1630 that was aimed specifically at Thomas, Earl of Haddington. He had been Earl of Melrose until 1627, but adopted a new title because he preferred being called after a county rather than an abbey (Haddingtonshire became East Lothian in 1921). This was rather ungrateful, because most of his family's land had been acquired from Melrose Abbey during its decline in the sixteenth century. Be that as it may, the Tax Roll lists a number of farms that he had leased to the Earl of Roxburgh, including Cocklaw and others nearby such as Sourhope, a mile or so the north, and Hownam Grange, on The Street over to the west. These farms, and others now lost, had initially been part of a Melrose Abbey estate first mentioned in 1309, so that suggests there may have been medieval activity at Cocklawfoot.

However, it's time to return to Clennell Street and follow it north and west alongside Bowmont Water.

Cocklawfoot to White Law (Map 4.3)

About a mile to the north, the now metalled road passes below the south-western slopes of Park Law. Here there is a reminder of the route's original purpose – an old milestone tells travellers they have 15 miles to go to Kelso. There is some confusion about the inscription on the other side; OS maps have consistently said that the single capital letter linked to a distance of 11½ miles refers to Morebattle, presumably because someone had read the letter as an 'M'. However, it is definitely a capital 'H' and given the way most milestones are configured, it must be a reference to a destination in the opposite direction from Kelso (Figure 4.21). It almost certainly means Harbottle, which is about the right distance to the south.

Figure 4.21 The milestone says 15 miles to Kelso and 11½ to 'H'.

There are traces of old cultivation and rig and furrow scattered across the side of Park Law, as well as an ancient enclosure with a later homestead built inside it. The main feature, however, is the large Iron Age camp on the crest of the hill.

This is an impressive, substantial and complex structure that shows clear signs of a long occupational sequence. At a height of about 1,000 feet, it overlooks Bowmont Water and the Sourhope Burn.

The heart of the camp is an irregular but roughly teardrop-shaped enclosure near the summit; this can be seen at the far end of the structure in Figure 4.22. About 300 feet long, it incorporates a natural ridge that may have supplied rock to help build the encircling rampart. Originally up to 12 feet thick, and with a single entrance quite near the point of the teardrop, there are places where the lower courses of the rampart's massive facing stones can still be seen. A second rampart surrounds this central bastion; built in a shape rather like a capital B, it also encloses a similar sized

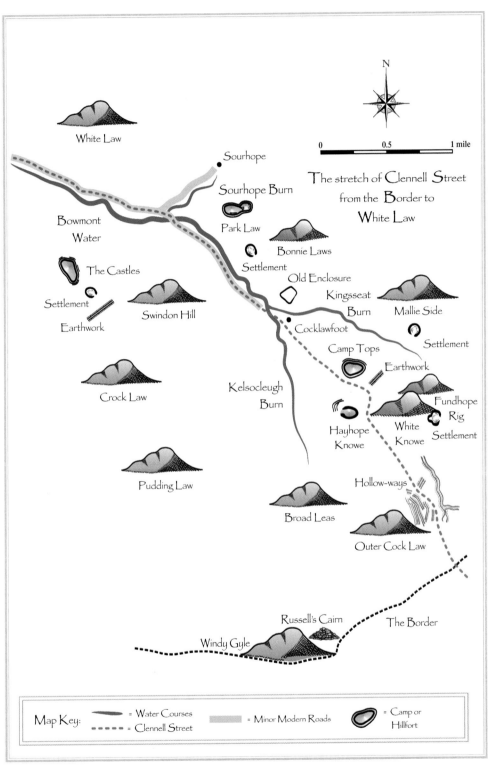

N

White Law

Sourhope

0   0.5   1 mile

Sourhope Burn

The stretch of Clennell Street
from the Border to
White Law

Bowmont
Water

Park Law

Bonnie Laws

The Castles

Settlement

Old Enclosure

Settlement

Kingsseat

Swindon Hill

Earthwork

Burn

Mallie Side

Cocklawfoot

Settlement

Crock Law

Camp Tops

Earthwork

Kelsocleugh
Burn

Fundhope
Rig

Hayhope
Knowe

White
Knowe

Settlement

Pudding Law

Hollow-ways

Broad Leas

Outer Cock Law

Russell's Cairn

The Border

Windy Gyle

Map Key: = Water Courses   = Minor Modern Roads   = Camp or
Hillfort
= Clennell Street

Cocklawfoot to White Law. (Map 4.3, repeated from page 77)

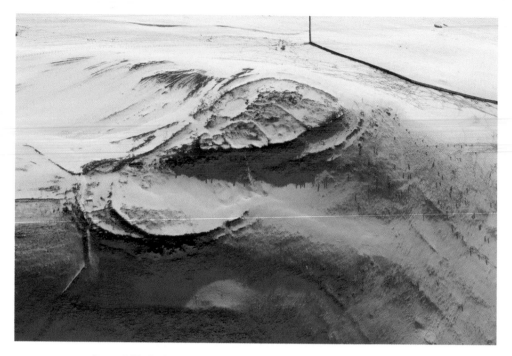

Figure 4.22 Park Law camp from the north-east. (Image © RCAHMS).

area to the east, thereby creating an annexe (in the foreground in Figure 4.22). The wall forming this rampart is slightly less robust than that around the inner enclosure; it's possible that the two were constructed at the same time but the balance of opinion is that the outer rampart is later. Finally, there is a third curved rampart at the eastern end of the annexe. This can be seen immediately adjacent to the base of the 'B' in the photograph and it may have provided additional protection against approach along the ridge from Bonnie Laws.

There are distinct traces of occupation inside both the bastion and the annexe, but these are probably not contemporary with the original structures, because in places they overlie the ramparts. In the bastion there are foundations for circular huts, together with the remains of walls enclosing three courtyards, and these have effectively obliterated signs of any original housing. Activity in the annexe may even have been medieval, with roughly rectangular foundations visible both inside and outside the ramparts. These remains are perhaps associated with a later phase of farming and the adjacent large enclosure abutting the camp, the straighter walls of which can be seen in the lower left of Figure 4.22. This enclosure extends over 400 yards along the ridge towards Bonnie Laws, encompassing an area of about 18 acres.

Just north of Park Law is Sourhope. As mentioned when discussing Cocklawfoot, this was probably the site of a medieval farm and, as at Cocklawfoot, there are the remains of old enclosures, field systems and rig and furrow in the valley. In the 1970s the farm became a land use research site, and analysis of the soils showed deficiencies in copper and cobalt. This would have resulted in poor quality pasture and may explain the disparaging name, the opposite of Sweethope.

The Sourhope Burn joins Bowmont Water just where Clennell Street's current route crosses the stream and continues on the north bank. There is now really just one track along the valley, but the OS survey of 1859 shows at least three, crossing and re-crossing the river. Here, at least, there was no single Clennell Street. After half a mile the road passes another large Iron Age camp, this time on the top of a hill to the south. Known as Castles, it bears several similarities to the structure on Park Law, which is clearly visible on the other side of Bowmont Water. Indeed, the positioning of this pair of camps across a valley is reminiscent of the two smaller ones which overlook the River Alwin above Alwinton.

Figure 4.23 Castles from the east. (Image © RCAHMS).

The original enclosure at Castles is probably the D shaped structure towards the north end of the camp (to the right in Figure 4.23). Up to 250 feet across, it sits on the top of a knoll at the north end of a long high spur and is surrounded by walls that were originally about ten feet thick, some of whose facing stones can still be seen.

As at Park Law, another set of ramparts has been built outside this inner enclosure. Since the inner and the outer sets never touch, it's not possible to say which was built first. The instinct of most archaeologists is that the outer ramparts reflect an expansion of the site, but it may be that the sequence was the other way round and indicates a contraction like the one suggested for Woden Law (see Chapter 8).

The outer double ramparts follow the line of the inner rampart quite closely, but they leave it to the south-east and, again like Park Law, sweep out to enclose another large annexe (to the left in Figure 4.23). These outer ramparts are up to ten feet thick and well preserved in places, with some original courses of boulders still visible. There are several entrances through them, and in places there are traces of what looks like a further encircling rampart. This is probably the result of spoil thrown up from the external ditch that was the source of the building material for the ramparts themselves.

There are traces of hut circles inside the bastion, but they are very hard to make out on the ground. At the south end of the annexe there are hints of walls forming small enclosures or yards, and it's generally assumed that these represent later use.

As with so many of these camps, the site has never been excavated. The only known find was that of a stone axe *'rather thicker than most implements of the same kind found in the district'*. This was reported in 1897 as being in the possession of *'Bailie Duns'* of Galashiels, who may have been John Dun, a banker and merchant who lived in a large house called Craigpark, now demolished. The whereabouts of the axe are not known.

There are cultivation terraces all round the hill on which the camp was built. To the south-east, back along the spur on which Castles sits, there are faint traces of old settlements and homesteads. After about 500 yards, there's a linear earthwork positioned across the top of the ridge leading to Crock Law. Some 200 yards long, it could be that this acted as a form of defence for the people living on the spur, or it might just have been a boundary marker.

White Law to Yetholm Law *(Map 4.4)*

Clennell Street now continues west and slightly north towards two hamlets based around farms. As Bowmont Water bends round to the north, Mowhaugh can be found on the north and east banks, while Belford is on the west and south. There is, however, one exception. About half a mile short of the bend, where the Calroust Burn joins Bowmont Water, there is a house above the south side of the road. This is the

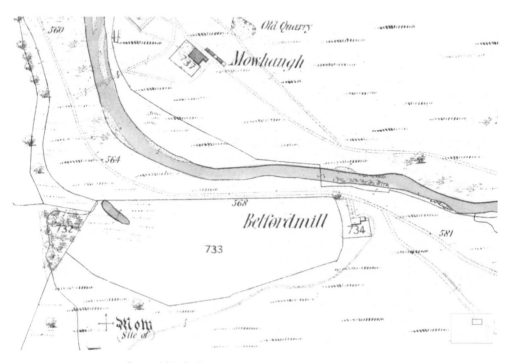

Figure 4.24 Belford Mill on the 1863 25-inch OS map.

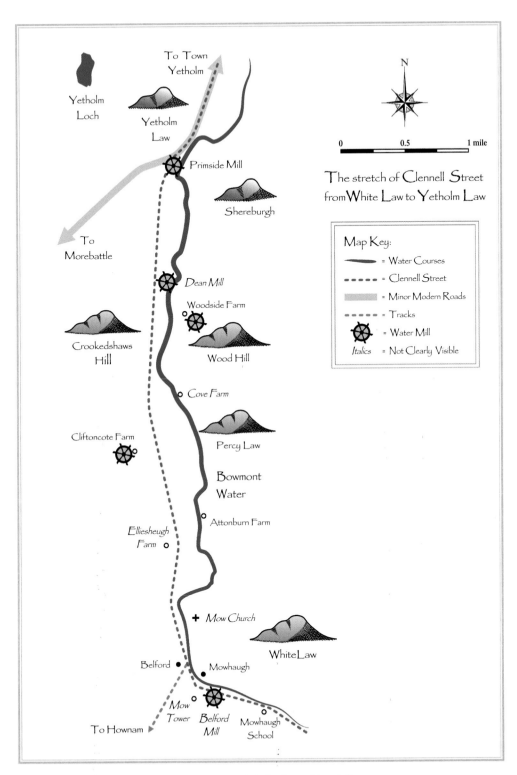

White Law to Yetholm Law. (Map 4.4)

old Mowhaugh school; established around 1830, it was closed in 1945. The Ordnance Survey maps of the 1890s show that it also served as a post office.

500 yards to the west of this is the site of Belford Mill, about which very little is known. It was marked on William Roy's map of the mid-eighteenth century and the 25-inch to the mile OS map of 1863 showed it some way from Bowmont Water on the south side of the road (Figure 4.24). There was no obvious leat or millpond to feed it, and it must have been disused for some time because the 1859 surveyors' book described it as a cottage with *'a mill at one time at this place, from which the house takes its name'*.

The 1898 map shows no sign of it at all, and only some indeterminate hollows are visible on the ground today.

Then there is the site towards the bottom left-hand corner of the map, marked Mow. Mow, or Molle, was the ancient parish for the area. Together with its church, it was granted to the monks of Kelso in the twelfth century, although the abbeys at Melrose and Paisley may have had interests here as well. It remained independent until 1672, when it became part of Morebattle.

There are references during this period to more houses than can be seen now, as well as a pele tower and a church. The site shown on the map is that of Mow Tower. Now part overgrown and part changed by agriculture, a report from 1985 described faint structures here that may have been the remains of village houses, as well as rectangular banks thought to be the pele itself. It has been suggested that the tower was one of those destroyed by William Eure, who as Warden of the East Marches campaigned in Scotland in the 1540s during the conflict popularly known as the 'Rough Wooing', a term coined by Sir Walter Scott in *Tales of a Grandfather* and repeated by Henrietta Marshall in *Our Island Story*.

At Belford, on Bowmont Water's west bank as the river turns north, an old road joins Clennell Street from the south-west. This was once the main thoroughfare between Belford and Hownam and it would have been the route taken by travellers crossing

Figure 4.25 The old farmhouse at Belford with crow-step gabling on the right.

the Cheviots on The Street. Just after this junction, the road passes Belford farm steading. In amongst the buildings here, on private land but visible from the road, is the shell of a late seventeenth-century house, now used for storage. One of the earliest domestic buildings in the area, it has a modern roof but is notable for a gable-end finished in what are known as 'crow steps' (Figure 4.25).

This architectural style originated in late medieval Europe, initially in the Low Countries and Denmark. The steps facilitated access to the roof and meant that squared masonry blocks could be used to cap the end wall without further finishing. The design first appeared in Scotland in the sixteenth century, in places like Fife that had trade links across the North Sea. Never disappearing entirely, from time to time it resurfaced in architectural revivals, notably in the nineteenth century in a style called Scottish Baronial.

About 400 yards to the north, and on the east bank of Bowmont Water, is the site of the old church of Mow. Reports describe the outlines of a nave and chancel, the two combined being nearly 70 feet long, but on the ground it's hard to make out more than a few low walls with some stone under the grass. A few gravestones and slabs are still visible, but earlier photographs suggest there were once more. Those remaining are in varying states of preservation (Figure 4.26); any inscriptions are now very indistinct, but past rubbings have dated the earliest of them to 1680, with others being some 50 years later.

The ruin is in a field bounded by a steep drop cut away by the river. One casualty of this erosion has been the western part of a low indistinct bank surrounding the

Figure 4.26 The last standing gravestone at the site of Mow church.

churchyard. It forms an approximately circular enclosure up to 70 yards across, but it's not clear if it was built to protect the church or an earlier structure on the site.

Continuing north, the road passes several active farms and two abandoned ones – Elliesheugh and Cove. The former is about three quarters of a mile north of Belford Farm; the remains of a rectangular building, an enclosure and other structures including a corn-drying kiln can be made out about 150 yards to the west of the road. It is thought to have originally been a monastic grange owned by Kelso Abbey in the twelfth and thirteenth centuries.

Figure 4.27 Dean Mill on the 25-inch OS map of 1863.

Cove is just over a mile further north. On the far side of Bowmont Water from the road there are traces of two quite large rectangular buildings with a curved enclosure wall on the slopes above them. They cannot be seen from the road, and access is not easy because there is no nearby bridge. The site is believed to be the remains of a medieval farm destroyed by the English in September 1545, being mentioned in the State Papers of Henry VIII among the structures 'brent, raced and caste downe' by the Earl of Hertford. The list for those along Bowmont Water starts 'Mowe, Mowe Meusles, Clifton Cote, Coleroste, Eleshenghe, Awton Barne, Cowe, Woodside, Owesnopside, Feltershawes, Clifton, Haihope, Kirke Yettam, Towne Yettam … '. If true, this represents comprehensive destruction, although it wasn't permanent; many of the names are recognisable as either later settlements or modern working farms.

Of these latter, Clennell Street passes first Attonburn, then Cliftoncote and Woodside. The last two were once the site of farm mills. Cliftoncote was a saw mill rather than a corn mill and although the outlines of the old millponds can be seen at both farms, they stopped working some time in the early twentieth century.

Just north of Woodside, on Bowmont Water, is the site of Dean Mill (Figure 4.27). The river has changed course over the years, and nothing is left of what was once a substantial building. First shown on Tennant's map of Roxburghshire in 1840, it was a corn mill described by the Ordnance Surveyors' book of 1859 as having two storeys with a cottage, garden and arable farm attached. The property was still in use in the early twentieth century, although perhaps not as a mill, but all that can be seen now is the channel that once delivered water to the wheel and then took it away to the north. Unusually, it doesn't feed back into the river, but rather runs parallel with it for over half a mile before delivering its water to the next mill at Primside. This was built where Clennell Street meets the road that connects Town Yetholm with Morebattle, and it was the only mill downstream from Belford shown on William Roy's map.

At this point, Clennell Street has essentially left the northern foothills of the Cheviots. Travellers to and from Kelso beyond this point had two options for their route, the main one taking them through Town Yetholm, with the Kelso road entering the village from the west. Alternatively, tracks to the west around Yetholm Loch offered a route that avoided the village completely.

In Chapter 3 we had a description from an old drover of how he had worked on Clennell Street. While one of the major markets that fed this business was probably that at Kelso[8], Kirk Yetholm, on the other side of the river from Town Yetholm, played a part as well. In the early nineteenth century, the cattle market there was reported as being frequented by dealers from Morpeth. These would certainly have taken their purchases south along Clennell Street, either going all the way to Alwinton and beyond or else turning east after the border ridge along the Salter's Road to Alnham.

That route is the subject of the next chapter.

---

[8]The autumn ram sales at Kelso are still among the most important in Europe

The Grey Yade of Coppath, next to the road up
to Ewartly Shank and west of Castle Hill.

Chapter 5

The Salter's Road

The Salter's Road is a path that runs north and west through the English Cheviots before joining Clennell Street just south of the border.

Often attached to roads, paths and places, the name *Salter* is usually connected with the salt trade. In Scotland, one of the main areas for salt manufacture used to be at Prestonpans, east of Edinburgh, while in Northumberland and Durham there were salt panning operations all along the east coast. There are references to salt extraction from seawater dating from the medieval period, but the industry in Britain reached a peak in the seventeenth and eighteenth centuries. It then declined as other sources and improved processes took over, but there was still some activity a hundred years ago.

Panning, as it was known, involved the continuous evaporation of seawater through the constant refilling of large, shallow iron pans that were maintained at almost white heat for days at a time (Figure 5.1). The process involved burning large amounts of timber or coal, so the local coal fields made the north-east coast an attractive area for the process. In the 1750s Reinhold Angerstein, a Swede who was essentially an industrial spy, visited Newcastle. He reported that there were over 100 pans in North

Figure 5.1 An eighteenth-century Tyneside salt pan, shown outside the building that held it. (Drawing from Reinhold Angerstein's diary).

and South Shields producing 10,000 tons of salt a year and noted that the government levied nearly £50,000 in tax on the result. Coal was brought down the river from Newcastle, with each pan consuming 40 tons a week[1].

The industry was visible for miles around. In the early eighteenth century Daniel Defoe reported that from the top of the Cheviot he could see the *'Smoke of the Salt-pans at Sheals...which was about 40 Miles South from this'*.

Although some of the salt from the east coast went for export, a lot of it was produced for domestic consumption and the Salter's Road would have been used by traders doing business in north Northumberland and southern Scotland. It's possible, though, that some salt came in from the other direction. In the eighteenth century, English salt was heavily taxed but rock salt was exported to Ireland duty free, creating a substantial refining industry there. An unintended consequence was that some of this cheaper Irish salt was smuggled back into England and Scotland. Most of this traffic was on the west coast, but some of the contraband made it across to the Cheviots. A tombstone in Elsdon churchyard dated 1778 records the burial of *'Thos Wilson, officer for the duty of salt, aged 51'*. He had lived at *Nether Houses*, just south of Rochester and less than a mile from Dere Street; the parish registers marked him as a pauper so he had not grown wealthy. The Salt Duties Act was finally repealed in 1824.

With the sources of salt ranging along the coast from Amble in the north to Bishopwearmouth and beyond in the south, there were clearly many routes to Scotland across the Northumberland lowlands. Alnham, however, was a major starting point for the crossing of the Cheviots, and so we will regard that as the southern end of the Salter's Road.

Alnham

The village now consists of a few farms and houses, one of which was a school that closed in the 1960s after nearly 100 years. Among the more notable buildings are the Vicar's Pele House and the adjacent church of St. Michael and All Angels. As the name implies, the former is built around a pele tower which was first recorded in 1415. By the eighteenth century it was in ruins, but it was rebuilt in its current form in the nineteenth century, complete with battlements and turrets. Now a private house, it served as a Youth Hostel between 1944 and 1958.

Alnham church was first mentioned in the twelfth century when William de Vesci gave it to the monks of Alnwick Abbey; the core of the current building seems to date from around this period, although there have been later alterations. However, some Saxon masonry blocks at the east end of the nave suggest that there was an earlier church here. There is a long-standing tradition that it was built on the site of a Roman camp or fortlet, a belief that seems to have originated with antiquarians some 200 years ago. Unfortunately, it's unlikely to be true. The theory seems to be based on the presence of a broad, flat-bottomed ditch now only visible on the east side of the church. Its profile is not Roman, however, and the nearest definite Roman activity in the area is the road to Rochester over three miles away to the south. It is more likely that the ditch is the remains of a medieval defence that protected both the church and the adjacent pele tower.

---

[1] He got less information elsewhere. In 1754 he was forced to beat a hasty retreat from Sheffield after apparently taking too much interest in the operation of a new steel works.

Alnham parish was extensive, stretching as far north as the River Breamish. This meant some parishioners faced a long walk over the moors, even though Ingram church was probably nearer for them and, in winter, more accessible. By the sixteenth century the parish was in the effective ownership of the Percy family; in the eighteenth century Hugh Percy became the Duke of Northumberland, and the history of the village is well documented in the archives at Alnwick Castle.

The clearest signs that Alnham used to be larger than it is now can be seen in the field opposite the church, on the other side of the small stream that becomes the river Aln. Here there are sets of low enclosure walls, a couple of house platforms cut into the slope and, at the top of the hill, a larger mound that is known as Alnham Castle. This is the site of another pele tower; owned by the Earls of Northumberland, it was recorded in the fifteenth century but was in disrepair by 1541, perhaps as the result of a raid by the Scots in October 1532. A letter to Henry VIII from the Earl of Northumberland, written in the spirit of the times, recorded that the Scots had burnt the village 'with all the corne, hay and householde stuff in the said towne, and also a woman'. It is alleged that in the first half of the nineteenth century a local mason, Edward Brown, built farm walls with stone taken from the ruins.

The area around Alnham is shown on an estate map of 1619 (Figure 5.2). Drawn within 20 years of the unification of the Anglo-Scottish crowns and the end of border raiding, it seems likely that the medieval layout of the estate was much the same as

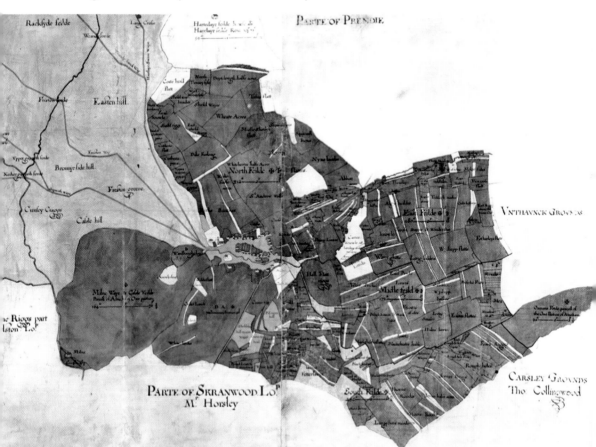

Figure 5.2 *Alnham and its field systems in 1619.* (Collection of the Duke of Northumberland).

Figure 5.3 Alnham village in 1619.
(Extracted from Figure 5.2: Collection of the Duke of Northumberland).

we see here. The green areas are the field systems and the village and the church form a nucleus just to the left of the centre of the map. Surrounding this are the large named fields – North, East, Middle and South – and each of these is subdivided into smaller fields and strips, some of which reflect the curved shape of ox ploughing. Judging by the names of some of these fields – such as *Wheate Acres* and *Broad Leatch Meadowes* – they were a mixture of arable and pasture, the latter presumably of a higher quality than the waste, shown in yellow. Tracks run across this, with the one heading north and then forking to the north-west following the route of the Salter's Road, although it is not called that.

A closer look at the village (Figure 5.3) reveals the few buildings whose remains can still be seen to the south of the stream, but the main part of the village was on the north bank and east of the church, with each house having a small plot of land. There are about 25 buildings in this cluster, but unlike those south of the river, most of them were sited on what is now a ploughed field and their remains cannot be seen with any certainty, even on aerial photographs. However, the plot belonging to the house nearest the east end of the church is larger than the rest and has a distinctive curved shape; a LiDAR image (Figure 5.4) shows lazy beds on a patch of slightly higher ground with almost exactly the same shape. A few other features can be recognised, particularly the structures and enclosures on the south bank, but also some of the shapes in the rest of the village, including that of the land belonging to the Vicar's Pele House west of the church.

The village fell into decline in the eighteenth century, with an estate map of 1726 showing about a dozen houses in two rows, one on each side of the stream. This depopulation ended in enclosure – a process whereby small landholdings were consolidated, purchased or legally taken from their owners to make larger farms. A map from 1776 (Figure 5.5) shows the result of this; while the large fields are still there, the subdivisions have gone.

A bill for the enclosure of the Alnham infields – those around the village – had gone through Parliament the year this map was drawn, and most of the village had

Figure 5.4 A LiDAR image of Alnham.
(Image under Open Government Licence 3.0).

disappeared along with the individual landholdings. In place of the village is a field called Penny Laws whose outline is almost exactly the same as its modern counterpart. The larger outfields are still there, although no longer subdivided, but 90 years later the first edition of the six-inch Ordnance Survey map shows that some of them had been abandoned as well.

Most traces of the old infields have disappeared under modern agriculture, although a few field boundaries can still be identified. However, large areas of rig and furrow

Figure 5.5 Alnham after enclosure.
(Extract from map of Alnham and Alnham Common: Collection of the Duke of Northumberland).

can be seen from the road to the west of the Vicar's Pele, most noticeably on the slope to the south. These are the remains of the field called Castles. Looking north from the same area, sets of gullies can be seen on the steep slope about 100 yards away (Figure 3.26 in Chapter 3). These are hollow-ways – the remains of the tracks shown heading north-west from the village on the 1619 map. Much eroded by water, they show where traffic came down off the moors from Scotland or, in the case of stock, went to the uplands for summer pasture. Their positioning is significant because it was the first opportunity to get to the moors without crossing the village fields. Droving traffic was probably heavy, because on the 1776 estate map the Salter's Road is called the *'Drift Road into Scotland'* and *'To Cocklawfoot'* has been added in ink next to it.

There are other documents that describe activities in and around the old village. The Quarter Sessions records of the early seventeenth century, for example, describe what was probably a normal set of crimes for a rural community. These were usually thefts of sheep, cattle and horses. Occasionally, money was stolen and once there was a knife attack; a John Olyver attacking a yeoman from Alnwick and stabbing him four times in the chest, stomach and arms with a dagger *'worth 12d'*. The report assiduously noted the value of the weapon, as it did for the assault at Murder Cleugh described in Chapter 4.

However, the name of one victim stands out: on July 16th 1604, John, Edward and Robert Howey were charged with riotous assembly *'in the fields of Alnum, striking Henry Guevarra with sticks and staves so that his life was despaired of'*. Guevarra survived, but it's an unusual name to find in a Northumberland village. It turns out that his family had come to England from northern Spain about 50 years earlier. Based in Lincolnshire, one of the children, John Guevarra, became Deputy Warden of the East Marches, an appointment arranged by a distant relative who was Governor of Berwick. Henry was John's brother and he acquired land near Alnham through marriage to a Collingwood. Whether he was attacked because he was a foreigner, a landowner who was over-zealous about rent collection, or just a figure of authority, we don't know. But this was not a one-off event. The next year about 50 villagers, including at least one of the original offenders, Edward Howey, armed themselves *'with staves, swords, knives, daggers, lances, bows and arrows and other offensive and defensive weapons'* and attacked one of Guevarra's properties or landholdings – Ewreden, which maps suggest was near the modern Ewartly Shank on the Salter's Road. He wasn't there, and three of his servants bore the brunt of the violence.

The Guevarra family continued to attract trouble. In the 1640s Henry's daughter Dorothy, by now married and living in Chatton, was accused of witchcraft, apparently because of a family dispute. The alleged victim, a girl called Margaret Muschamp, had periodic fits, claimed she was being attacked by *'the Rogue'*, and once vomited *'stones, coles, brick, lead, straw, quills full of pins, with straw full of pins, tow, and Virginall wire, all full of pins'*. Coincidentally, this happened just before seeing a hitherto unsympathetic judge. In short, although an arrest warrant was issued for Dorothy, and although one of her alleged accomplices confessed and said that the Devil had twice had *'carnall knowledge of her'*, no serious action was taken.

Census records of the nineteenth century are a valuable source of information, shedding light, for example, on itinerant labour. The entry for Alnham in June 1841 lists the extended McMillan family, who are described as Scottish tinplate workers and who may have been camped near Ewartly Shank. There are 14 of them with ages ranging from 60 to three months; we don't know if they were heading back north or coming south for a summer's work, selling pans and mending metal utensils, but it seems almost certain they were using the Salter's Road to travel between Scotland and England.

*Figure 5.6 **The camp on Castle Hill, showing the multiple ramparts and the rectangular buildings.*** *(Image © 2016 Google, Getmapping plc).*

Before leaving the village, there is a notable site just over half a mile to the west. This is the Iron Age camp on Castle Hill, close to the single-track road that leads west from Alnham up to Ewartly Shank (Figure 5.6).

It's a complex structure, in good condition with ramparts up to ten feet high, and it was almost certainly built in a number of phases. One suggested sequence is that it started life with a single low rampart, most of which can still be seen encircling the one-acre central area. Subsequently, two larger sets of ramparts and ditches were built outside this, although less care was taken with ditches on the west side, where the ground falls away steeply to the Spartley Burn. At least one entrance was constructed on the east side. In the next phase a third external rampart was added, which was later strengthened on the north-west side and around an entrance to the south-east. The objective of this final project is not entirely clear. From a point of view of defence, the camp is most vulnerable to an attack from along the spur from the north, but this section of rampart was not improved. Steep slopes give the north-west side much better natural protection but it was nevertheless upgraded. However, it would be the first part of the camp seen by someone coming down the valley, while the south-east ramparts, also upgraded, face the open country beyond Alnham. Perhaps the work was done as a declaration of status and strength.

Finally, clearly visible in the photograph as well as on the ground, sets of rectangular enclosures were built all along the east side of the camp and over some of the ramparts in the north-east quadrant. Remains of roundhouses, sometimes sheltered between the ramparts, are associated with some of these enclosures, and while there has been no excavation, this final development is probably Romano-British in origin. However, there is little sign of any earlier activity inside the camp.

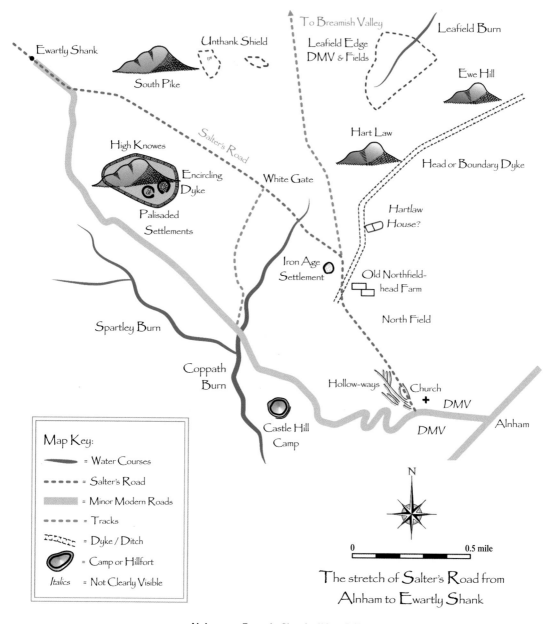

Map Key:

- —— = Water Courses
- - - - - = Salter's Road
- ▬▬▬ = Minor Modern Roads
- - - - - = Tracks
- ⌁⌁⌁⌁ = Dyke / Ditch
- ◯ = Camp or Hillfort
- *Italics* = Not Clearly Visible

The stretch of Salter's Road from Alnham to Ewartly Shank

Alnham to Ewartly Shank. (Map 5.1)

Figure 5.7 Old Northfieldhead farm, with one part of the building just left of centre and the other beyond the stones on the right.

Alnham to Ewartly Shank *(Map 5.1)*

Returning to the village and the Salter's Road, the age of the road and the first use of its name are both unclear. The 1619 map shows a track passing the North Field and following the current path to Ewartly Shank; this was called the *Weandy banck Way,* and where it crosses the Coppath Burn is called *Weandyforde.* In the 1770s there was significant work done to improve this route; the Enclosure Award designated it as a public highway for anyone to use on foot, on horseback or with coaches or carts. People could also *'lead and drive all manner of Cattle along the same'* and the landowners who had benefitted from enclosure had to contribute to its improvement and maintenance.

The modern Salter's Road heads along a wall up the hill behind the church and the Vicar's Pele House, and then runs along the west of a large field. About 150 yards beyond the field's north-west corner are the remains of a substantial stone structure with a few blocks of masonry showing the lines of original walls in among random tumble (Figure 5.7). This is marked on the first OS map as a sheepfold, but a comparison of its position with buildings on the 1776 estate map (Figure 5.5) suggests that it is in fact the remains of the original Northfieldhead Farm, last referred to in the parish registers in 1771.

The ruins are much disturbed. It looks as if the original building consisted of two offset sections, one a rectangle about 40 feet long and 14 feet wide, with the more irregular second one being some 33 feet long and 16 wide. This may have been a byre. A later Northfieldhead Farm was built lower down the slope and about 100 yards to the east of the modern Salter's Road path. There is still a building there and a small area of rig and furrow, in among the larger fields.

When the vegetation is low, areas of rig and furrow can also be seen on the now uncultivated land to the east and north of the old Northfieldhead farm. Whereas modern ploughing has destroyed it on the lower slopes, it survives up here, albeit interspersed with modern drainage ditches and some forestry. Some of the fields shown on the 1619 map can still be identified (Figure 5.8), such as one called *Toftes flatt* on the eastern edge of the field systems at the top of the map in Figure 5.2.

Starting close to old Northfieldhead Farm, a substantial dyke (Figure 5.9) heads north-east; with an accompanying ditch it runs along the edge of the nearby plantation and then sweeps round in a large curve before continuing along the side of the hill. North of the plantation it passes a small oval enclosure within which aerial photographs show very faint traces of walls. These may be all that's left of Hartlaw House, which is at the top of the 1776 map in Figure 5.5 and was last mentioned in the parish registers in 1774.

This dyke seems to fulfil two related functions; firstly, it acts as a head dyke that protects the fields shown in green on the 1619 map and also Hartclay (later, Hartlaw) Field. However, it continues past the field system; although it gets lower and more indistinct, it runs for about a mile before petering out above the neighbouring settlement of Prendwick. It is likely, therefore, that it also acted as a general boundary marker between the moors and the cultivated valley slopes.

Returning to Northfieldhead, the old farm shares its name with a low hill to the north-west. Nothing we've described so far has been much more than 1,000 years old, but on the top of Northfieldhead Hill are the remains of an Iron Age settlement (Figure 5.8). Until they are pointed out the remains are very indistinct; people have walked across them without realising they were there. Official descriptions say that it's a palisaded settlement surrounded by a low bank forming a circle about 60 yards

Figure 5.8 The outline of the field called Toftes flatt (Figure 5.2) is on the right and the Northfieldhead Hill Iron Age settlement is on the left. The old Northfieldhead Farm (Figure 5.7) and the western section of the head dyke (Figure 5.9) are also shown.
(Image © 2016 Google, Infoterra Ltd. & Bluesky and an extract from Figure 5.2: Collection of the Duke of Northumberland).

Figure 5.9 Looking west along the head dyke above the Alnham fields to the east of Salter's Road.

across. This bank is extremely hard to see at ground level, but definite traces of some 15 roundhouses show up as circular grooves, most about 25 feet in diameter.

Although the hill is steep in places, especially to the south, the site is not very defensible, because the hilltop is really a projecting ridge along which an attack from the moors to the north would be quite easy. However, with a beautiful view across the valley to the south and east it was probably occupied for some time; quite a few of the roundhouse grooves overlap, suggesting several generations of building. Other people may have had the same idea about the position and the view because there is another very similar settlement on top of Hart Law, about half a mile to the north-east.

The Salter's Road continues past Northfieldhead Hill and heads north-west up onto the moors, leaving a well-maintained farm track and dropping through some hollow-ways towards a distant gate in a boundary fence. However, before heading through the gate we'll describe a site further along the farm track and just to its east.

This is the deserted medieval village (DMV) of Leafield Edge. Situated at a height of about 1,000 feet, the settlement itself covers a rectangular area measuring some 150 yards from north to south and 50 yards east to west. This contains the remains of several building platforms for houses or barns, the low enclosure walls of small paddocks and a shallow sunken track running along the length of the area.

What is more remarkable, however, is the field system to the east. Covering about 120 acres, several sets of rig and furrow lead down to a stream at the bottom of a shallow valley and then continue up the slope towards a ridge on the other side (Figure 5.10). Near the top, these fields are bounded by a sizeable head dyke, but there are traces of later cultivation beyond it. Apart from a small plantation at the northern

Figure 5.10 The central part of the Leafield Edge field system.

corner of the system, the structures are almost completely undamaged and are one of the best-preserved arable areas in the Cheviots.

It is not known for how long the fields were productive in the face of a deteriorating climate, or when the village was finally abandoned. The cultivated area appears on both the 1619 and 1776 maps of the Alnham estate, although no buildings are shown, but the parish records list the baptism of an Adam Oliver *(Olepher)* in 1743 and the burial of an Ann Scott *(Scot)* in 1760, both described as being *'in the Lee Field'* (which is the same as the spelling on the 1776 map).

Back on the Salter's Road, the route passes through the gate mentioned above (known as the White Gate) and continues north-west towards the farm at Ewartly Shank, which is over a mile away. There are two interesting sites along this stretch.

500 yards beyond the gate, as the path passes a hill called High Knowes on the left, a long low dyke can be seen running parallel with the track about 100 yards up the slope. This is actually the north-eastern section of a roughly oval enclosure bank that encircles the upper slopes of the entire hill at around the 1,200-foot contour. The structure is about a mile and three quarters around and enfolds some 120 acres; in some places, especially to the north-west of the hill, it's very indistinct, but elsewhere is nearly two feet high. For a stretch of about 400 yards along the south-west side it seems to split into two. Towards the top of High Knowes are structures that may explain why this dyke was built.

On the south-eastern shoulder of the hill are two palisaded settlements about 150 yards apart that probably date from the Late Bronze Age or the Early Iron Age and which were investigated by George Jobey in 1962 and 1963 (Figure 5.11).

The western settlement, High Knowes A, is roughly circular, about 50 yards across and surrounded by ditches which represent the remains of a double palisade. These have obviously been eroded but the space between them consists of a low mound six

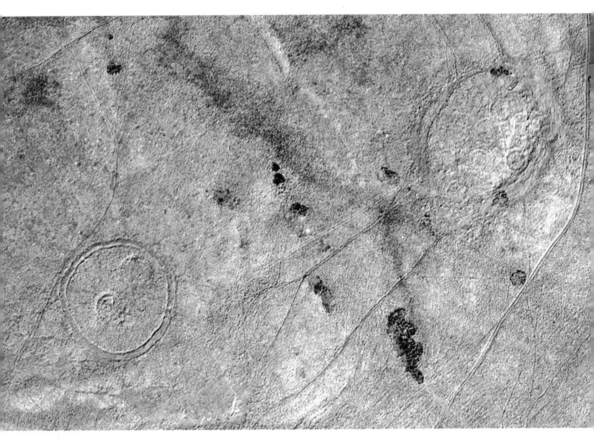

Figure 5.11 **The High Knowes settlements.** (Image © 2016 Google, Getmapping plc).

Figure 5.12 **The trenches of the double palisade around the western settlement at High Knowes.**

feet across (Figure 5.12). Remarkably, after 2,500 years or more, the nature of the grass between the ditches still differs from that outside them, perhaps because the soil there mainly came from the palisade trenches. The palisades have been breached in several places, but the original entrance was about six or seven feet wide and on the east side. Jobey excavated this and found closely-set postholes for timbers that would have been about eight inches in diameter.

Inside the palisades are the remains of four roundhouses. The biggest of these, and the one Jobey focused on, is about 40 feet across. He discovered that the edges were formed by a narrow trench about a foot wide that had been cut to take closely-set timbers secured in place by stones. Two larger postholes flanked the building's eastern entrance. Inside the building there were additional postholes that may have held roof supports; there were also sets of scoops or short ditches, which Jobey suggested could have had several different functions, ranging from the mucking out of cattle to the creation of sleeping accommodation.

The eastern settlement, High Knowes B, is slightly larger and somewhat different. The palisade trenches are less obvious, but the interior contains the remains of 16 roundhouses ranging from 24 to 38 feet in diameter. This makes it more of a village; few of the houses seem to overlap so it's possible that the majority were in use at the same time, providing homes for a considerable number of people. Jobey excavated the remains of one of the smaller ones and exposed the stone foundations of a hut with a central hearth. A wall extending from the hut cut across the groove of another roundhouse; this, together with the discovery of some fragmentary pot sherds, led to the suggestion that it was a later Romano-British structure exploiting an existing, slightly sheltered position.

Aerial photographs show signs of cultivation on the slopes of High Knowes to the east and south-east of the settlements, as well as field boundary banks running downhill. These are very hard to see on the ground, but appear to stop at the dyke encircling the hill. So although there's no definite proof of a connection, it may be that High Knowes was once home to a Bronze Age or Iron Age community living in defended settlements on the upper slopes, with some fields below them protected by a boundary dyke around the hill.

On the other side of Salter's Road from High Knowes, and about 400 yards to the north-east, is a second site of interest. This has no modern name – the only thing marked on Ordnance Survey maps is a sheep stell – but on the 1776 Alnham estate map it's shown as an area of just over four acres called *Unthank Shield*.

On the ground there's an irregular-shaped area of rig and furrow surrounded by a dyke up to three feet high (Figure 5.13). Inside there are two fields separated by another low dyke running across the whole enclosure; the larger field to the north, has rigs aligned east to west, while in the southern one they run from north to south. The rigs are straight and about 18 feet from crest to crest. There are no signs of headlands, either between the two fields or at their edges by the dyke, so this suggests that the structure was either ploughed by a horse that could turn sharply at the end of each pass, or else built by hand. The size of the enclosed area is as noted in 1776; there may be the remains of a building in the north-east corner but at ground level it's hard to see. A large entrance has been cut through the dyke on the east side but this is modern, providing access to the sheep stell built on top of the rig and furrow.

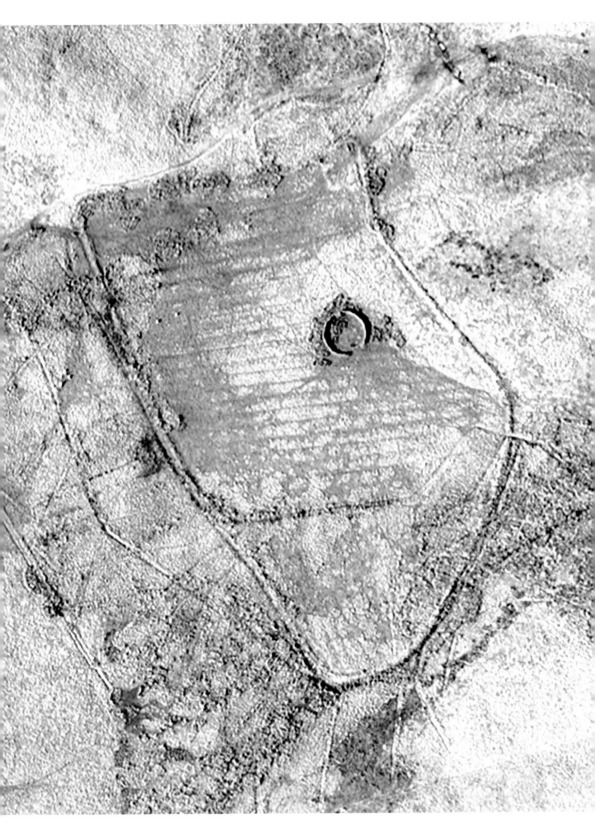

*Figure 5.13 **The main area of cultivation at Unthank Shield.***
(Image © 2016 Google, Infoterra Ltd. & Bluesky).

About 200 yards to the east is another area of rig and furrow, which is not marked on any map. It's smaller, at just over an acre, and surrounded by a low dyke on a south facing slope above a small burn. The rigs run across the slope, are less distinct than in the main enclosure and vary in width between seven and ten feet. This looks as if it may well have been built by hand.

Little is known about this site. One of the few definite conclusions is that the name connects it with the hamlet, now just a farm, of Unthank[2]. This was about a mile to the east of Alnham, and the use of the word *Shield* implies that the community there took their stock along the Salter's Road and used the site as a shieling for summer pasturage.

However, although it's unusual to find this amount of rig and furrow next to a shieling, it's unlikely that it was a proper farm. Smaller than six acres, it probably wasn't big enough to be a going concern, especially with the reduced crop yields at this altitude. At nearly 1,100 feet it's between 100 and 250 feet higher than the fields at Leafield Edge, and those were 20 times the size. Six acres here might have provided 50 bushels of oats per year, or just enough to support two people. Any diet would have been supplemented by milk and cheese from stock grazing on the moor, but it's hard to see how the result would have been enough to keep even a small family. However, it must have been used enough for it to be considered a home for some people; in June 1746 the Alnham registers record the burial of a Robert Hall of Unthank Sheall.

We don't know when it was built. Although it doesn't appear on the 1619 map, there is a hint that it may have been in use by then, because the name of a now-lost track that leads to the area from Leafield is *Shield Rig Way*. If it was there then, it may have its origins in the Middle Ages, before the border troubles started. A 1726 estate map has an unnamed patch of green of exactly the right shape in the right place, and it must have been abandoned sometime between 1776 and the 1861 survey for the first six-inch Ordnance Survey map, which doesn't show it.

The dyke would have protected any crops from stock that were grazing on the surrounding moorland, but we don't know what was being grown. Given the altitude and the exposed conditions, it may well have been a robust variety of oats, but it could have been a forage crop such as vetch that was used to feed sheep in the winter. Whatever was grown must have just added to a diet rather than supported it completely. With the likely yields and the gradually deteriorating climate, it's possible that the eastern field was developed to increase – or just maintain – output.

Finally, just beyond the eastern end of that field is something rather sad. On December 3rd 1863 Nellie Heron, who had been visiting a friend in Alnham on her way home from Rothbury, ignored pleas from locals to spend the night there and set off home, over the moors to Hartside in the Breamish valley. She was last seen disappearing into a snowstorm, singing a popular hymn. A small memorial stone marks the spot where her body was found the next day (Figure 5.14).

Nellie was not the only person to die like this. Nearly 100 years later, in November 1962, two shepherds, Jock Scott and Willie Middlemas, were on their way from Rothbury to Ewartly Shank and took the track from Alnham that headed west past Castle Hill. Driving a tractor, they dropped a friend, Willie Bulloch, after less than a mile at Castle Hill Farm and went on their way. They must have lost the route; with

---

[2]This unusual name derives from the Old English *unthances* meaning 'without permission', implying that the farm's original occupiers were squatters.

*Figure 5.14 **Nellie Heron's memorial stone.***

no phone at Ewartly Shank the alarm was not raised for two days, and their bodies were discovered about half a mile from their destination. In 2007 a memorial cairn was placed on the western slopes of High Knowes near where they were found.

The origins of the farm at Ewartly Shank are uncertain. The 1619 map of the Alnham estate does not show any building on the site, but the name *Ev-erlawe* is written nearby, and the crossing of the watercourse (now the Shank Burn) just to the west is identified as *Ev-erdeane forde*. The report of the attack on Henry Guevarra's property quite probably referred to this location, so the area was certainly in use in the early seventeenth century. The 1726 map shows nothing, but the Armstrongs' county map of 1769 shows '*Shank*' and the more detailed 1776 enclosure map has a building called *Shank House*, with the moor to the north called *Ewerlaw Shank*.

Most of the buildings there now are relatively modern, but there is one older one (Figure 5.15). This was probably used for stock rather than people because there is no sign of a hearth or a place for a fire inside.

It is very hard to date accurately, and the best that specialists can say was that it was originally built between the seventeenth and early nineteenth centuries; it has been updated and altered at least once, and maybe periodically. The roof, in particular, is probably relatively recent because the timbers appear to display circular saw-marks; it is, however, deteriorating quite rapidly.

The building is rectangular, about 30 feet long and 16 wide, with walls seven feet high. Made of unfinished stone with few discernible courses and no mortar, the construction

*Figure 5.15 **The central part of the old building at Ewartly Shank.***

is not unlike that of a large sheep stell, but perhaps not as good. There is one main door and two windows; a second door has been knocked through in the west end of the structure, and the interior is just a single space.

Stock being driven along the Salter's Road *(The Drift Road to Scotland)* would have passed right by Ewartly Shank. There are no records of how the droving was managed, but it is possible that animals coming south would have spent the night in the relatively sheltered upper Breamish valley before heading on to Alnham. Whether they would have stopped here and grazed at the farm or been driven on through, we cannot say.

Ewartly Shank to the Border *(Map 5.2)*

After leaving Ewartly Shank and crossing the Shank Burn, the track continues north-west up to higher ground, eventually reaching some 1,400 feet as it passes north of Cushat Law. *Cushat* is a regional word meaning pigeon, but it's open to misunderstanding; in his map of 1750 Thomas Kitchin unfortunately labelled the hill as *Cowshit Law.*

Apart from the occasional sheep stell, there is little of archaeological interest along this stretch until the descent into the Breamish valley. Here, about half a mile apart, we find two farms; High and Low Bleakhope – as the Ordnance Survey refers to them – or Blakehope, an older spelling and one closer to local pronunciation.

The name may be derived from the Old English *hope* meaning valley and *blaec* meaning black or dark. As with Ewartly Shank, the origins of the farms are uncertain. No

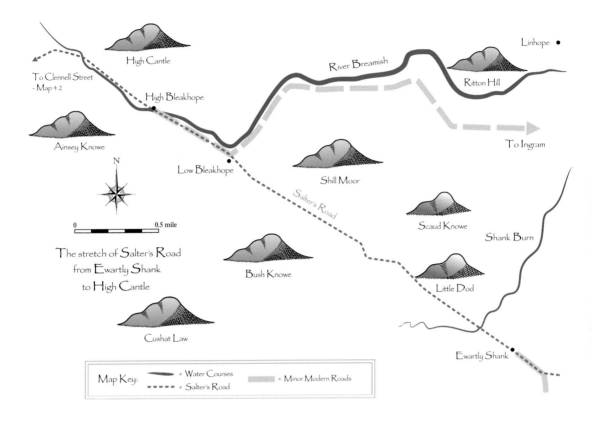

Ewartly Shank to High Cantle. (Map 5.2)

buildings are shown on the 1619 Alnham map, but the name was already in use. The burn leading down to the Breamish from the south-east, now Hope Sike, was called *Blakeup Burn*, while the higher ground to the west of the modern Low Bleakhope had the delightful name of *Wallopping Knowle*. At least one farm was probably functioning by 1697, because in that year a William Burne of Blackhope made his will, splitting his estate between his wife, his children and a grandson. At least 54 pounds of *'inglish money'* are specifically identified, so he was by no means a poor man.

The 1726 estate map shows two farms in operation – an *Upper Blakehopp* and an *Under Blakehopp*. In April 1771 marriage banns were read in Ingram church for a Mary Davidson of *High Blackup* and George Douglas of Linhope, a bit further down the valley. Both farms – called High and Low Blakehope – are shown on the 1776 enclosure map.

The age of some of the buildings is hard to assess. The old house at Low Blakehope was replaced by a bungalow in the 1950s; as is often the case the older building was kept for uses such as a hay store and a generator house. The main house at High Blakehope is modern as well.

Past the farms, the track continues up the Breamish valley for a short distance, before heading west for about three miles to the junction with Clennell Street just south of the border. The route is across moorland and through forestry and in among the latter is the most spectacular sight in the area, a remote waterfall on the Usway Burn called Davidson's Linn. It isn't the largest waterfall in the Cheviots, but in the right conditions it's probably one of the most attractive (see Map 4.2).

About 400 yards further down the Usway Burn, at the junction with a stream running in from the west through a small valley called Inner Hare Cleugh, are the remains of a whisky still – the one named after Black Rory who was mentioned in Chapter 3. Never excavated, and well-enough hidden to make it hard to find without good directions, a now-ruined rectangular building about 18 feet long and nine feet wide has been cut into the hillside. The wall against the upslope (to the left in the picture) is about three feet high, and there's little or no visible tumble from it. Less survives of the downhill wall, although random blocks suggest it was quite substantial. Beyond the firehole in Figure 5.16 is the circular kiln; about five feet across it now hosts a tree, but there is still some interior stonework visible.

The building was probably a working area, used for both malting and distillation. The walls may have had a wooden superstructure to provide more headroom and the building probably had a turf or heather roof for additional camouflage, with the water supply coming from the adjacent streams. Although very remote, it was well positioned for the distiller to take his product either down Clennell Street to

Figure 5.16 Rory's still – looking along the rectangular building to the firehole for the kiln.

Alwinton, or west to Alnham on the Salter's Road. He might have sold refreshment to local farmers and passing travellers as well.

Unlike the still at Wholehope described in the previous chapter, no signs of domestic activity have been identified here. There may have been some other building nearby that has disappeared, or perhaps the people that worked here lived at Uswayford and walked to work.

Half a mile further on, the Salter's Road joins Clennell Street, and the traffic between Scotland and England would have used that as the route over the border and down to Cocklawfoot – a path that was described in the previous chapter.

A standing stone on The Street above Hownam.

Chapter 6

The Street

Unlike some of the other Border Roads, in particular Dere Street, where we have a reasonably good understanding of the history and the origins of the route, information about The Street is rather more tenuous. However, its route through the hills, following a long ridge from the border extending south to the Coquet and another north-west towards Hownam, means that it must have always been an attractive way to cross the Cheviots.

The name was in use by the middle of the nineteenth century, appearing on the first edition of the six-inch Ordnance Survey maps. Surveyed in 1859, these also label it as a *'Drove Road'* and the route shown is almost identical to the modern path.

Figure 6.1 Roy's map: the label 'Clattering Path' is written across the border. Calroust farm is at top left.

However, the Greenwood map of 1828 does not give it a name but shows a track that leaves the Coquet to follow the valley of the Rowhope Burn east of the current path before making its way to the high ground beyond Loft Hill and thence to the border.

Many earlier maps don't mark it at all, although in the middle of the eighteenth century William Roy showed a path that was close to the current route south of the border and for about a mile to the north, before dropping down the slope to the east to the farm at Calroust and heading north along the valley to Belford (Figure 6.1). There's still a footpath that follows this line. Roy called this route the 'Clattering Path', a name that Greenwood assigned to a Northumbrian path to the east of The Street that passes Ward Law on its way to the border just west of Windy Gyle.

The origin of the name *Clattering* is unclear, although there are claims that it comes from the noise of either stock or troops moving along the road. There is another Clattering Path about 35 miles to the north-west, a track that crosses the southern slopes of Minch Moor south of Traquair; elsewhere there are Clattering Burns, Clattering Sikes and at least one Clattering Ford.

Some two hundred years before Roy, in 1543, the border crossing-point at Black Braes was listed in Henry VIII's papers as one of the *'ingates and passages forth of Scotland upon the Middle Marches'*. Black Braes is where the modern Street reaches the border.

Even earlier, between 1165 and 1185 the charters of Melrose Abbey refer to a gift of Scottish land (specifically, a peatery) bounded on the west by *Herdstrete*. This seems to have been the boundary between Hownam and the old parish of Mow that was centred on Bowmont Water, a line close to that of the current track. In Old and Middle English, *herd* was also *hierd* or *heord*, meaning a shepherd or a herdsman – which may be a clue as to who used it.

However, even allowing for inaccuracies and misattributions, the impression that old maps give is one of a route that is more of a general direction than a fixed path. Nevertheless, with the rich set of Iron Age structures that lies along the current track in Scotland, it seems likely that the modern Street has at least been one of the choices for the route since prehistoric times. This path still carried commercial traffic as late as the end of the nineteenth century; in 1956 a shepherd at Mainside, a farm south of Hownam, was recorded as remembering cartloads of oatmeal being taken up The Street for customers south of the border some 60 years earlier.

Modern Ordnance Survey maps first use the label 'The Street' as the path leaves the Coquet and heads up to the border. North of the border, and coming in the other direction, the name is first used just south of the track that connects Hownam with Belford. When it was a working thoroughfare, travellers could have made choices about their route at these two points. In the Coquet valley most would probably have taken the road to Alwinton and beyond, although a minority might have turned upstream towards Dere Street at Coquet Head. On the north side of the border, the route to Hownam would have served Morebattle and Kelso, while that to Belford opened up opportunities towards the Yetholms. Indeed, there is still a shortcut in that direction that leaves The Street further south near Blackbrough Hill and joins the track from Belford to Hownam about a mile from Belford.

For the purposes of this book, however, we will start on the Coquet at Wedder Leap, near the farm at Barrowburn, head up to the border and then take the route that goes down to Hownam, finally looking at a few sites north of there on the road to Morebattle.

Wedder Leap to Slymefoot (Map 6.1)

According to local antiquarians, the name Wedder Leap is based on the story of a sheep rustler who made off with one of his prizes (a wedder) tied round his neck. Pursued and trapped, he tried to jump the river but the sheep's weight was too much for him and he fell into the pool below; some versions of the story say he drowned. This may be true, but it should be remembered that there are several places in the Cheviots where someone allegedly made their escape – or tried to – by jumping over an unlikely chasm.

Now very peaceful, not long ago this was a busy area; the building next to the car park, now a hay barn, is actually equipped with a dance floor. Built in 1935 and called Askew Hall after its benefactor, it was used for social events of which the best known were probably the dances. People came to these from as far afield as the Breamish valley and Cocklawfoot, over the border in Scotland. Sometimes arriving on horseback, they would dance through the night to bands like Jimmy Shand's, leaving at dawn to go back to work. But a declining population and improved transport reduced the need for the building; it was sold not long after the Second World War and is now used for quieter purposes.

Opening much earlier than Askew Hall, and surviving it as well, was the school. Throughout the early nineteenth century, local children were often educated by travelling teachers who moved from farm to farm, providing lessons in exchange for board, lodging and a few pence. The 1861 census recorded one of these, a 26-year-old teacher and lecturer called Robert Julyan, staying at Uswayford. But by 1879, local parents felt that this was no longer satisfactory and a public subscription

Figure 6.2 *The old school above Barrowburn, probably taken in the 1920s. To the left is the teacher's house, and left again are the ruins of the farm of Lounges Knowe.*
(Image courtesy www.rothbury.co.uk).

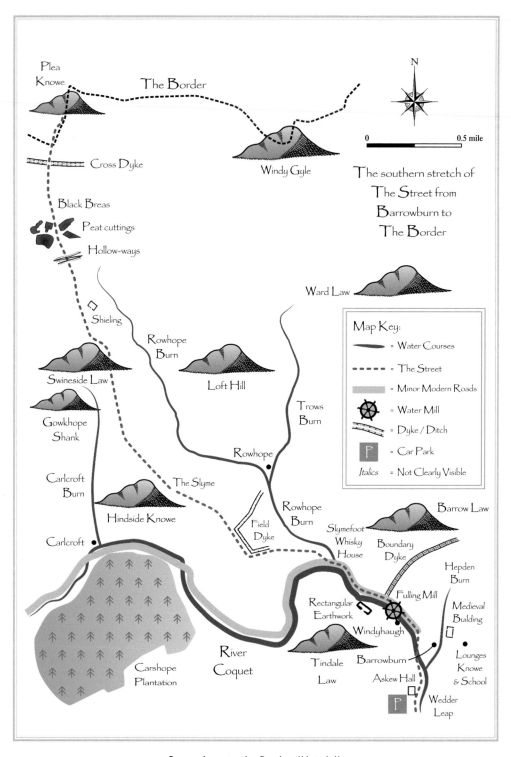

Barrowburn to the Border. (Map 6.1)

was organised to set up a school in a building at Lounges Knowe, a now-abandoned farm on the slopes above Barrowburn (Figure 6.2). Boarding at the nearby farm of Windyhaugh, the teacher appointed was Andrew Faa Blythe, who had lost an arm in a childhood shooting accident.

Reputedly a gypsy, he may have been related to the Blythe family who for over 100 years provided the popular kings and queens of the gypsy community in Yetholm – a sequence ending with Esther Faa Blythe who 'reigned' from 1861 to 1883, and her son Charles who, perhaps to encourage the tourist trade, was persuaded to accept the crown in 1898. However, although any formal connection is unclear, Andrew may well have been of gypsy stock; early Scottish census records show he was indeed born in Yetholm and that his mother and his grandfather were 'hawkers of crockery'.

The census of 1911 listed his formal name as Andrew Richardson Blythe. Aged 59, he was living in the three-room house recently built for him next to the school. Robert Dixon, the local postman, was boarding with him, an arrangement that may have helped boost Blythe's income. In 1903 this had been set at £87 a year; because of his disability he was unable to teach the full curriculum and so five pounds of this was set aside to pay for a sewing mistress.

Blythe retired in 1919 after 40 years' service. Despite having to battle with problems with the water supply, the plumbing and the sanitary arrangements, the teachers that followed him ensured that the school prospered and got good reports from inspectors. In the 1920s there were about two dozen children enrolled; in the early 1960s there were still some 20 pupils, but it was becoming clear that the building was no longer fit for purpose. After prolonged discussions, a new school was built next to Askew Hall, finally opening in 1971. But falling rolls meant that its days were numbered; it closed in 1978, the building was demolished and the current car park built.

It's not clear when the road up the valley from Alwinton was first metalled, but the area had always been isolated. At Barrowburn, the route of the modern road

Figure 6.3 The old farmhouse at Barrowburn, with Windyhaugh beyond it.
(Image courtesy www.rothbury.co.uk).

probably dates from the 1930s, when the bridge over the Coquet was built and the road beyond was improved. Before that, maps show it looping round the east end of the old farmhouse (on the right in Figure 6.3) and then heading north-west along what is now a farm track to meet the current route again. Barrowburn acted as a hub for the farms in the upper valley, with deliveries of food and supplies being left there for collection, and church services sometimes being held in the farm's kitchen. In severe winters access was almost impossible; even local pupils were unable to get to school and the doctor sometimes used skis to get to patients.

The three farms in the immediate area are all old. Barrowburn dates from at least the first half of the eighteenth century and if Lounges Knowe is the same as *Lounderingknow*, then it was operating in 1663 when an entry of that name appears in a list of rentals and rates for Kidland. There is certainly a will dated 1684 for a John Pratt of *Loungers Knowe*. His three young daughters were left orphaned, and their uncle Cuthbert Pratt of Carlcroft, just up the valley, was appointed their guardian. John's estate was valued at £170 and the items in the inventory range from 420 sheep valued at £100 to 'one Candlestike a Quart pott one Tankett one potting dishe' worth three shillings.

The 1604 Survey of Debateable and Border Lands lists *Windie Haugh* as one of the *'Summer and Shieldinge Grounds'* in the Manor of Harbottle, and it was an active farm by the middle of the seventeenth century. When its owner, John Potts, died in 1662 his possessions were valued at £540; well over half of this was made up of stock on the farm. But he had also lent money to people; the inventory lists 80 debtors with liabilities ranging from £160 down to nine shillings. In all, his estate was worth £1,125, which made him wealthy in comparison with his neighbours.

There are medieval references to the area as well. Barrowburn is on the Hepden Burn, and in 1233 'Heppeden' is listed as paying tithes to Alwinton, while in 1296 a *John of Hepden* was one of the 40 people paying tax in the parish.

Around this time, one particular family was having a major influence on the area. The Umfravilles had come to England soon after the Norman invasion and were initially based in Prudhoe. Subsequently, they were given land in Redesdale and Coquetdale and built castles at Elsdon and Harbottle. In 1181 they started to grant large land holdings north of the Coquet to the Cistercian monks of Newminster Abbey near Morpeth, first through leases and then gifts. This land, the Kidland estate, came down to the banks of the Coquet in the Barrowburn area.

The monks were diligent businessmen, keeping detailed reports of their transactions; the chartulary in which some of these were recorded has survived. One entry shows that between 1226 and 1244 they negotiated with the Umfravilles, who still owned the land south of the Coquet, about building a pond for a fulling mill on the river near Windyhaugh. Not only was sheep farming an important part of the upland economy for milk and cheese, but it seems that the monks were planning to process wool in the area as well.

Fulling was an important part of the cloth production cycle, following shearing, spinning and weaving. When first woven, especially if by hand, cloth is very loose, like sacking, and too greasy to be dyed. The fulling process soaked the cloth and pummelled it in water together with an agent such as fuller's earth. If this was not

Figure 6.4 The mill's wheel pit.

Figure 6.5 The remains of the washing area below the wheel pit.

available, then substances such as urine and burnt bracken were used instead. This tightened the cloth and removed grease. After fulling, the cloth was rinsed and stretched out on tentering frames to dry and bleach in the sun; the word 'tenterhooks' comes from the way the cloth was attached to those frames.

In 2010, members of Coquetdale Community Archaeology (CCA) walked the riverbank when the water levels were low looking for clues to the mill's whereabouts. Finding two or three blocks of masonry and some timber which testing showed was medieval, a full excavation was mounted.

The most notable find was the wheel pit buried in the bed of the river (Figure 6.4.) 16 feet long and made of high quality stonework, it had presumably been built by the masons responsible for the abbey in Morpeth. Some of the blocks were missing, either

Figure 6.6 *The location of the mill machinery.*

Figure 6.7 **Late sixteenth-century fulling machinery.**
(Image from Biblioteca Nacional de Madrid).

washed away or taken for use elsewhere, but abrasions on those that were left established the position of the wheel and its diameter, which was about 11 feet. The curved shape of the block at the entry to the pit showed that it had been of a low breast shot configuration; this means that the water did not hit the blades of the wheel at the bottom, but rather part way up one side. This made it more efficient, with the wheel being turned both by the impact of the water and its weight on the blades; it's the earliest known such configuration in the country.

A wooden structure was found on the river bed just downstream from the wheel pit (Figure 6.5).

It seems that it originally consisted of a floor enclosed by low, timber walls and was probably where workers washed the cloth after the fulling process. The outflow from the mill would have provided constant clean water and the agents used in the fulling process could have been removed before the cloth was dried.

Figure 6.8 The upstream 'floor'. It is about 15 feet long.

With the position of the mill wheel known, excavations on the bank revealed associated structures. Low walls bounded an area with some cobbled and paved surfaces that yielded medieval finds such as pottery, coins and a key. Near the river, a revetment protected the site of the mill machinery (Figure 6.6).

This might have been very lightweight (see Figure 6.7 for a later example), and no trace of it was left. Nor was there any sign of a building, and there may never have been one. Unlike a corn mill, where the product has to be kept dry, fulling is a process based around water and so shelter is unnecessary.

About 60 yards upstream from the wheel pit, investigators found what looked like a wooden floor lying on the riverbed (Figure 6.8). Also medieval, it consisted of three large timber baulks placed across the stream, with a total of ten heavy wooden planks fastened across them.

Mortices showed there had been vertical posts mounted in each baulk; three of these were still in position. There are several theories about the structure's function; it might be the remains of an early corn mill powered by a horizontal wheel or it could have been the floor of a sluice system feeding water to a leat for the mill downstream.

The monks must have made a major investment in building this remote mill. The pit probably contained at least five tons of masonry; there is no suitable quarry close by and all the stone would have been brought up the valley. And then there was the timber, much of which would not have been available locally; indeed, some of it showed signs of re-use and may have come from earlier buildings elsewhere.

Why did they go to all this effort? It may have been because the local population provided them with cheap labour, and contemporary documents show the monks had a farm just up the valley at Rowhope, so the steward there could have managed the business. The remote location also put them beyond the influence of the guilds in Morpeth. These would have had considerable control over the monks' operations, with rules about the number of apprentices and restrictions on who could be a weaver.

However, the venture was not successful. The Anglo-Scottish troubles started in 1296 and may well have caused the monks to abandon both the mill and the Kidland estate;

their last documented presence in the area was in 1304 and records for nearby settlements a few years later refer to '*destruction and burning by the Scots*'. Other factors, such as plague (the Black Death came in 1349), an increase in sheep disease and the famine caused by a series of disastrous harvests between 1315 and 1317 may also have made the location less attractive. In 1538, when Henry VIII dissolved the abbey, his surveyors described the area as '*lying waste*' and being '*ravaged by the Scots each year*'.

Unlike many other mills the site was never redeveloped, and this explains why so much of the original structure was found. Very few medieval mills have been excavated in England, and there are none where a masonry wheel pit has survived in such good condition. Although the excavations on the bank have been filled in, part of the wheel pit can still be seen in the riverbed by the bank opposite Windyhaugh Farm.

The project provided a valuable insight into life in the medieval valley. With some 17,000 acres of rough grazing, the Kidland estate could have supported up to 5,000 sheep. These would have needed a lot of shepherds; there were still wolves in the area, so they had to take good care of their stock as well as milking them every day. And the shepherds' families must have been sufficiently numerous to support a cloth production industry, with activities ranging from clipping through to spinning, weaving and fulling.

All this meant that there must have been a substantial population in the area. There are few immediate signs of this, but there are one or two sites that hint at their presence. One of these, about 200 yards up the Hepden Burn behind Barrowburn Farm, has been the subject of a second excavation by CCA.

Close by the burn, the site initially consisted of a set of low banks forming a roughly rectangular enclosure about 60 feet long and 20 feet wide. Excavation revealed several phases of construction, and showed that for much of their length these banks

Figure 6.9 The medieval floor and the later cobbled floor beyond.

contained crude but substantial walls, while a cobbled floor covered a good part of the area inside the enclosure. Finds included fragments of pottery and a piece of a drinking glass, but for dating purposes the most useful discoveries were clay smoking pipes. The makers' stamps on these showed that they came from both Tyneside and Edinburgh, with the earliest being from the middle of the seventeenth century. This was at the time when the Kidland estate was being revived after the end of the border conflicts.

The cobbles extended through the entrance and on to land outside the enclosure. Beneath them and extending even further was an earlier floor of large, irregular flagstones; these were flat on their upper surfaces but of varying thicknesses and each had been laid carefully in order to make a smooth surface (Figure 6.9). Fourteenth-century pot sherds were found on top of it, strongly suggesting the floor was medieval.

These floors were clearly inside buildings of some sort, but we don't know what they were for. There were no traces of hearths, so they probably weren't residential, but the earlier floor, in particular, is of surprisingly high quality for an agricultural structure and suggests it was commissioned by the Newminster monks. It may have been required for jobs such as weaving that needed a clean, flat surface; however, no discarded loom weights were found. A possibility is that it was the floor of a storage shed for the wool from a summer's clip, which would have rapidly become unusable if it got wet. The building was probably abandoned because of the border conflicts and then rebuilt, with a new floor, in the seventeenth century. It certainly looks as if some of the flagstones from the medieval floor were used in the walls of the later building.

About half a mile up the Coquet from Barrowburn is a similar, but larger structure. This is on the far side of the river from the road and is harder to investigate, because it's in the Controlled Area of the ranges. Its agricultural provenance is slightly more obvious, because there is an entrance in its east end which opens out into what looks like a stock enclosure. It's not known if this too has medieval origins, but a structure that almost certainly does lies practically opposite. Here, running down the slopes of Barrow Law above the road is a prominent dyke and ditch that can be linked to a description of an estate boundary in the Newminster records. It can be traced up the hill for half a mile or so, to a point just beyond the track that runs up Barrow Law heading north from Barrowburn. This is probably an old path, because it doesn't just cut through the dyke but rather uses what appears to be a man-made opening.

A tributary enters the Coquet some 600 yards further upstream. This is the Rowhope Burn; now crossed by a bridge, there used to be a ford here and the remains of the old track leading down to it can be seen a few yards below the bridge. This spot is marked on old maps as *Slymefoot* (or *Slimefoot*), so called because the long ridge leading down to it from the border is the *Slyme*, with the area at the top sometimes being referred to as *Slymehead*.

The Street runs up the Slyme, but Slymefoot is best known for being the reported site of an old drinking house. The earliest reference to this was in Eneas Mackenzie's book *A View of the County of Northumberland*, published around 1820. His writing was, to put it mildly, subjective and it contains more than a modicum of moralising: he refers to the people of the area as being *'devoted to a tame, languid and insipid occupation'* and

Figure 6.10 **The dyke showing some exposed stones.**

therefore *'fond of strong liquors which ....by a temporary madness vary the uniform circulation of thought'*. He then describes the Slymefoot whisky-house as being built on a whinstone rock on the north bank of the Coquet and being *'the winter rendezvous of all the neighbouring sheep-farmers'*. This is followed by references to *'gambling and hard drinking'*, *'a whirl of dissipation'* and *'days passing by unheeded'*. He reports that, when news of this reached the rector of Rothbury, Thomas Sharp, he closed the establishment down, thus putting an end to *'riotous assemblies'*.

Sharp was appointed rector in 1720. He was a busy man, also being chaplain to the Archbishop of York and then Archdeacon of Northumberland and canon of Durham Cathedral, as well as holding clerical posts in Yorkshire and Nottinghamshire. Despite this, he kept the Rothbury appointment until he died in 1758. This means that Mackenzie was writing about events that happened many years earlier, so his reports must have been based on hearsay or on a now-lost source. Subsequent writers who have referred to this establishment as a pub or an inn are probably providing it with a degree of formality it never really had.

While no sign of it can be seen today, this is not necessarily surprising. There has been road construction and other work in the immediate area, but if a local entrepreneur wanted to sell whisky to local farmers and to travellers along The Street then it would have been a good site to choose.

On the lower slopes of the field immediately to the west of the Rowhope Burn and just upstream from the bridge are the remains of low banks that form three sides of a small rectangle measuring about 80 by 50 feet. This enclosure may be linked to a now-lost building down by the burn itself. Early maps show one there, and the Harbottle Presbyterian Church records list a William and Margaret Hall of *Slime foot* having two daughters (Isibell and Anne) baptised in July 1737.

Slymefoot to the Border (Map 6.1)

As it climbs away from the Coquet, The Street passes two sets of old boundary dykes. The first of these is a low bank that defines a triangular field in the space between the river and the Rowhope Burn. The second, more interesting one, is a larger bank parallel with the path that becomes apparent after a few hundred yards (Figure 6.10). As The Street, which has been heading broadly west, turns north-west, so does this bank, and it then runs next to the track for another 400 yards before turning again and heading downhill towards the farm at Rowhope.

At various points erosion shows that the bank has a stone core. Its age is uncertain, but it is tempting to think that it's another of the boundary dykes built by the Newminster monks in connection with their grange in the valley below, with The Street following a route outside it on its way up to the ridge. There are certainly several similar structures in the area and a set of them can be seen from the track leading up from Rowhope to Uswayford.

After leaving this dyke, The Street crosses an area that from an archaeological perspective is relatively barren. It first passes Hindside Knowe and then Swineside Law, which may refer to animals that lived here. Along this stretch, a fine area of rig and furrow can be seen to the west, draped over the spur of Gowkhope Shank on the other side of the Carlcroft Burn.

Just north of Swineside Law, as the path drops to cross a saddle, about 80 yards to the east are the remains of a small, one-room building and an enclosure about 70 feet square. It seems likely that this is an old shieling, but it's not clear whether the enclosure was built to hold stock or to keep them out. Just beyond this, a track zig-zags down the slope on the west of the Rowhope Burn, crossing it at a ford and ending up at a modern shed on the other side. The track is well-defined and has clearly had considerable use; next to the modern shed there are the vestiges of an earlier building, but these may be all that's left of a sheepfold marked on the Ordnance Survey map of the 1860s.

Leaving the saddle, The Street climbs towards Black Braes. It's a relatively steep ascent and the slope is criss-crossed with old tracks made at various times by travellers avoiding eroded areas and finding new ways up. While the saddle is quite well-drained, the terrain reverts to peat bog at the top and there are cuttings on either side of the path that show that at some stage this has been exploited. They are particularly extensive to the east where a series of them spreads over some 20 acres. It's not known if local people dug these to get fuel or if they were made by passing travellers who saw a business opportunity. Maybe it was both.

At Plea Knowe, just short of the border, The Street cuts through a well-defined cross dyke that, with its accompanying ditch, is about 150 yards long. Most of this lies to the east of the path, because to the west the ground drops quite sharply to the Easthope Burn.

On reaching the border, which just here runs almost north-south, the track follows it for about 500 yards. Then, as the border turns sharply east, so The Street heads north-west into Scotland.

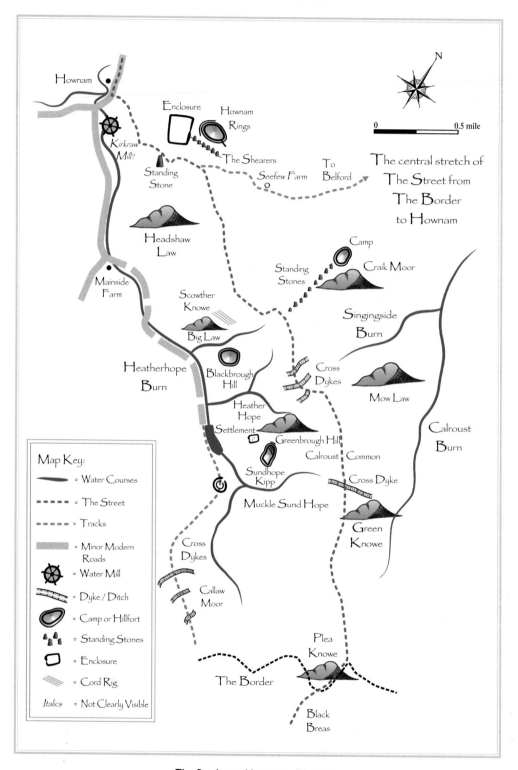

The Border to Hownam. (Map 6.2)

The Border to Hownam (Map 6.2)

In contrast to the stretch of The Street just described, once over the border the route passes through an area full of intriguing sites.

The track runs down the centre of a wide, flat-topped ridge known as Calroust Common, with the Heatherhope Burn below it on the west and the Calroust Burn on the east. Overlooking these burns are a series of spurs projecting from the ridge, on several of which are Iron Age sites. One of the first of these spurs – Greenbrough Hill – is just over a mile north of the border and a few hundred yards west of The Street; on it lies Sundhope Kipp (Figure 6.11).

Sundhope Kipp

This has been variously called a camp or a fort, but it could equally well be described as a defended settlement. Positioned on the end of the spur, around most of it are steep slopes that drop some 500 feet to the Heatherhope Burn and a side valley called Muckle Sund Hope. With a gradient of nearly 30 degrees, these make the settlement almost invulnerable from anyone trying to climb them; an attacker could only really have approached from along the spur – but four earth and stone ramparts, three large

Figure 6.11 Sundhope Kipp from the east, showing the hut circles packed into the interior, the ramparts across the approach and one of the (later) bothies and stack stands. The entrance and the path leading to it are in the lower centre of the picture. (Image © RCAHMS).

and one small, have been built across it. They are still many feet high and between 20 and 40 feet across; with the ditches between them they would have formed a very effective barrier.

These ramparts curve as they wrap around the settlement and the steep slopes at either end. The main entrance to the interior is along a sunken track on the east side, ten or 12 feet wide, that picks its way between the ends of the ramparts and the drop below.

This was clearly a busy place. The oval interior is about 250 feet long and 170 wide and covered with the remains of roundhouses. They are so closely packed and overlapping that it's hard to count them precisely, but there are probably about two dozen with diameters varying from 25 to 45 feet. Although some of the earlier ones have been almost obliterated by later building, archaeologists have identified a minimum of four phases of construction. Some houses look as if they have been shoehorned in between existing structures, and others are contiguous with a neighbour, effectively making one house with two rooms.

Sundhope Kipp has never been excavated but is almost certainly Iron Age in origin. There are, however, signs that the site has been used more recently. Sheltering within or near the ramparts are the remains of three rectangular huts or bothies, each measuring about 20 feet by ten. There are also traces of lazy beds in the area, suggesting small volumes of crops were grown, but more obvious are three circular structures in a line about 400 feet long leading north from the ramparts. Each one is between 40 and 50 feet across and none has any sign of an entrance, so they are probably the remains of stack stands where fodder was stored for stock. The huts,

Figure 6.12 *Looking along one of the cross dykes to the west.*

the lazy beds and these stands are probably medieval or later, but it is not known if they were all in use at the same time.

About 300 yards to the west of Sundhope Kipp and below the top of Greenbrough Hill is a second, smaller settlement. Protected on all sides apart from the east by steep slopes, it now consists of a well-defined but shallow trench laid out in a rough rectangle that once would have held a single palisade, with the resulting enclosure measuring about 90 feet by 70. On the north-east side is what appears to be the only entrance – a break in the palisade with a track leading through it; the fact that the track is slightly sunken may indicate quite heavy use. It leads towards the centre of the enclosure where a circular ditch about 25 feet across shows the position of a roundhouse. Next to it, to the south and apparently squeezed in between the central house and the palisade is the fainter ditch of a second, slightly smaller house, with a diameter of some 20 feet.

The structure probably dates from some time in the first millennium BC, but a more precise estimate is impossible. There are traces of cord rig nearby, some quite near the enclosure entrance, and so the relatively small number of people that lived in the two houses would have spent at least part of their time farming.

Both Sundhope Kipp and this settlement are well protected by the drops that surround them. But there has also been activity in the valley below. Clearly visible to the south from Sundhope Kipp, on the lower slopes of Church Hope Hill on the other side of the Heatherhope Burn, are the remains of a circular earthwork about 180 feet across. In places it's been damaged by cultivation and by a farm track that has been driven through it, but elsewhere it's quite well preserved and it clearly consists of two banks on either side of a ditch. On the southern, uphill, side of the interior are two flat courtyards scooped into the hillside that may once have held dwellings.

Much more recently, about 100 years ago, a dam was built across the Heatherhope Burn downstream from here to make a reservoir supplying water to Kelso. Partly drained, it is now just used for fishing.

Three cross dykes

As The Street continues to the north-west, it leaves Calroust Common and drops quite sharply to a saddle of land overlooking the Singingside Burn to the north. Over the years, travellers have cut several different routes down the slope to the saddle; the modern track skirts round it to the north, but on some of the steeper parts the old routes handle the gradient with sharp curves marked by hollow-ways. The banks around these can be confused with more significant archaeology on the saddle in the form of of three parallel cross dykes.

Working from the south-east to the north-west, the three dykes each consist of a single bank and a ditch (Figure 6.12) and are separated first by 125 yards and then 160 yards. The south-eastern dyke is about 230 yards long; it only drops a little way down the slopes on either side and the different paths that form The Street skirt it at either end.

At about 370 yards in all, the central dyke is longer and slightly curved as it crosses the middle of the saddle. Up to 15 feet thick, in places it stands some five feet high when measured from the bottom of the adjacent ditch. It is divided by two gaps, each some 50 feet wide, through which pass the tracks of The Street.

The third dyke is on the next upslope as The Street climbs towards Craik Moor. It is of a similar length to the central one, starting by the small watercourse in Green Cleugh to the north and then heading broadly south until it terminates on a small spur below Blackbrough Hill. It is bisected by a large gap about 150 feet wide through which all the paths of The Street pass.

The age and function of these dykes is completely unknown. They have been cut through by at least some parts of The Street so they are clearly older than that, but this doesn't help because we don't know when those tracks were made. As pointed out in Chapter 3, the dykes might be of different ages and they might have fulfilled different functions – perhaps a mixture of stock control, boundary demarcation and route management.

Sets of three dykes are generally unusual but there are others in the area. One is about two miles to the south on Callaw Moor where three linear earthworks cross a path leading from the west side of the Heatherhope Burn up to the border between Lamb Hill and Beefstand Hill. Then about a mile and a half to the south-west of that there's another set. This one is on Raeshaw Fell and the dykes there intersect paths, deeply worn in places, that lead up to the border from Buchtrig Farm (Map 8.2). Their function is far from obvious and their date is unknown but there's a fourth dyke at right angles to them that runs along the eastern edge of the fell above the valley below. Cutting through the others, and clearly newer, it's been suggested that it's the boundary of a hunting park built in the twelfth century. This, with its accompanying ditch, was referred to in the charters of Melrose Abbey. The text there reads *'fossatu int raweshauue et cuithbrithishope'* and Cuthberthope Rig is immediately to the north of that end of the dyke.

Blackbrough Hill

About 500 yards to the north-west of the cross dykes on The Street, another spur projects to the south-west from the main ridge. Overlooking the main stream of the Heatherhope Burn, some 700 feet below, it is bounded by small, steep-sided valleys on either side – Cribs Hope to the north-west and Heather Hope to the south-east. It is known as Blackbrough Hill, and at its end is an imposing camp (Figure 6.13).

The steep drops down to the burns below mean that it can only be approached along the spur from the north-east, but despite these natural defences there is an impressive single rampart all the way round the camp. Oval in shape, this is about 280 feet long and 215 feet across.

Up to 40 feet wide, the rampart is surrounded by a V-shaped ditch between ten and 15 feet across and, in places, four or five feet deep. Standing in the bottom of the ditch, the top of the rampart can be 15 feet above you.

The path along the spur passes through the original entrance. Here, the ends of the ramparts on each side are turned out through 90 degrees, having the dual effect of blocking access to the ditch and turning the entrance into a narrow corridor about ten feet wide and 50 feet long. A few boulders embedded in the side of the ramparts

Figure 6.13 Blackbrough from above. Note the ramparts turned out around the entrance (top right). The interior palisade trench is visible in places (red arrows).
(Image © 2016 Google, Getmapping plc).

hint at some sort of structure, but elsewhere the defences seem to be largely built from earth and rubble.

Directly opposite this entrance there is a clean gap in the south-west section of rampart. This looks much more modern, probably cut by a farm track running through the middle of the camp.

Unlike Sundhope Kipp, there is little to see inside the camp. The most obvious feature, and even this is only visible from ground level after some searching, is a shallow trench forming an oval around the centre of the camp, about 110 feet long and 80 feet across. This may have once held a palisade and it's been suggested that the enclosure housed the people who were building the main structure; alternatively, it might have been used to hold stock. In addition to this, there are very faint remains of four roundhouses, each about 20 feet across. These can only be seen in some aerial photographs: the palisade trench seems to cut through one of them, so it's possible they represent an earlier phase of activity. There has been no excavation, so no reliable sequence is known.

Like some other camps described in this book, such as that on Castle Hill near Alnham (Chapter 5), Blackbrough joins the group of structures whose function is hard to determine. With little sign of activity inside it, was it overtaken by events? Was it abandoned because it was no longer needed? Was it just used for occasional, ephemeral events such as trading or stock gathering? Was it a stronghold only used in times of trouble? Or was it built as a display of status or even a subtle form of defence to deter or distract aggressors – like the dummy airfields and battleships of the Second World War?

Craik Moor

On the other side of The Street from Blackbrough Hill lies Craik Moor, an exposed area of moorland with another Iron Age camp and the remains of palisades at the far end. This is half a mile from The Street, but it's certainly worth a detour and is essentially on the same ridge as the route, just on a long spur jutting out to the north.

Starting at The Street and leading along that spur is a line of small standing stones. Nine in all, the gaps between them range from about 60 yards to 140, so it's possible some are missing; they run almost parallel with the modern fence and although one slightly larger one has fallen over, the others stand up to two feet high (Figure 6.14).

It's not known how old they are, and there seems to be no record of them; there is no lettering or marking on any of them. Did they define an old boundary, or were they early route markers? If the latter, though, they'd soon by covered by snow in winter.

The site of the camp at the end of the spur was surveyed in the 1980s by archaeologists from Edinburgh University and they probably did some limited excavation as well. They found that the approach crosses a number of structures built across the spur, stretching between the steep drops on either side. Presumably intended for protection, they consist of a series of single trenches – and one double one – that almost certainly held palisades. There is also a line of boulders and stones that may be the remains of an earth and stone dyke and finally a more substantial wall

*Figure 6.14 **One of the line of stones leading across Craik Moor.***

Figure 6.15 Remains of masonry facing on a rampart at Craik Moor.

or rampart. At various points between these structures there are ghostly hut circles; with one exception they are really only visible from aerial photographs, but they hint at a series of settlements that occupied the ridge before the final phase of building.

It is likely that at least some of the palisades and ramparts along the spur would have been in place when the stone-walled camp at the end of the spur was constructed, so they would have protected it from the south, while steep slopes on every other side provided natural defences.

Perhaps because of this there are no visible ditches surrounding the camp. Its south wall is fairly well preserved and up to 12 feet thick, consisting of a core of tightly-packed, small stones faced on either side by blocks of masonry (Figure 6.15). This section contains more visible stonework than many camps in the Cheviots. Elsewhere, however, the position of the original wall can only be traced by lines of debris or tumble. Its absence is probably best explained by a combination of robbery – there is, for example, a drystone wall running up to the fort from the north – and the steepness of the surrounding slopes, down which any collapsing material would soon disappear. A track runs along the east side of the spur, and this may have caused damage as well. It's not now clear where the entrance to the fort was, but inside there are two adjacent hut circles, each about 30 feet across.

Craik Moor's defining characteristics, however, are its commanding position and its views. At 1,500 feet, it's the highest camp in the Cheviots. To the west you can see The Street and the camp at Hownam Rings further along it; Hownam Law dominates the view to the north, while below and to the east Clennell Street follows its route along Bowmont Water past the settlement at Mowhaugh. On a warm, sunny day, there's no better place to be.

Returning to The Street, for a time the track heads in a more westerly direction. Within half a mile of this turn and about 150 yards to the south of the track are three circular structures in a line about 200 yards long. They are each between 40 and 50 feet across, and although eroded in places they have no clear entrances. It seems likely that they are the remains of stack stands, holding food for local stock or for animals being driven along The Street.

Scowther Knowe

South of the stack stands lies the farm of Scowther Knowe. Probably of Iron Age origin, this is on the east of Big Law; the first sign of it from a distance is a large area of cord rig in a slight hollow between the main ridge holding The Street and the upturned end of a small spur on the other side of the valley from Blackbrough Hill.

In all, there's about one acre of well defined cord rig, with the most of the rigs being between four and five feet apart (Figure 6.16). It's at a height of 1,200 feet, which would have made it less than ideal for agriculture, even if the climate were warmer. At the very far end of the spur, as the ground rises slightly to a small summit, are the remains of what must have been the farmhouse. Only one circular outline of a hut can be seen from ground level, but an aerial view shows a second and hints at a third. The most obvious one is about 30 feet across, with the second about five feet smaller. Around them is a shallow ditch only a few inches deep that may once have held a palisade enclosing an area about 80 feet across. The ditch is most obvious to the north-west; erosion on the south side seems to have destroyed it with debris sliding down the steep slope towards the Heatherhope Burn in the valley below.

The fields are well-preserved, but what's intriguing is the position of the farmhouse. At this height any dwelling is going to be open to the elements, but there are several places in the immediate area where there's more protection. It looks as if the people

Figure 6.16 Part of the cord rig at Scowther Knowe. Blackbrough Hill in the background.

Figure 6.17 The ruined farmhouse of Seefew.

who farmed here didn't care about that. Living above the slopes on the very edge of Big Law certainly had defensive benefits, but they may have traded exposure to the weather for the dramatic views to the south and west. Perhaps for the designers of Scowther Knowe it really was all about location, location, location.

Back on The Street and heading towards Hownam, the ruined farmhouse of Seefew can be seen in the valley below the path and about half a mile to the north (Figure 6.17). Abandoned in the 1880s, it is situated on the old track connecting Hownam with the Bowmont valley and Belford, a hamlet on Clennell Street described in Chapter 4.

The Street joins this track a little further on, and about 400 yards north of this junction is the last, and best-researched, of the Iron Age camps along this stretch – Hownam Rings. As part of the project in the Borders mentioned in Chapter 4 which would include Hayhope Knowe on Clennell Street, the site was investigated by Margaret (Peggy) Piggott in 1948.

Hownam Rings

At a height of about 1,000 feet, the camp is positioned at the north end of a flat-topped spur that feels more like a plateau. On three sides it is bordered by slopes down to the surrounding valleys, but these are not as steep as those around the other camps we've described. Oval-shaped, 430 feet from east to west and 300 feet north to south, the first impression that the visitor gets is one of complexity, but walking over the structure several times helps make things clearer.

There are ramparts all around the camp, particularly on the west side; in some places they seem to have been damaged, mostly by building work carried out on top of them. There are remains of 20 or more roundhouses throughout the interior and at least one bank has been built across it.

The excavation identified the main reason for this complexity; the site went through four phases of occupation spread over a considerable period, with each successive

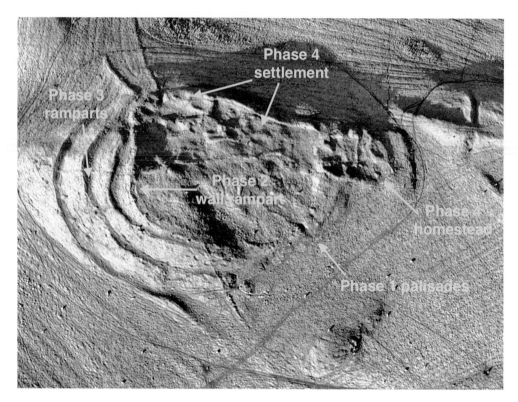

Figure 6.18 Hownam Rings from the air showing some of the surrounding rig and furrow.
(Image © RCAHMS).

phase re-using or building on top of earlier structures. Elements of these four phases are highlighted in the aerial photograph in Figure 6.18. In summary they consisted of:

Phase 1: The construction of two wooden palisades, the second replacing the first. Traces of these were found over a stretch of about 40 yards along the southern walls of the camp. How far they extended to the north was unclear; they might have encircled the entire camp or could have just acted as barriers across the approach along the spur.

Phase 2: The building of a defensive wall, about ten feet thick at the base, around the high ground on which the camp stands. This had an entrance to the south-east, which had subsequently been blocked by a quern that Piggott dated to the first century AD.

Phase 3: Some stones from the Phase 2 wall were used to build an inner kerb for sets of multiple ramparts that surrounded the site. Parts of this kerb can still be seen. The ramparts are most obvious on the west side of the camp and in places are four or five feet high and up to 30 feet across. The majority of them seem to have been built by scraping together surface rubble and earth, but the inner two probably also used material from ditches connected with them.

Phase 4: A settlement was built that accounts for at least the majority of the roundhouse remains that are visible today. The main area of activity was in the northern part of the camp, where houses were constructed on top of the reduced ramparts or scooped into them, possibly to provide protection from the weather. There was also a homestead surrounded by a rectangular enclosure built on the east side. When excavated, a hut in the north-west area of the camp turned out be about 20 feet across with stone walls five feet thick, and finds of British and Roman pottery showed it was in use in the late third century AD. Investigation of the homestead did not reveal a reliable date, and so it's possible that what was described as a single phase was actually spread over a considerable period.

Piggott concluded that the site had been in use for up to 500 years, with the earliest occupation dating from the first or second centuries BC. Her observation that the structure of the camp progressed from a single palisade to a single rampart and then multiple ramparts was very influential; it became known as the Hownam sequence and for a long time it was regarded as the blueprint for hilltop camp development. More recently, this generalisation has been questioned; while it undoubtedly holds true in some cases, other sites seem to be more complex. At Woden Law, for example (Chapter 8), the single innermost rampart was probably built later than the ones outside it.

Interesting as the Hownam Rings site is, it's not the only archaeology in the immediate area. Walking along the spur to the camp, the visitor is almost certainly aware of crossing rig and furrow, and the aerial photograph shows it clearly.

This picture shows not only the complexity of the camp itself but also the mixture of paths, field boundaries and the remains of agricultural activity surrounding it. The rig and furrow extends over a large number of fields and covers more than 100 acres. Some of it is curved and some straight, so it may not all be of the same date. And we

*Figure 6.19 **The Shearers looking west.***

don't know what that date was. Piggott's team found a George III penny in one of the huts in the camp, but this might have been dropped by a shepherd, a ploughman or a just an inquisitive visitor.

South-west of the camp, and intermixed with the rig and furrow, is a large rectangular enclosure bounded by now-low turf walls. Covering about eight acres, it's not immediately clear whether it predates or postdates the surrounding ploughing, but it may have been built with cultivation in mind because there are occasional small clearance cairns along its edges and in the corners.

Finally, 100 yards south-east of the camp, is a set of upright stones called the Shearers (Figure 6.19). There are 28 of them laid out in a straight line about 120 yards long running from east to west. Spaced fairly irregularly, none of them is more than two feet high. Only eight are now upright, but a rough site plan from 1938 implies that more were standing then, and the OS map of the 1860s calls them the '11 Shearers'. Their origin is unknown, but it's been suggested that they are the remains of a core of an earth bank built to mark a boundary or to provide some form of defence. This may be the case; erosion of the outer wall of the enclosure around the homestead at the eastern end of Hownam Rings shows that it was constructed in much the same way. A report of 1897 in the *History of the Berwickshire Naturalists' Club* mentions only 11 stones, but says they were in the *'centre of an ancient division mound'* which had been weathered away.

In the interest of balance, we should mention that an older and more interesting tradition says the Shearers are the remains of people who were turned into stone for reaping corn on the Sabbath.

Hownam to Morebattle (Map 6.3)

Passing the standing stone shown in Figure 3.25, The Street drops down into Hownam, a village first mentioned in the twelfth century with documents describing grants and transfers of land. Some of these grants were substantial; one involved a William of Hownam giving Melrose Abbey an area of land identified as being bounded by Whitton (a mile or so to the west), Grubbit (downstream along the Kale Water and near Morebattle) and Clifton (on the Bowmont Water to the east). This is at least 3,000 acres, and could be double that. The gift may have been the cause of some dispute, because in 1207 the monks of Melrose Abbey complained that William was attempting to *'injure'* lands he had given them. This resulted in the involvement of no less a person than Pope Innocent III, who set up an investigation with quite wide-ranging powers: *'If the witnesses named shall have withdrawn out of favour, hatred or fear, they shall compel them by a similar stricture, without appeal, to provide testimony of the truth'.* The result was that although William admitted he had given the Abbey the land, he was granted use of it during his lifetime, with the Abbey getting it on his death.

Even though this has never been a large village, in the nineteenth century it must have been busier than it is now. An early Ordnance Survey map shows two inns and a school, which was still operating in the 1940s.

The church at the north end of the village was first mentioned in 1185; by 1220 it was owned by Jedburgh Abbey. There is nothing left of this early building, but a doorway in the south wall of the current structure probably dates from the end of

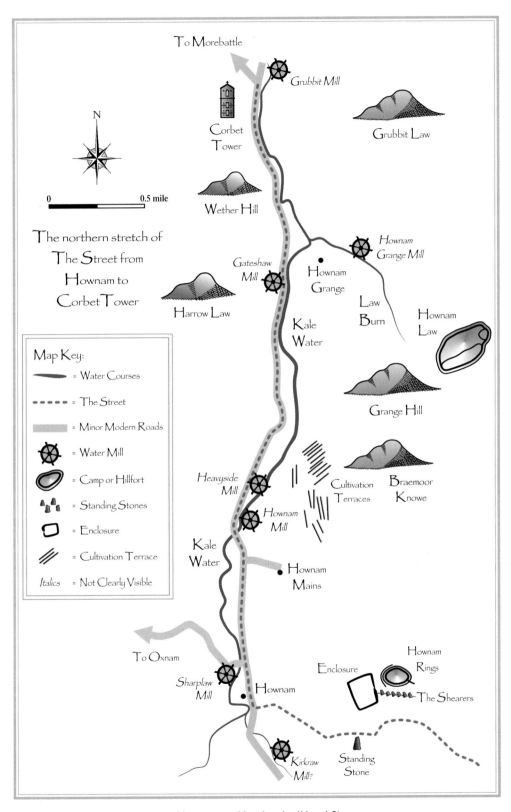

N

0   0.5 mile

The northern stretch of
The Street from
Hownam to
Corbet Tower

To Morebattle

Grubbit Mill

Corbet
Tower

Grubbit Law

Wether Hill

Gateshaw
Mill

Hownam
Grange Mill

Hownam
Grange

Harrow Law

Kale
Water

Law
Burn

Hownam
Law

Grange Hill

Map Key:

= Water Courses

----- = The Street

= Minor Modern Roads

= Water Mill

= Camp or Hillfort

= Standing Stones

= Enclosure

= Cultivation Terrace

Italics = Not Clearly Visible

Heavyside
Mill

Hownam
Mill

Cultivation
Terraces

Braemoor
Knowe

Kale
Water

Hownam
Mains

To Oxnam

Sharplaw
Mill

Hownam

Enclosure

Hownam
Rings

The Shearers

Kirkraw
Mill?

Standing
Stone

Hownam to Morebattle. (Map 6.3)

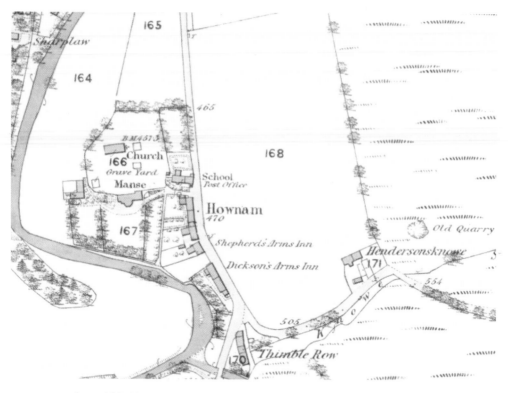

Figure 6.20 Hownam on the 1859 OS map: original at 25 inches to the mile.

Figure 6.21 Death is inevitable.

the fifteenth century. It's believed that the building was originally in the shape of a cross, but in the middle of the eighteenth century its core was reduced to the current rectangle, with further additions and repairs in the nineteenth century. To the passer-by, one of the more interesting features can be found outside, where an old gravestone has been cemented into one of the walls (Figure 6.21).

Although it looks macabre to the modern eye, the skull and crossbones was really just a reminder of the onlooker's mortality; like everyone else he or she was going to die one day.

After reaching Hownam, most travellers would have continued north towards Morebattle, using the road that follows Kale Water. There are farms all along this valley, and old maps show a number of water mills. This is not surprising because most of the Cheviot rivers are sufficiently fast-flowing to be attractive sources of power. In the sixteenth century the Scottish cartographer, Timothy Pont, noted five mills before the river reached Morebattle. Blaeu's map of 1654, which was based on Pont's work, actually identifies seven, and around the end of the seventeenth century some of them were listed as owned by the Duke of Roxburgh. Most, if not all of them, were probably corn mills.

Working towards the north, the first is Kirkraw Mill. John Thomson's map of 1832 shows this on the east side of the Heatherhope Burn just upstream from Hownam. In about the right place, about 400 yards from the village, there is a rectangular platform cut into the slope above the burn, with a track leading down to it (Figure 6.22). It's hard to be certain, but this is at least a plausible site for the mill.

Immediately north of Hownam and on the west bank of Kale Water, is a farm called Sharplaw (top left in Figure 6.20). The adjacent sheet of the 1859 Ordnance Survey map shows a mill pond almost on the edge of the road that goes past it on the way to Oxnam. It has been filled in, and there are trees growing on the site, but this was probably the source of power for a simple farm mill. These sometimes operated farm machinery but more often produced flour for the farm and its immediate dependants.

Less than a mile further north, Thomson's 1832 map shows Hownam Mill near the bridge where the road crosses Kale Water, and then Heavyside Mill just beyond that. Both of these seem to have disappeared by 1859, and neither has left discernible traces. Then, about a mile to the north again, and on the west side of the road, there's

Figure 6.22 The possible site of Kirkraw Mill. The Heatherhope Burn is near the bottom of the picture.

Figure 6.23 This is believed to be part of Grubbit Mill – perhaps the miller's house.

Gateshaw Farm, the site of another farm mill. The pond was still there as late as 1918; it's now been filled in and although the farm has expanded, nothing substantial has been built on top of it.

At Hownam Grange, on the eastern side of Kale Water, the remains of a mill pond are still visible about 200 yards beyond the main buildings and 60 feet uphill. Here the Law Burn, which rises near Hownam Law, was dammed on its way down to the river; it's not clear if the mill was near the pond or further downhill.

The last mill on this stretch of Kale Water was Grubbit Mill. About 500 yards south of where the road between Morebattle and Yetholm crosses the river, the 1859 Ordnance Survey map showed this as a set of buildings, with a mill operated by a 600 yard leat fed by the river and running parallel with it. The surveyors described it as *'a corn mill two stories high, with a cottage, garden, and arable farm attached, the property of the Marquis of Tweeddale'.* Although still there in the 1890s, it had disappeared from maps by 1918; of all the Kale Water mills, however, it is the only one of which we may have a photograph (Figure 6.23). Despite this, it may also be one of the oldest, being mentioned in the list of properties destroyed by the Earl of Hertford in his attacks on Scotland in 1545.

Blaeu's map of 1654 shows two towers on the other side of the river from Grubbit Mill, *Grubethous* and *Corbetthous*. The first of these has vanished, but the latter still stands in the gardens of Corbet Tower House – a private dwelling.

A small rectangular structure, with three storeys and a garret, it's built of random mortared blocks with masonry quoins. The site may well be of medieval origin, because the estate at Clifton, about three miles to the east on Bowmont Water, passed to the Corbet family in 1241. The tower was burnt by the English about 300 years later and the current doorway contains a block with the date 1575. It seems to have fallen into disrepair after that, but was restored by another local family, the Kers, early in the nineteenth century.

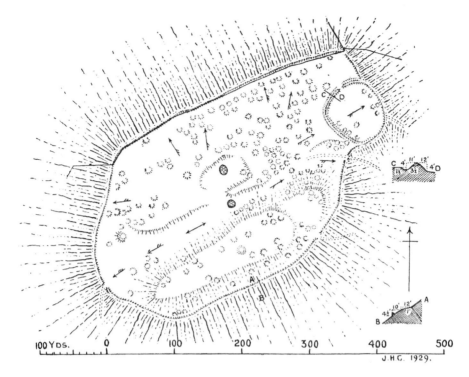

Figure 6.24 A plan of the Hownam Law structures drawn in 1929 by J. Hewat Craw. He identified 187 hut circles.

As Kale Water flows down the valley from Hownam, there are two other sites of note clearly visible from the adjacent road.

The first of these is the imposing presence of Hownam Law. On the east side of the valley and visible for miles around, it is one of the most conspicuous of the Cheviot outliers. Nearly 1,500 feet high, the whole of the summit ridge and some of the slopes around it are surrounded by a drystone wall enclosing an area of over 20 acres. Originally some ten feet thick, it can be traced along much of its three-quarter mile circuit, although in places it's been badly damaged, particularly to the north where a modern wall has been built on top of the original footings (Figures 6.24 and 6.25).

If the wall was a defensive structure, it was a very simple one. Inside the area it encloses are hollows that are probably the remains of quarries and two ponds that are thought to be artificial. A second enclosure is tucked into the eastern end of the larger structure. Roughly circular and some 250 feet across, the dyke surrounding it is built of earth taken from an adjacent ditch. Its eastern side follows the line of the main enclosure, and here it seems to have been built on top of the wall, suggesting that it's of a later date.

Different surveys have identified between 110 and 187 hut sites inside the main enclosure, with the variations in the numbers probably caused by different states of vegetation. These sites are either simple saucer-shaped depressions between 20 and 30 feet across or circular platforms cut into slopes to provide a level floor.

Beyond a description of the visible remains, little is known of the site. There has never been an excavation and as far as we know no reliable artefacts have ever been found

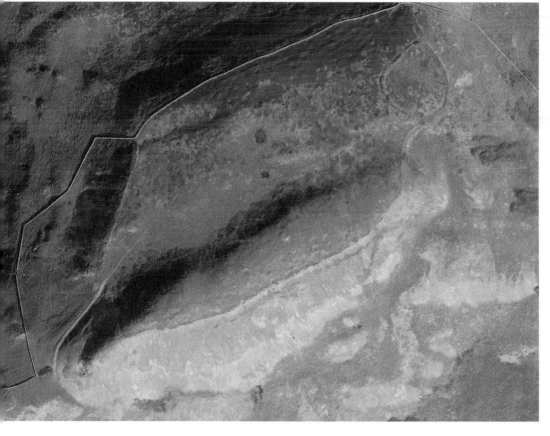

Figure 6.25 Hownam Law. The original wall is clearest just below the summit ridge in the lower part of the picture and then running north-south to its left. On the north side it is covered by a modern wall, and is partly covered by the enclosure on the right.
(Image © 2016 Google, Getmapping plc).

to help date it, although there is an eighteenth-century account of an iron gate being found at the top of the Law and put on display at Cessford Castle. This is some four miles to the west, but since it was probably already in ruins, it's not clear how big an audience it attracted.

Archaeologists used to believe that large sites like this appeared in the late Iron Age and acted as focal points of resistance to Roman incursion. However, investigations at broadly similar places like Trapain Law (in East Lothian) and Eildon Hill North (above Newstead) have suggested that their original occupation actually started in the late Bronze Age, with a hiatus during the Iron Age followed by reoccupation during the Roman period.

South-west of Hownam Law, on the lower slopes of Braemoor Knowe and on the east side of Kale Water, is the other striking site in the area. Clearly visible from the road are some 45 acres of combined agricultural terracing and rig and furrow. Sometimes it's hard to distinguish between the two, because when the latter follows the contours of a slope it turns into terracing if the slope gets steeper (Figure 6.26).

The structures are extremely well-defined and must rate as one of the most impressive of their type in the Borders. On some of the adjacent fields later

Figure 6.26 **The terracing and rig and furrow on Braemoor Knowe. Kale Water runs across the top of the picture.** (Image © RCAHMS).

agricultural activity has removed nearly all trace of them, but they reappear to the east of the farm at Hownam Mains, where terracing can be seen on both the northern and southern slopes leading down to Hownam Burn. It is not known how old this system is, or if it was all in use at the same time, but it's a sure sign that there was once intense agricultural activity in the valley.

In the next chapter we turn to an area on the southern slopes of the Cheviots. Here there were farmers as well, but they were mostly managing stock rather than growing crops.

A gable end in the ruins
of Yearning Hall.

Chapter 7

Buckham's Walls

This chapter is not about a track that crosses the Cheviots, but rather about an area in Upper Coquetdale where a circular route passes through a landscape rich with history. The archaeology here is not spectacular in the conventional sense of the word. While there are some signs of a prehistoric presence with objects such as cairns, there are no intriguing Bronze Age farms, imposing Iron Age forts or important Roman camps. Rather there are the relics of farming communities and hundreds of years of agricultural activity that have left their mark on the hills.

The area would have had connections with an old Scottish track that passed through the triple set of earthworks on its way across Raeshaw Fell up to the border. This route is shown both on the Crawford and Brooke map of Roxburghshire of 1843 and on William Roy's nearly 100 years earlier; on the northern side of the border it led down to Buchtrig Farm and thence to either Dere Street or Hownam. And as we shall see, the people that lived at Buckham's Walls farm and others nearby often came from Scotland, or married people from there.

The area's southern edge runs along the Coquet, from the farm at Blindburn in the east to Fulhope in the west, while to the north it extends to within a few hundred yards of Scotland, about two miles from the river.

Blindburn and Fulhope are still working farms, and it is the name of the latter that provides one of the earliest

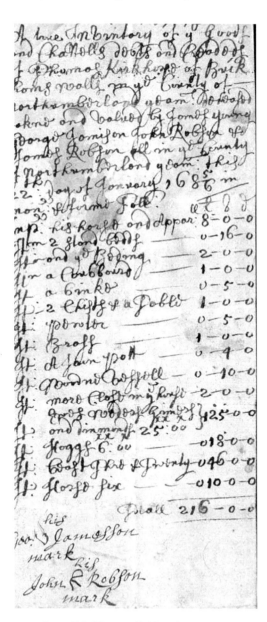

Figure 7.1 Thomas Kirkhope's inventory.

written references to the neighbourhood. The 1604 survey of the Debateable and Border Lands listed 16 *sheylding grounds* associated with the parish of Elsdon. The last of these was *Phillipe*, one of the many ways in which the modern name was written. A later list set the rent for *The Phillippe* at two shillings. Presumably this was for the season; it was one of the cheaper deals available.

Over the next hundred years or so, sets of records such as rental assessments, tithe lists and leases mention other farms or settlements in the area. The names include places such as *Erlingborne, Comesmerebanck, Fair Fillup* (alias *Halarickburn*) and *Ettrickburn*. *Phillipe* is also called *Fillup* and then *Foul Philip*; it seems to have been one of the more important farms, because on one occasion other places are described as being *'in the hamlet of Phillip'*. It's possible that some of these names (such as *Halarickburn* and *Ettrickburn*) actually refer to the same place; most if not all of them seem to have been north of the river. Did they start as shielings that became farmsteads once the border troubles died down?

Buckhoms Walls farm was first mentioned in an inventory for a Thomas Kirkhope who died there in 1686 (Figure 7.1). He had livestock worth £199 out of a total estate of £216, a sum which was much in line with that of other farmers in the area. Some eight years earlier Elsdon parish records listed a Thomas Kirkhope from Greenchesters, a farm in Otterburn about two miles from that of Davy Shield, where a family called Buckham lived a little later. Was this how the name appeared in Coquetdale? Were these the people that built the farm?

But with the exceptions of Blindburn, Fulhope and Buckham's Walls all these farms are now lost. There are ruined and abandoned sites which we will describe as we follow the route round the area, but we have no way of knowing which ruin was which farm – if indeed there was an exact correspondence. Early maps are no help; those of Warburton and Roy in the first half of the eighteenth century are either insufficiently detailed or do not extend far enough south, while the Armstrongs' map of 1769 only has the three farms we know about.

Sites near the Coquet (Map 7.1)

A 1642 list of tithes includes Blindburn Farm, at the south-eastern corner of the area covered by this chapter. The current farmhouse is clearly not that old but is of an attractive late Georgian appearance. Indeed, there is a reference to a cairn by the road to Buckham's Walls being *'dug out'* around 1826 on the instructions of a Thomas Telfer in order to provide stone for a building project, but whether this was for the farmhouse itself or other buildings on the site is unclear.

At the south-western corner of the area is Fulhope. The farm dates from the same period as Blindburn, but the current house is even more recent. There has been less development on this site than at Blindburn, and the remains of old enclosures, and possibly buildings, can be seen just to the west as the road climbs away from the farm.

There are points of interest along the course of the river between the two farms. About 150 yards downstream from Fulhope, clearly visible on a small haugh across the river from the road, are the remains of what may be another farm. There's a set of earthworks forming a rectangle about 14 feet by 40 with some facing stones. This

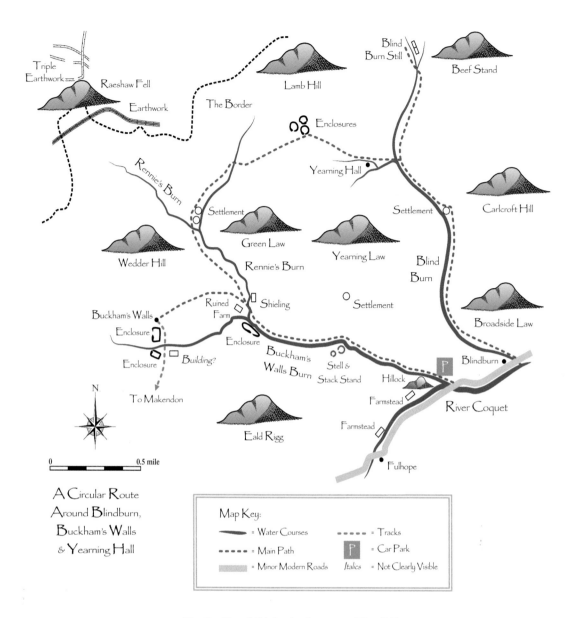

The Buckham's Walls circular route. (Map 7.1)

looks like a building, while beyond it further sets of earthworks are arranged along the river with a stack stand at the end. In all, the remains cover a stretch of bank about 80 yards long. The site has never been investigated; it may be medieval, or it may be later.

Further downstream again, just over 100 yards to the west of the Buckham's Walls Burn car park and between the north bank of the river and the track leading up to Eald Rigg, is a second abandoned farm. Again, there are a few facing stones that help define a set of rectangular earthworks and a couple of nearby enclosures. Just to the west of this, a low earth dyke cuts across the ridge between the Coquet and the Buckham's Walls Burn. Then about 50 yards further west, and extending for another

100 yards, is an area of partly enclosed disturbed ground that contains the remains of yet another small building, some lazy beds and various indeterminate low banks and ditches.

There may be some relationship between these sites. Given their position on the end of Eald Rigg, it's possible that one or both of them represent the now-lost *Erlingborne* or *Elrigburn* farm(s) mentioned above.

Finally, there is an interesting small ruin near the car park itself. In the previous chapter we discussed the now-vanished drinking house at Slymefoot that was described as being built on a rock.

There is a large rock (or small hillock) about 100 yards up the Buckham's Walls Burn. About 150 feet long and 30 or 40 feet high, on its southern end are the remains of a small building about 12 feet wide and 25 feet long. Apart from being too small and in an unsuitable place to be a stock enclosure, we know nothing about this. It could be an old shieling or the remains of a domestic building on the same sort of site as the Slymefoot drinking house.

The Coquet to Rennie's Burn *(Map 7.1)*

Leaving the Coquet and heading slightly north of west up the Buckham's Walls Burn, the signs of past agriculture continue. After about half a mile, for example, there's a small area of haugh land to the south of the burn that is home to an old sheep stell and a bigger turf stack stand that looks for all the world like a giant green doughnut (Figure 7.2).

*Figure 7.2 **The stell and stack stand beyond.***

Figure 7.3 The hollow-way leading down to the ford.

There are signs here that the current footpath along the north bank of the burn used not to be the only route along the valley. A short but pronounced hollow-way leads down to a spot where the stream is easy to ford (Figure 7.3); its width is such that it might have taken wheeled vehicles. Other hollows and fording points along the burn suggest that this early track crossed and re-crossed the watercourse as it headed upstream, exploiting the flat areas of haugh land on either bank.

Opposite this area, about 350 yards to the north of the burn but over halfway up the steep valley side towards Yearning Law, is an abandoned settlement or shieling. Here, a ditch has been dug around a small hillock, with the upcast soil being used to build a bank on its downhill edge. The result is an oval enclosure with a long axis of about 50 yards and a possible entrance on the east side; here another bank, to the side of the hillock, forms a D-shaped enclosure some 30 yards across. This enclosure may be later than the one around the hillock because the western section, the straight line of the D, seems to overlie the hillock's ditch.

There are the remains of what is probably a building along the southern part of the D. About 50 feet long and ten feet wide, traces of two interior walls divide it into three bays. The two at each end are some 12 feet long, while the larger central one is much decayed. There are also indications that there was once a smaller, single-bay structure at the north-west corner of the D.

It's impossible to provide a date for these constructions. Indeed, they may date from several different periods, and the ditch and bank around the knoll may even be prehistoric. Some indistinct marks on the slopes down towards the burn may be the remains of lynchets or agricultural terracing, and aerial photographs hint at the presence of rig and furrow, but this is not apparent on the ground. In bad weather it's in an exposed position, with westerly winds howling down the valley. Sheep corralled on the hillock would have felt the full force of these, but they probably weren't consulted.

Half a mile further upstream is the point where the Rennie's Burn flows into the Buckham's Walls Burn from the north. Although we made a suggestion earlier about the origin of the name Buckham, we have nothing to offer on Rennie – if indeed it refers to a person at all.

A ruined building sits in the fork where the two burns meet. Marked on the current OS map as a 'Farmstead', in the 1863 version it was described as a sheepfold. There are, however, some signs that it was once more than that.

Firstly, there is the structure itself. At a casual glance it looks like a rectangular set of walls forming an enclosure of about 24 by 30 feet, but it's actually more complicated than that. An old wall runs down to the burn from the southern corner of the ruin (towards the bottom left in Figure 7.4) and there are more low banks to both the south and the west of the building. To the west there are also the indistinct remains of a rectangular enclosure, and further west again are three or four ridges of lazy beds. In the photograph, these can be seen beyond the ruin about halfway to the modern fence that drops diagonally down to the burn. Then, just downstream from the junction of the burns, on a haugh on the south-west bank of the Buckham's Walls Burn, low banks form a thin oval enclosure about 370 feet long and 80 wide with a sheep stell inside it (Figure 7.5).

*Figure 7.4 **The ruin at the junction of Buckham's Walls Burn and Rennie's Burn.***

Figure 7.5 The long oval enclosure alongside the burn.

All this suggests that the building at the fork was more than a sheepfold and was perhaps once lived in and used as a farm. The only argument against that is its size. Although it's quite possible to build a roof 24 feet wide, this would have been unusual for an old upland building. However, the ruin is divided by another wall about two thirds of the way across it. This can be seen in Figure 7.4; it is quite well finished, with faced edges, and might have once been an external wall. It is possible, therefore, that the original building on the site was a farmhouse consisting of the northern two-thirds of the current rectangular ruin. This would have been a more manageable 16 feet wide; when abandoned the site was extended and remodelled to make a stock enclosure or sheepfold.

We know nothing of the history of this site, not even its name. The Armstrongs' map of 1769 shows a farm called Buckham's Walls here, but this has to be treated with considerable caution. Their accuracy in these remote regions is often questionable; in this area, for example, the line of the Buckham's Walls Burn running down to the Coquet is recorded as being about 20 degrees west of north. In fact, the angle is more than 70 degrees; this is a substantial error, but extensive copying meant that other cartographers followed suit. Pottery sherds that may date from the eighteenth century have been found in the stream bank, and so it's possible that there was activity on the site at that time.

Fortunately, William Roy's map of Scotland extends just far enough south to pick up this area. It shows nothing at the junction of the burns but has the farm of Buckham's Walls in its current position about half a mile to the west (Figure 7.10). His survey was conducted about 20 years earlier than that of the Armstrongs and it seems likely that he or his staff actually visited the area, whereas the Armstrongs may not have done.

In summary, the ruin might be an earlier site for Buckham's Walls farm, but it could equally be one of the other farms or steadings listed in the seventeenth century for which there is no known location.

Hollow-ways can be seen in Figure 7.4 running up the spur of Wedder Hill to the north-west of the ruin. Towards the top these curve round to the west and lead to Buckham's Walls farm.

Buckham's Walls Farm (Map 7.1)

At the start of this chapter, we established that the first known reference to this farm dates from 1686. The 1724 will of Robert Henderson of Blindburn provided John Clark of *Backham's Wals* with a small legacy, while in the census in 1841 the tenant was a Scottish shepherd, Hugh Lilico, with his wife and six children.

Figure 7.6 Buckham's Walls from the south when it was still being farmed.
(Image courtesy www.rothbury.co.uk).

The first map to mention the site was earlier than Roy's, being that of John Warburton[1], published in 1716. However, it is impossible to establish its position from this. Buckham's Walls Burn is not shown at all, and the name of the farm is actually written north of the border in Scotland.

Isolated as it was, the farm was still operating well into the twentieth century (Figure 7.6); the last tenants we know of were John Little, from Hownam, and his wife Margaret; both were in their early 60s and living there in the summer of 1940. The 1939 register lists their 38-year-old son Walter and Ninnian Anderson, a 66-year-old

---

[1] Warburton (1682-1759) was an absent-minded, London-based antiquarian and collector who apparently once left a pile of manuscript plays in his kitchen. Returning to collect them about a year later he found that his cook, appropriately called Betsy Baker, had used most of them to light fires or line pie dishes. Some 50 plays were lost, including two which Shakespeare had allegedly written or co-authored. Some commentators have cast doubt on this account, but even if it's not true it still makes a good story.

Figure 7.7 Buckham's Walls from the south-east in the 1990s.

shepherd, as well. It also shows that there were younger generations of Littles working as shepherds at Blindburn and at Carlcroft, less than a mile down the valley. The farm was probably abandoned soon after this, and John Little died in 1944.

Buckham's Walls was serviced from the east by the track described at the end of the previous section, although old OS maps show its route as being nearer the burn than the hollow-ways suggest. Those maps also show a path leading up to the site from the Coquet at Makendon, the westernmost farm in the Coquet Valley and upstream from Fulhope. This may have been the main access route; a description of a visit in 1940 referred to it as the *postie's road*. As it approaches the farm, this track follows a burn with the unusual name of Foul Whasle (or Whazle). This is a dialect term for wheezing, or breathing with difficulty, but there is no apparent reason why a stream should be called this.

Low earth banks define the boundaries of three enclosures or fields around the farm – one uphill from the building and two downhill. These two are larger than the first, but still only cover a quarter and half an acre respectively. There's a large stack stand about 80 feet across to the east and, although the farm was only about 150 yards from the burn, old OS maps show a now-vanished well just to the west of it.

The building itself was basically rectangular, nearly 70 feet long and 15 feet wide. It was single-storeyed and well-built, with walls consisting of mortared andesite rubble with corners reinforced by sandstone quoins. There was also similarly dressed stone around the windows and doors in the form of sills and lintels. The eastern third of the building consisted of a byre, whose entrance can just be seen at the right of the structure in Figure 7.6. In Figure 7.7, a photograph taken in about 1990, the main part of the building was relatively intact, but the byre (at the near end) had either collapsed or been destroyed.

Parts of the slate roof were still intact at this time, although there had been some patching with corrugated iron. One distinct feature in this photograph was an

Figure 7.8 The interior of the farmhouse 25 years ago.

entranceway to the farm built out to the south. Having an inner and outer door would have protected the interior, with the outer door opening to the east (towards the camera) out of the prevailing wind. The area between these doors could have been used for storing wet clothes and tools.

Turning to the interior, a still-visible fireplace at the eastern end of the house appears to have been blocked with stone while the farm was still in use, and so all heating must have come from the range at the western end of the house (behind the camera in Figure 7.8). Also taken about 1990, this picture shows the entrance on the right. The roof joists were still in place, although we don't know if the space above was used

Figure 7.9 Buckham's Walls today.

for anything. It must have been tempting, however, especially in warmer weather. The 1901 census shows ten people at the farm: parents David and Margaret Wilson, with six children aged from six to 19, a 16-year-old niece and an 81-year-old boarder.

Over the last 25 years the building's condition has deteriorated to a point where it consists mostly of piles of stone and masonry; it's possible that this change has been at least partly due to deliberate action.

The farm's concrete floors are still visible, and these probably date from the late nineteenth or early twentieth century. The two most obvious standing structures are the gabled entranceway described above and the remains of a scullery or larder built out at the back of the farm (to the right in Figure 7.9). This was equipped with wooden shelves, the remains of which are still embedded in the walls. A wall separated this annexe from the main building, presumably to protect it from the heat of the nearby range, and the doorway through to it can be seen at the extreme left of Figure 7.8. There are no real signs of other internal walls, although a small step in the concrete floor towards the eastern end, and the remains of house-bricks amongst the general rubble, suggest that there may have been a built partition. Whatever its nature, it seems likely that it separated a living area in the western end of the house from a sleeping area at the eastern end with the now-blocked fireplace. The 1911 census notes three rooms, which could mean the scullery and a divided main area.

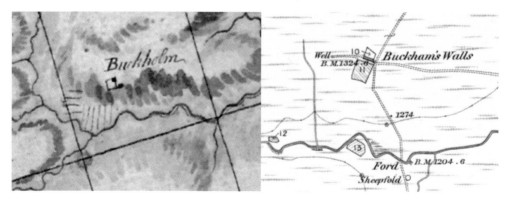

Figure 7.10 William Roy's map (left) and the 1st edition OS map (right).

Aspects of the present ruin suggest a building that was probably constructed in the first half of the nineteenth century. A tell-tale building technique can be seen at the corners of the entranceway, where slate has been used as a levelling layer between rough andesite foundation blocks and the finished masonry quoins above them. There also appear to be remains of gutter attachments in some scattered stone blocks, and ceramic roof ridge tiles have been found nearby, particularly in a nearby slit trench that must have been dug by military personnel.

This dating raises questions about the location of the original farm building, if the farm was on this site in the seventeenth century. Figure 7.10 compares the area as shown on William Roy's map of around 1750 with the version on the first edition of the six-inch Ordnance Survey, based on work carried out in 1863.

What follows is a somewhat tentative suggestion, and relies heavily on the accuracy of Roy's map, although he is usually quite reliable. If the small enclosures by the farm on the two maps are one and the same, then the position of the farm building on its north side in the 1860s is compatible both with the farm's current position and the suggested date of the building. While Roy's map shows a black mark close to the site of the current building, it has a red mark just outside the south-east corner of the enclosure. Red was a colour he normally used to indicate a house or dwelling, so although there is nothing there now, was this the site of an earlier farm? Was there, indeed, more than one building on the site? The term Walls is sometimes used to describe just such a situation; there is an example of this in the next chapter, where we will see that the medieval village at Chew Green was referred to in the sixteenth century as Kemylpeth Walls. Similarly, there is today a farm called Cote Walls near Netherton that consists of at least four old buildings.

There was certainly some activity 200 yards away on the south side of the Buckham's Walls Burn, which runs across the bottom of the OS map in Figure 7.10. Near where the Foul Whasle Burn joins it are the faint outlines of two buildings, stones from which may have been used to build the nearby sheep stell. And the irregular shaped enclosure to the west, due south of the farm, is still quite prominent. Inside it are the remains of a horse-drawn tedder, a device that turned over cut grass during hay-making.

Rennie's Burn and beyond *(Map 7.1)*

Returning to the point where Rennie's Burn joins Buckham's Walls Burn, there are traces of more farming activity upstream along the former. These include the remains of a small rectangular building or shieling some 70 yards from the fork where the two burns meet. It's just over 20 feet long and 12 wide; at the southern end there's an entrance, and near that another smaller building. Close to another crossing-point on the burn, traces of an old track pass by on its western side. This path heads north along the burn, passing abandoned sheep stells and the remains of what were probably stock enclosures or folds.

After about half a mile, the burn splits again, with Rennie's Burn being joined by an unnamed burn from the north-east. On the high ground between these two burns and by the side of Rennie's Burn are traces of more concentrated activity.

Spread over an area of two acres or so are the remains of a settlement consisting of perhaps as many as five steadings or shielings, at least one of which is attached to a yard or garth, together with some free-standing enclosures. The banks defining these structures are now rarely more than a foot or 18 inches high and stock trampling is probably partly responsible for their condition. There are no exposed stone faces, but in some places stones can be seen in the banks, although it's not clear if these were structural or just a by-product of the banks' construction.

The largest steading is some 70 feet long and 12 feet wide. It doesn't appear to have any internal cross walls, but at least one of the smaller buildings does. In some of the buildings entrances can be made out, but it's not always clear if these are original or caused by later activity.

It isn't possible to provide a date for these structures, but it seems reasonable to suggest that they are part of a medieval or post-medieval pastoral economy. And there is at least one other example of this sort of thing nearby.

A track follows the line of the unnamed burn and then crosses it and turns slightly more to the east. After about half a mile, the keen-eyed walker will see a stack stand

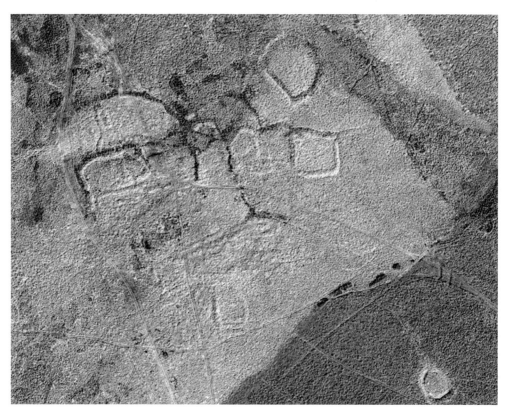

*Figure 7.11 **The Lamb Hill enclosures, shieling and stack stand.***
(Image © 2016 Google, Getmapping plc).

off to the north, and shortly afterwards will arrive at an even larger complex of enclosures on the southern slopes of Lamb Hill.

Here, an aerial photograph (Figure 7.11) shows the remains of at least a dozen enclosures in various states of preservation covering an area of about four acres. Some are broadly rectangular while others are more irregular, and several appear to have later structures built on top of them. In addition, there are one or two

*Figure 7.12 **The stack stand showing the prominent ditch.***

freestanding banks; these might have been built for defence but could also be the remaining fragments of even earlier enclosures.

There is also the outline of at least one shieling. Sited just below the curved bank at the top left of the picture, it consists of a small rectangular set of earthworks about 30 feet long. Precise measurements are misleading because it seems to have been built from turf and over the centuries the walls have collapsed and spread extensively.

All this hints at a period of protracted and possibly intensive use; but we don't know who the users were. It's possible that the site was part of the shieling grounds at *Phillippe* listed in 1604, but equally there were earlier reports of Scottish farmers coming into England for the summer to graze their stock on the south-facing slopes, and this site is less than half a mile from the current border.

There is a second outlying stack stand near the enclosures. About 130 yards to the south-east, and at the lower right of Figure 7.11, it's about 50 feet across and is notable for a distinctive ditch surrounding it (Figure 7.12). There is a low bank outside it and the interior platform seems to be slightly raised, so the spoil from the ditch may have been used in both these places.

Some authorities believe that stack stands originated with agricultural practices of the eighteenth and nineteenth centuries, and so it may be that this one was built later than some of the nearby enclosures, perhaps reflecting a more recent phase of usage,

The Blind Burn *(Map 7.1)*

Continuing to the east from these enclosures, the track leads to the Blind Burn, which defines the eastern edge of the area we are describing. It rises close to the border ridge and flows south and east, before joining the Coquet near Blindburn Farm.

Figure 7.13 The ruins of Yearning Hall looking south-east. On the right is a single, partial gable-end next to the entrance to the byre on the far side. The living area is on the left.

Just before the track meets the burn it passes another abandoned farm. Built on a spur between two small streams, Yearning Hall is marked on few if any maps until those of the Ordnance Survey in the 1860s. However, the Harbottle Presbyterian records show a Weir family (John and Margaret) living here in the late eighteenth century, with six children being born between 1777 and 1790. They may have been Scottish because a John Weir had married Margaret Rutherford in Yetholm in 1775. These baptismal records refer to an *Earning Hall*, rather than the more evocative *Yearning*, and this may provide a clue as to the origin of the farm's name. *Earning* (sometimes actually spelt *yearning*) is a dialect word in Northern England and Scotland for the rennet used in cheese-making, so perhaps it's a reference to the business conducted here.

Figure 7.14 Yearning Hall circa 1980.

In 1841 the farm was lived in by a shepherd, William Davidson, with his wife Hazel, four children and another shepherd. This family had also come from Scotland; judging by the ages and birthplaces of the children, they had probably moved south between 1831 and 1833. Like the farm at Buckham's Walls, Yearning Hall was abandoned in the 1940s. It was then being lived in by a George Lowes and his wife Gladys Evelyn, whose daughter Barbara was born here on 6th April 1940.

Now ruined, the remains are those of a rectangular building about 40 feet long and 17 feet wide aligned on a roughly east-west axis. Single-storeyed, it was built of mortared rubble with dressed stones at the corners and around the doors and windows. An interior stone wall divided it into two, with the eastern part (to the left in Figure 7.13) being almost square. This was the farm's living area; it had a south-facing front door (on the far side in the photograph) and two large windows on either side, the openings of which were splayed out internally to maximise light. It's possible that the roof space above this area was used for sleeping; the 1911 census noted that there were three rooms and it's hard to see how they could all have been at ground level.

A photograph from *circa* 1980 (Figure 7.14) shows that the farm once possessed a slate roof and that its walls had external rendering; there are still traces of this at the eastern end. It also shows a chimney at that end of the building, above the site of a fireplace. There is still an arched, cast-iron fire insert *in situ*, with the remains of a brick-lined flue, some masonry and a few loose Pegswood colliery bricks.

Even though the dividing wall across the building is now badly damaged, there is no sign of a doorway through it to the western section. This has a large opening in its ruined south wall, and the 1980 photograph clearly shows one wide south-facing entrance to this part of the structure and hints at another. Both, however, seem to have been blocked up, and on-site inspection of the remaining walls confirms this. Nevertheless, like its equivalent at Buckham's Walls, this was almost certainly a byre rather than a room.

There are conifers planted near the building, two to the east of the house itself, while another four about 100 feet to the south are on the western end of a rectangular enclosure now bounded by traces of low earth banks. These trees may have been planted after the house was abandoned, because they were quite small in 1980.

Figure 7.15 *The Blind Burn still about 50 years ago. The kiln is on the left.*
(Image courtesy Julian Philipson).

The condition of the building has deteriorated substantially since then; like Buckham's Walls this may not be entirely due to natural causes. At the foot of the trees in Figure 7.13, stones from the house have been used to build a small circular structure that looks like the footings of a campsite or a military emplacement, and there are masonry blocks embedded in a marshy area over 100 yards away.

About half a mile north on the Blind Burn are the remains of an illegal whisky still sited on a small area of haugh land below the steep slope of Beef Stand to the east of the watercourse. Never excavated, if other stills are anything to go by it probably dates from the eighteenth or early nineteenth centuries.

It is not shown on any old maps, but the modern 1:10000 Ordnance Survey marks a small rectangle on the site. Access is not easy, because unlike the other stills described in this book, it's not near an obvious track. And in summer, when the vegetation (mostly nettles) is prolific, the site can hardly be seen at all. Even at other times, a certain amount of careful probing may be necessary.

Built on a north-west to south-east axis, the rectangular building measures about 18 feet by 11 and consists of a turf-covered rough wall up to two feet high in places with a few stone courses still standing (Figure 7.15). There is a good inner face and the outer one is clear along the south-facing sides but elsewhere obscured by the natural slopes. An entrance can be made out at the downstream end of the south-west wall.

The kiln is about six feet across and is outside the north-west end of the rectangle. A certain amount of its stonework is still visible but only a little of the outer face is clear because the rest is covered by the slope of the ground. A small opening through the end wall of the building is still visible and would have acted as a firehole, with fuel being pushed through it.

Depending on rainfall, the water quality and volume in the adjacent burn can be low. If that supply failed, Ordnance Survey maps mark a spring in the hillside just downstream from the site.

Turning back down the burn, and nearly half a mile after passing Yearning Hall, are the remains of a settlement of uncertain date on an area of haugh land. The most obvious feature is a set of low turf and stone banks outlining a rectangular building on the north-east bank and set at right angles to it. In all, the structure is about 40 feet long and 15 feet wide, with an internal wall dividing it into two roughly equal parts. There are traces of an entrance to the building through the south-east wall, while immediately next to it are even fainter traces of a doorway between the two halves of the structure.

There are what may be the remains of two or more irregular enclosures next to this building. Very hard to see except in winter, but definitely there, is a long low dyke downstream from the building. To the east it's tucked in under the slopes of Carlcroft Hill, and with the burn acting as a boundary on the west, it encircles an area about 100 yards long and 50 yards wide.

Some 70 yards upstream there are two sites on the other side of the burn. One is another rectangular building; longer and narrower than the one just described, it measures about 50 feet by ten, with the remains consisting of heavily turfed, low stone walls. From the position of some of the tumble, it is possible that the structure had one, and perhaps two, cross-walls. South of this is a roughly rectangular area scooped into the hillside. About 25 feet square, it could have been dug to hold a now-vanished building, or else it might have been intended for some activity that needed a level floor.

There is no documentary evidence linked with this site, nor is it shown on any old maps. The best that can be said about it is that it was once a small set of shielings or steadings that may have been built at any time between the medieval period and the eighteenth century.

Continuing downstream, the burn meets the Coquet near the farm at Blindburn at the south-eastern edge of our area, and the modern metalled road heads west to the Buckham's Walls Burn and Fulhope, sites that we covered at the start of this chapter.

Detail of Roman masonry
in a wall at Bremenium.

Chapter 8

Dere Street

The roads through the Cheviots have never existed in isolation, connecting as they did with the early tracks and routeways that threaded their way through the Scottish Lowlands and the Northumbrian plain. However, the names by which we know the Cheviot roads are predominantly linked to their presence in the hills; we rarely have names for the lowland routes.

The one exception is Dere Street. Its name is probably of Anglian origin, borrowed from the kingdom of Deira that stretched from the Humber to the Tees and which later became part of Northumbria[1]. Its origins as a Roman road linking York with Scotland were in the years around AD 80 when the military governor Agricola campaigned in the north of Britain. Parts of its route are well known. From York it headed to Aldborough, where it turned north along what is now the A1, the Great North Road. After Catterick it continued through County Durham to Corbridge, crossed Hadrian's Wall and followed the modern A68 to Rochester. From there it traversed the Cheviots, passed Jedburgh and headed to Newstead. Near Melrose, this was the site of the Roman fort of Trimontium – the *tres montes* being the three peaks of the Eildon Hills. Beyond that, its exact course towards Edinburgh is sometimes less certain; medieval charters identified part of its route south of Soutra and it would have linked up with the road systems that serviced the Antonine Wall.

The Romans, however, should probably not get all the credit. It was once thought that they laid out the British road system on a blank canvas, but this was not always the case. While the existence of some major prehistoric trackways has been known for a long time, recent discoveries hint at a more substantial Iron Age road system. For example, work at Bayston Hill in Shropshire has revealed that a Roman road was built on top of a sequence of earlier metalled surfaces, some of which may have dated back to 200 BC. Analysis of the A1 corridor in Yorkshire has revealed that it is lined with structures such as Neolithic henges, Bronze Age barrows and Iron Age settlements. Here there are traces of early trade with mainland Europe, so on occasions the Roman Dere Street may well have re-used existing tracks, particularly in the Cheviots where the number of viable routes is limited.

This chapter focuses on the stretch of Dere Street that starts at Rochester, about 25 miles north of Hadrian's Wall. We follow the Roman route as it heads away from the modern A68, crosses the border north of Chew Green and, for our purposes, ends at Whitton Edge, east of Jedburgh and some four or five miles into Scotland. Between Rochester and Chew Green, Dere Street crosses the Otterburn artillery ranges, first established in 1911, where its path is largely the same as that of the modern metalled road. The Ministry of Defence publishes live firing times for the ranges and while you can use this road when there is no activity, *ad hoc* exploration in the area is not

---

[1] Confusingly, parts of Dere Street were often labelled 'Watling Street' on maps as late as the twentieth century. This error may result from a misreading of the Antonine Itinerary, a document that described roads in Britain and mainland Europe as they were some time around the third century AD.

permitted. So while we can describe the archaeology along the part of the route entitled 'Crossing the Ranges', it may be hard to visit it.

Rochester (Map 8.1)

At Rochester a Roman fort next to Dere Street is generally identified as the Bremenium listed in Ptolemy's *Geographia*; written in about AD 140, he suggested that before the Romans arrived this was a centre for the British tribe now referred to as the Votadini.

The language the Votadini spoke has not survived, but it is generally accepted that it was from the early Celtic family – a precursor, for example, of modern Welsh. There are indications that in these languages *brem* meant 'roar', so the name may be a Romanised version of a British one meaning *'place of the roaring stream'*, presumably a reference to the nearby Sills Burn.

The fort covers just over four acres and is almost square in shape, with interior sides of between 420 and 440 feet. Much of the stonework from the walls has been robbed and later buildings have been constructed in the interior of the camp; the best surviving stretches of original masonry are on the west side (Figure 8.1).

Of all the archaeological sites covered in this book, Bremenium is among the best studied and, as Roman forts go, is quite well preserved. The site was first excavated in the 1850s with the involvement of Thomas Taylor, the Duke of Northumberland's *'very able mining engineer'*, and then again in 1935 by Ian Richmond, who was later a professor at Oxford. In the 1990s, there was a series of geophysical surveys and excavations overseen by James Crow of Newcastle University, then more surveying in 2003, while in 2010 a planning application within the fort gave rise to yet another dig.

It is likely that the first Roman building at Bremenium consisted of a turf-walled enclosure constructed in the first century AD, probably at the time of Agricola's

Figure 8.1 The west gate of the Roman camp at Bremenium. The wall blocking the entrance, and the one on top of the masonry blocks are modern.

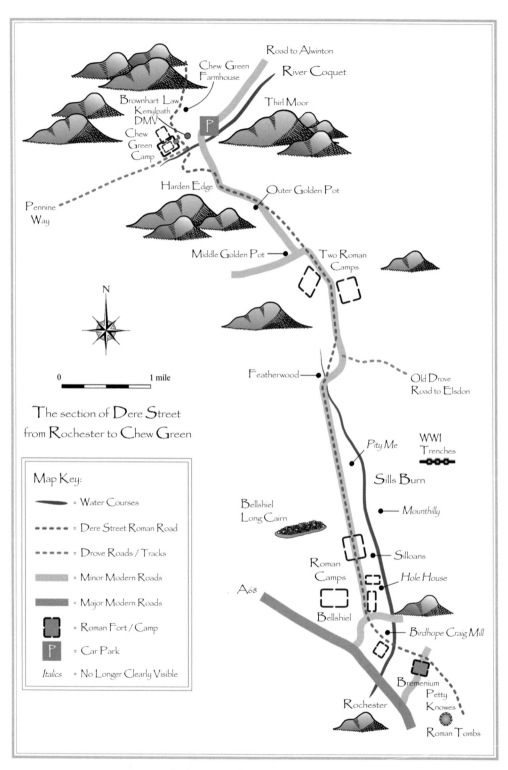

Rochester to Chew Green. (Map 8.1)

campaign. It isn't known if it was abandoned when the Romans subsequently withdrew south before Hadrian's Wall was built soon after AD 122, but stone inscriptions found at the site help track later activity.

For example, it is almost certain that the first stone fort was constructed under the direction of Quintus Lollius Urbicus, the governor of Britain between AD 139 and 142 (Figure 8.2). Having refurbished the fort at Corbridge further down Dere Street, he moved north to start work on the Antonine Wall; perhaps he broke his journey at

Figure 8.2 *This inscription was found in 1852. Heavily abbreviated, it reads 'Imp(eratori) Caes(ari) T(ito) Aelio H[a]d(riano) Antonino Aug(usto) Pio p(atri) p(atriae) sub Q(uinto) Lol(lio) Urbico | leg(ato) Aug(usti) pro prae(tore) coh(ors) I Ling(onum) eq(uitata) f(ecit)'. For the Emperor Caesar Titus Aelius Hadrianus Antoninus Augustus Pius, father of his country, under Quintus Lollius Urbicus, emperor's propraetorian legate, the First Cohort of Lingones, part-mounted, built this.*

Bremenium, or else just managed the work from a distance. Later inscriptions describe sequences of rebuilding in the early third century, probably after a period of abandonment following a series of local uprisings around AD 180. One such text provides an insight into the complex patterns of service that Roman officers experienced. Now in Elsdon church (see Figure 2.2), it was commissioned by one Julia Lucilla to commemorate her husband Rufinus, the commander at Bremenium who died at some time in the third century. Before this posting, he had held positions in Egypt, Morocco and Italy, so Rochester winters must have come as a bit of a shock.

Other inscriptions confirm the cosmopolitan nature of the Roman army. There are references to a cohort of Varduli being at Rochester *circa* AD 240, possibly around the time Rufinus died. These were troops from what is now the Basque country in Spain and they also show up on Hadrian's Wall and at Cappuck, further north on Dere Street and east of Jedburgh. There is also a reference to spearmen from Raetia, a Roman province sited mainly in eastern and central Switzerland.

The fort's walls were more than 16 feet thick in places, with a core of clay and a substantial masonry facing; surveys have identified sets of multiple ditches outside them, although it's not clear if these went all the way round the fort. The interior had a network of narrow, paved streets and pathways separating densely packed stone buildings which included what was apparently a headquarters, some barrack blocks with hypocausts, a bathhouse and two grain stores; at least a number of these structures were apparently visible on the surface at the time of the first excavations (Figure 8.3). It was unusual to have granaries and a bathhouse actually inside an early Roman fort, and the reason may have been the precarious frontier nature of the location.

The granaries could have stored imported wheat. We have no direct evidence about the diet of the people at Bremenium but analysis of latrine waste from Bearsden, an Antonine Wall fort on the edge of Glasgow, shows that the soldiers there were largely vegetarians (as well as suffering from fleas and worms). Different grains were used to make bread, porridge and pasta, with durum wheat for the latter maybe coming from southern Spain. Although some local fruit and vegetables were consumed, such as berries, wild celery and turnips, other imports included figs, lentils and coriander.

The troops at Bremenium probably consisted of mixed infantry and cavalry regiments known as *cohortes equitatae*. Up to 1,000 strong (a *milliaria*), these were miniature armies, sometimes accompanied by scouts, and this sort of number could probably

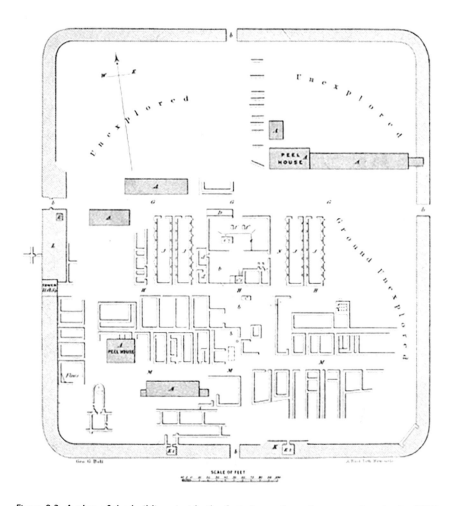

Figure 8.3 *A plan of the buildings inside the fort, drawn from the excavations in the 1850s.*

have been accommodated inside the fort. However, it would have been difficult to handle any visiting troops and this may account for some of the other camps along Dere Street.

Geophysical surveys and investigations have located the surface of the Roman road about a foot below ground level to the north of the fort, and identified other structures outside the walls. One of these was an extensive area of cobbling, perhaps used as hard standing for passing troops and wagons. To the west there were annexes covering an area similar to that of the fort itself. There may have been some prehistoric earthworks among them, but it is likely that these mostly consisted of extensions to the early fort and buildings and workshops for military applications. One building might have been another bathhouse.

It is not clear how many phases of Roman occupation there were at Bremenium and how often rebuilding took place, but although there were undoubtedly periods of abandonment and reoccupation, the main function of the fort was to act as one of a series of outposts for the main body of troops at Hadrian's Wall. The site appears to have been abandoned in the early fourth century, although the 2010 dig referred to above found hints of continuing activity on the site.

The ramparts and some areas of exposed stonework are now best viewed from a path that encircles the fort, but very little can now be seen of the other features described. However, some of the fort's masonry may survive in the two houses in the interior. Much modernised, these may be based on strongholds or bastles dating from around the sixteenth century; past inspection has revealed walls that contain both rubble and squared Roman stones.

The nineteenth-century excavators believed they had found a comprehensive water distribution and drainage system inside the fort with its supply delivered by an aqueduct from Petty Knowes. This is about 500 yards to the south-east; it's an area where a Roman cemetery with about 100 barrows and four more substantial tombs has been identified.

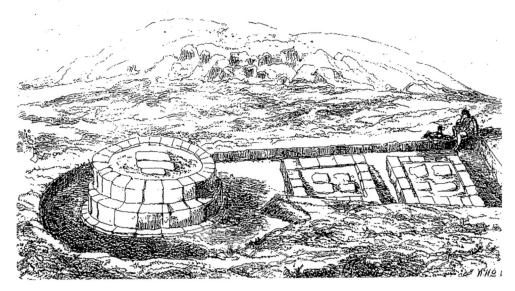

Figure 8.4 Three of the original high-status tombs at Petty Knowes drawn in 1854.

*Figure 8.5 **The officer's tomb.***

In 1978 and 1979 some of the barrow burials were investigated by Margaret Mitchison and Beryl Charlton, who did extensive work for the Ministry of Defence on the archaeology of the ranges. Many of the graves consisted of low mounds surrounded by a ditch and an outer bank, although a few were discovered that were undetectable on the surface. About half the burials contained the remains of burning, suggesting that cremation had taken place *in situ*; in almost all the cases investigated the cremated bones had been placed in pots prior to final burial. It was possible to identify the origin of many of these, some coming from as far afield as Kent, Dorset and Suffolk.

The four more substantial tombs, one circular and three square, were immediately next to Dere Street. The 1866 Ordnance Survey map shows that two of the square ones were near the circular structure, with the fourth a few yards away to the southeast. They were investigated in 1850 by William Coulson, an excise officer. He lived in one of the houses inside the fort and was presumably stationed there to control smuggling along Dere Street. There are few details of his work, although there were reports of finding burnt soil, a broken urn and a coin of Severus Alexander, who was Emperor from AD 222 to 235. A useful contemporary survival is a drawing made in 1854 (Figure 8.4).

In 1886 the area was managed by John Dixon, a colliery owner who lived just to the west at Hopesley House. Fed up with trespassers visiting the tombs, he did the logical thing and started to destroy them. The Society of Antiquaries in Newcastle got wind of this and persuaded him to stop, but not before the circular tomb was the only one left. Dixon then wrote to the Society, assuring members of his '*desire to preserve and protect it from destruction'*, which seems a bit rich. Some masonry from the other tombs has found its way into a sheep stell about 100 yards to the north, while low mounds mark the site of the demolition.

Known as the officer's tomb, the surviving structure is about 15 feet across with two main courses of masonry remaining, although in places a foundation course can also be seen (Figure 8.5). Two of the blocks carry very worn carvings; one is of the head of an animal, perhaps an ox, while the other may be a pine cone. The latter, in particular, was a symbol the Romans associated with death; it falls from an evergreen tree but in the cycle of death and rebirth it contains seeds that create a new one. These carvings are best seen on a clear day around noon, when the sun shines across them rather than on to them, and they are thrown into relief.

Charlton and Mitchison concluded that the cemetery was definitely associated with the fort, and said there might be others as yet undetected. The condition of the bones they found was poor and only two tentative identifications of their source could be made; one set came from a female or a juvenile that had been buried with a small animal, perhaps a lamb, while another appeared to be from a child aged between five and ten.

A similar mixture of burials is reflected in Rochester's Roman tombstones. Most of these were unearthed during the eighteenth and nineteenth centuries and it is not clear exactly where they were found, but they include memorials to a freedman, a child and someone's foster child. It would seem that, at certain times at least, there were civilians and families living in or near the fort as well as troops and military staff.

Crossing the ranges *(Map 8.1)*

As it leaves Bremenium, Dere Street follows a line to the west of the Sills Burn. On the burn, less than half a mile from the fort, is the site of Birdhope Craig mill. Now vanished, apart from the possible remains of a leat or race that fed the wheel, it was first mentioned in parish records in 1705, but may well have been built in the seventeenth century at a time when the number of mills increased substantially. Last recorded in 1817, it was probably abandoned when grain prices fell after the Napoleonic Wars.

Corn milling was not the only industry here; as in many rural areas there is also evidence of coal mining. On the other side of the road from the mill site and about 400 yards south of Dere Street there are clusters of depressions and mounds that are the remains of old bell pits, shafts and spoil heaps. There are similar remains elsewhere in the area.

In the eighteenth century local wood supplies became depleted and people turned to peat and coal, the latter being more efficient and sometimes fairly accessible. In addition, coal was needed for the developing practice of burning limestone to make quicklime for land improvement.

The output from these pits must have been quite substantial; in the 1790s there are records of it being carried on horseback over the border to Hownam, a journey that must have taken it through the Cheviots on Dere Street and then along the track north-east from Pennymuir. Ten years later the Newcastle mining engineer, John

Watson, estimated that the cost of building a colliery at Birdhope Craig with a five-foot shaft 100 feet deep, together with pumps driven by a water wheel, would be over £500.

There are additional Roman camps in the area as well; the first one, before the line of Dere Street joins the modern road over the ranges, is Birdhope Craig (Figure 8.6). Just 500 yards north-west of Bremenium, it consists of a well-preserved rectangular set of ramparts inside a much larger, earlier, and now very faint trapezoidal structure covering between 20 and 30 acres.

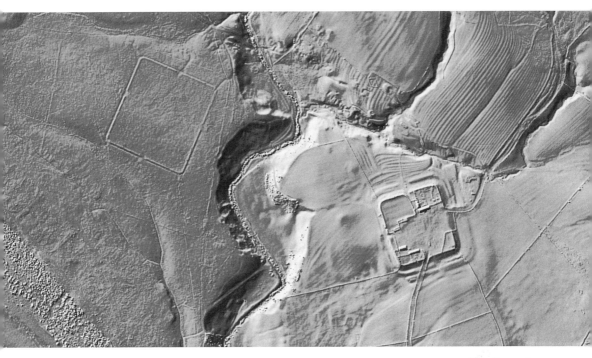

Figure 8.6 A LiDAR image of the fort at Bremenium (on the right of the burn) and the Birdhope Craig camp. The line of the larger outer camp also be seen in places.
(Image supplied under Open Government Licence 3.0).

Then about a mile from Bremenium, just after Dere Street has joined the modern road, there's a camp at Bellshiel. With low, turf-built ramparts, this is on top of a gentle hill to the west and covers nearly 40 acres – big enough for two legions. Nearly opposite, just to the east of the road and in a field leading down to the Sills Burn, is a smaller camp in the form of a long thin rectangle that is clearly visible from a passing car. Probably only large enough for a few hundred troops, some of its ramparts have been damaged by ploughing and much of the interior is full of rig and furrow. And about 200 yards further on, again to the east of the road, there's another small camp. This has suffered more damage, but its western rampart and gate can still just be seen.

These camps may have housed visiting troops, but they could also have been used to provide soldiers with building practice; they are, however, larger than most of the camps generally recognised as pure training sites. Nearly 2,000 years later the area was definitely used for military building practice. Further on, beyond Silloans farm and about a mile east of Dere Street, is a set of well-preserved World War I trenches

(Figure 8.7). They consist of both front and reserve lines, linked by communication trenches built in zig-zags. There are no records of exactly when they were built or who built them but an excavation showed that parts of them conformed to construction standards described in a 1916 Field Fortification Manual.

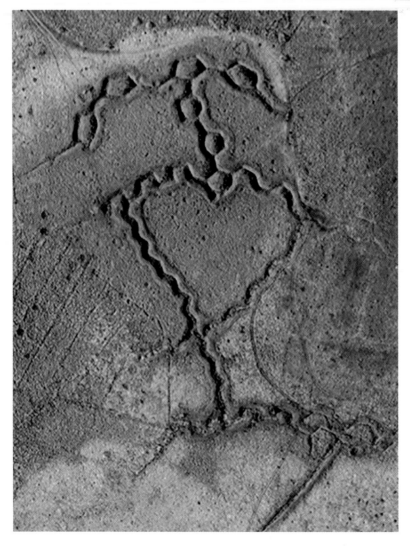

*Figure 8.7 **The WWI trenches at Silloans.** (Image © 2016 Google, Getmapping plc).*

There is another non-Roman military connection with Silloans. In 1987, while a field at the farm was being cleared of ordnance, investigators came across the remains of a medieval sword. It was clearly a high status object and one possibility is that it was a relic from the Battle of Otterburn in 1388, with a victorious Scotsman dropping it on the way back north.

Just 25 yards south of the turning to Silloans, the road cuts through a low bank. This is a rampart of yet another camp, even bigger than Bellshiel; Dere Street passes neatly though its southern gate and exits via the northern one after 500 yards, where the rampart is more visible to the west of the road. Some observers have suggested that this intrusion means it was an early camp, built and abandoned before Dere Street was driven through it. However, William Roy's map of the fort at New Kirkpatrick, now Bearsden, on the Antonine Wall, shows exactly the same characteristic, with the structure bisected by the military way that connected the forts along the wall.

A little further on, a clump of trees is visible towards the top of a hill to the west; beyond that, about half a mile from the road, lies Bellshiel Long Cairn (Figure 8.8). This dates from the Neolithic and is one of only a few of this type in Northumberland; probably some 5,000 years old, it's 360 feet long, up to 50 feet wide and five feet high in places. It consists largely of exposed stones, some of which have been rearranged to form shelters inside the structure. A dig in 1935 conducted by Nancy Newbigin revealed that it had been considerably damaged: a sheepfold had been built into its south side, it had been probed in pursuit of rabbits (she found a snare deep inside it) and, worst of all, the eastern end had been robbed as recently as 1912, with stones being removed for building local roads. Examination revealed a kerb around the cairn, with stones then being piled up fairly randomly inside. Long cairns are typically burial monuments, and cut into the underlying rock at the east end was a six-foot long pit which was interpreted as a grave.

Despite this, it was clearly a frustrating dig. With a rare display of archaeological anger, Nancy Newbigin described the structure as having '*no courts, no chambers, no ditches, no revetment, no structures, no secondary burials, no forecourt, crude and spasmodic attempts at coursing. It is a monster of degeneracy*'.

There are more Neolithic and Bronze Age cairns still further to the west, so it's possible that there were early paths across the moors in that area and that the Romans ignored them when they followed their normal practice in building the straight stretch of road north of Bremenium.

Dere Street continues north towards the farm at Featherwood, passing the sites of other, abandoned farms. The first of these, 'Hole House', is actually south of Silloans and just to the west of the burn; the last definite reference to it was on the

Figure 8.8 Bellshiel long cairn from the east.

Armstrongs' map of 1769, while the earliest we can find is in 1687 when a yeoman, William Hall, died there leaving just over £20. He was not a wealthy man, with over half of this consisting of two oxen and two cows. There's now no sign of the farm, but the name appears elsewhere along the border, sometimes being used for bastles or other defended houses.

Just over half a mile north of Silloans, and across the burn to the east of the road, is the Mounthilly tank training area. Less than 100 yards from the burn is a sheepfold, but on the 1866 Ordnance Survey map it is described as 'Mounthilly (in ruins)'; low earthworks show it was once more than just a fold but nothing else is known about it.

Finally, north of the tank training area and about 200 yards east of the road is a site with the evocative name of Pity Me. Some remains of the house that stood here can still be seen; a working farm in the nineteenth century, but abandoned because the site was dangerously close to artillery fire, it was demolished by the War Office in 1927. There are several theories about the origin of the name, but the simplest and the most likely is that it was a cry for sympathy from the people that farmed in such a bleak spot.

Figure 8.9 The Featherwood blast shelter.

The two current buildings at Featherwood date from the 1950s and the nineteenth century – although Elsdon parish records show that people lived here in the seventeenth century. The farm has not been inhabited since 1982, and life here must have been hazardous when live artillery was in action on the ranges. There's a substantial blockhouse across the burn to the west; built for civilian use and with walls about two feet thick, it was designed to be shellproof. In the 1960s, when the army started testing a new anti-tank missile nearby, it was replaced by a reinforced-brick blast shelter at the rear of the farm (Figure 8.9).

Having been dead straight for about three miles, beyond Featherwood the route starts to submit to the terrain, picking its way between gentle hills and finally climbing to over 1,600 feet, with the metalled road not always following the Roman one. For example, after crossing the Sills Burn at Featherwood the modern road runs north-east for about 300 yards before following a branch to the north. Dere Street itself heads north almost immediately after the burn, and can be seen in the fields to the west of the road before the two meet up half a mile further on.

There are more items of note along this stretch – such as two large Roman camps just over a mile north of Featherwood. The first of these, to the east of the road, is almost square and occupies some 40 acres, while the second, slightly further north and to the west, is lozenge-shaped and a bit smaller. The closest part of the square camp is only 100 feet from the road, and its western gate is protected by a *titulus*, an external bank and ditch placed opposite the gateway in order to protect it from direct attack. The north-eastern gate of the second camp is about 200 feet from the road, and also sports a *titulus*. Each of these structures could have handled at least one legion.

Figure 8.10 The Outer Golden Pot. Each side is about three feet long.

Counting these two, there are the remains of eight Roman camps along a six-mile stretch of Dere Street north of Bremenium – and there are three more within three miles further south. Even if they were not all in use at once, there was clearly the capacity to handle a considerable number of troops. It's interesting to note that a similar concentration of camps is found near Wroxeter in Shropshire, which may have served as a mustering point for campaigns into Wales.

The other items of interest in this area are the Golden Pots – large shaped stones with holes in their upper surfaces (Figure 8.10). Modern Ordnance Survey maps show two – the Middle, just beyond these last two camps and the Outer, nearly a mile further north.

It is unclear how many Pots there originally were; in the mid-eighteenth century William Roy said that there were at least five, but some have now vanished, others may have been moved and names may have been changed. The Armstrongs' map of 1769 shows one, presumably the hypothetical Inner Pot, to the north of Featherwood just where the old drove road leaves Dere Street to the east and heads to Elsdon. Maclauchlan also shows this on his 1851 map but his commentary implies that he copied it from the Armstrongs and didn't actually see it[2]; however, he did see and record the current Middle and Outer Pots, the only two that remain. Now damaged, they were once thought to be the remains of Roman milestones, and it has also been suggested that they could have been markers for an early boundary between the parishes of Elsdon and Holystone. However, they are more likely to be the sockets for medieval wayside crosses. Often found on isolated moorland tracks these served both to guide and reassure travellers.

From its high point at Harden Edge, north of the Pots, the road descends the hillside to the headwaters of the Coquet. There has been a lot of erosion on this slope – and a lot of traffic over the centuries – but with a bit of imagination and the right lighting, segments of what was probably Dere Street can be made out as it loses height in a series of switchbacks to the west of the modern road.

Chew Green

Apart from Bremenium itself, the camp at Chew Green is the first set of Roman remains north of Rochester that can be examined at leisure. As well as coming along Dere Street, the site can be reached by driving up Coquetdale to the car park just before the road turns south and enters the ranges. If you've approached from this direction then it's worth passing the car park, crossing the river and going up the hill to the south to see the camp from above; this view helps clarify what can often be a confusing set of earthworks at ground level (Figure 8.11).

A third way of reaching Chew Green is to walk along the Pennine Way, which joins Dere Street from the west and then follows it for a couple of miles until it heads north-east towards Kirk Yetholm. The first National Trail, it was finished in 1965 but had been a long time in the planning.

After the Second World War, a group of Labour politicians used to organise an annual walk along a section of what would become the Way; by May 1950 they had reached the Cheviots. The party included Hugh Dalton, the minister for Town and Country Planning and president of the Ramblers Association, and Barbara Castle – then an MP but later a cabinet minister in the Wilson governments.

After a surprise visit to the school at Barrowburn (politicians never miss a trick), the group planned to walk up the Coquet and then on to Cottonshope, a farm near the ranges to the west of Dere Street. It had been agreed *'at a high ministerial level'* that the army would not be firing that day, but the arrangement had not been communicated to the actual gunners who were pounding the area[3]. A detour was made.

The modern name Chew Green may have been adopted from the area around an almost-lost farmhouse at the north end of the site, of which more later. The camp is sometimes identified with the Roman name *Ad Fines*, which can be loosely translated as 'at the limits' or 'at the end'. But this label has to be taken with a large pinch of salt,

---

[2] He wrote: *'This we presume is the spot where the Golden Pot stood … as drawn in Armstrong's map'*
[3] The Minister for Defence was Manny Shinwell; he was new to the job.

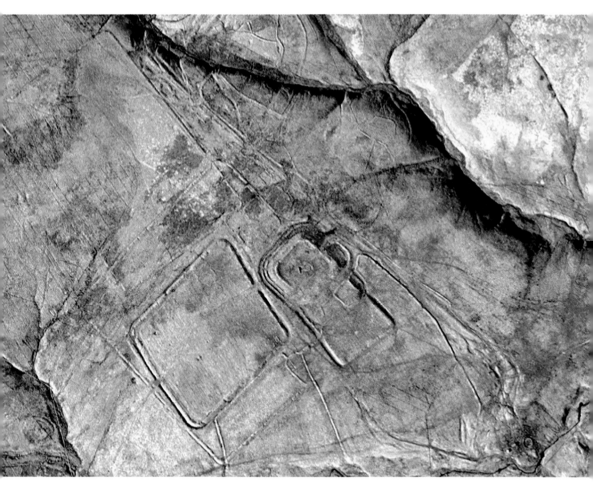

Figure 8.11 An aerial view of Chew Green. The boundaries of the field systems are above the sike at top centre. (Image © 2016 Google, Infoterra Ltd. & Bluesky).

originating as it did in a book called *De Situ Britanniae*. Purporting to contain a medieval manuscript incorporating a hitherto lost account of Britain written by a Roman general, it turned out to be a forgery created in the middle of the eighteenth century. Its author, Charles Bertram, lived in Copenhagen; this made access to his source material difficult and it took over a hundred years for his chicanery to be generally accepted, partly because it was a clever blend of fact and fiction. It deceived the great and the good, influencing first William Roy and then site descriptions in the Ordnance Survey. The fictitious name *Ad Fines* is still perpetuated on the web and elsewhere.

The only major published excavation at Chew Green was carried out in 1936 by Ian Richmond and George Keeney. They showed that there were four visible Roman structures on the site, and they believed they had found the buried remains of a fifth.

Dere Street runs along the eastern side of these structures. The earliest component of the Chew Green complex is the south camp (red in Figure 8.12). Some 19 acres in size and large enough for a legion, it is overlapped by the later north camp which covers about 14 acres. Each of these camps has gates, and there are two on the longer sides of the latter. Richmond and Keeney found *tituli* opposite some of these, but they are now very hard to see. They detected *claviculae* in some places; these are curved banks on the inside of the gates that also served to discourage direct charges, but they are now invisible on the surface, as are the few stretches of internal streets they described.

The other two structures are better preserved. They consist of a six-acre camp with ramparts sometimes several feet high that is completely inside the original south camp, and a small square fort or fortlet to the east of this that measures about 200 feet on each side. The smaller camp is almost certainly later than the southern camp encompassing it, since a *titulus* outside its western gate appears to block access to the gate of the larger structure. Parts of the fortlet are surrounded by an impressive

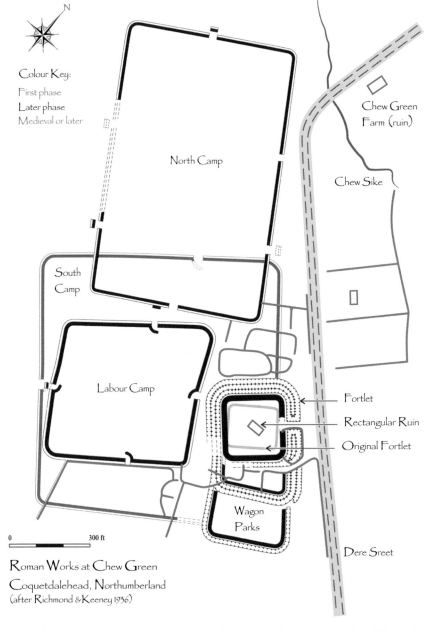

N

Colour Key:
First phase
Later phase
Medieval or later

North Camp

Chew Green
Farm (ruin)

Chew Sike

South
Camp

Labour Camp

Fortlet

Rectangular Ruin

Original Fortlet

Wagon
Parks

0   300 ft

Dere Sreet

Roman Works at Chew Green
Coquetdalehead, Northumberland
(after Richmond & Keeney 1936)

Figure 8.12 **Plan of the main structures at Chew Green (after Richmond and Keeney).**

triple ditch, but this doesn't encircle it completely, perhaps because of intervening bedrock. The fortlet was apparently built on top of an earlier one, which can no longer be seen; to its south are earthen banks forming sets of enclosures.

In 2010, the Ministry of Defence commissioned a geophysical survey of the site. With the exception of a rectangular building within the fortlet, no substantive remains were found inside the camps, although ground conditions were not ideal. Perhaps not surprisingly, this suggests that the site was not used as intensively as Bremenium, a conclusion reinforced by the number of finds from the 1936 excavation, when just a single sherd of first-century pottery was identified in the remains of the first fortlet, and a few pieces of second-century pot from the later one. From this, and from the relationships between the structures, Richmond concluded that the south camp and the original fortlet had been built around AD 80 during Agricola's campaign in Scotland, while the north camp, the second fortlet and the smaller camp inside the original south camp followed in the next century, at the time of the Antonine wall. It was suggested that the smaller camp housed labourers who were responsible for building the second fortlet and maybe maintaining Dere Street, while the adjacent enclosures acted as wagon parks, making Chew Green the equivalent of an armed service station.

Given what we know of Roman activity in the north of England and Scotland, this is a plausible scenario, although there is limited evidence to support it. The situation has been complicated by later activity on the site. Richmond and Keeney found fragments of medieval pottery dating from between 1250 and 1450; more obviously there are several dykes and earthworks around the camps that they did not investigate, probably because they thought these were medieval as well. They do not appear to be part of the Roman configurations, and their construction could have disturbed any remains in the area.

We don't know when the site was abandoned, but Dere Street must have continued as a civilian thoroughfare and a trading route. There are no specific records of this for a thousand years but in the thirteenth century, as the concept of an Anglo-Scottish border started to become a reality, albeit a disputed one, Chew Green emerged from the mists.

It became known as a place where opposing groups would meet to try to settle border disputes – and sometimes hear criminal cases about border raiding. People from Redesdale, Coquetdale and Roxburghshire could easily travel here for such a purpose; of course, Dere Street was also a similarly useful thoroughfare for the raiders themselves.

The stretch of Dere Street around Chew Green became known as *Gamelspeth* – a name that persisted well into the post-medieval period, even appearing on twentieth-century Ordnance Survey maps as Gammel's Path. *Gamel* is a Norse word also found in Old English. Sometimes used as a name, it originally meant 'old'; in modern Danish and Norwegian the equivalent word is *gammel*. The reason for the label is obvious: when it was adopted the road had been in use for over a thousand years.

A settlement grew up next to the Roman camps, although it's not clear whether this was the result of the meetings there, or because its presence made it a convenient place to hold them. Known by variations on the name *Kemylpeth*, it first appeared in records in the thirteenth century and was listed in inquisitions *post mortem* for the Lords of Redesdale up to the late fifteenth century. A 1550 survey referred to houses 'built in times past called Kemylpeth Walls' and thereafter the name seems to be more associated with the road than the settlement. Some of its house platforms and enclosures can still be seen on either side of the current Dere Street track, most clearly just to the north of the Roman fortlet. The outlines of old field systems are also visible further east beyond Chew Sike. These may be medieval too, but they could be connected with the Chew Green farmhouse a few hundred yards further north, which was almost certainly functioning much later. Of course, they might be both.

Finally, we should describe an earlier dig at Chew Green carried out in 1883 and 1884 by Clement Hodges, an architect from Hexham Abbey who had been hired by the landowner, Ralph Carr-Ellison, to find Roman antiquities. He failed in this and he never published his results, but we know from later reports that he investigated the remains of the building in the centre of the fortlet and found pieces of worked masonry that he thought looked Norman. If he kept them, these are now lost and there is no drawing of them.

A few years later, Thomas Glendinning, a shepherd from the nearby farm of Makendon, found a small sandstone cross nearby and Hodges suggested that it might have decorated what he had come to believe was a chapel built in the fortlet to serve the medieval community. However, careful reading of the shepherd's account raises doubts about this connection. He described the cross as being found 20 yards from 'the Chew Green', which sounds like the farmhouse, especially as at the time the Roman site was often referred to as the 'Makendon camps'. He also said it was 'about 40 or 50 yards from where you were digging on the north-east side of the camp'. This suggests that the cross was found near where the current footbridge crosses Chew Sike and over 400 yards from the site of the building in the fortlet, which is much nearer the south-east of the camp than the north-east. It may be that the cross was a medieval wayside marker rather than from a chapel.

Although the evidence is circumstantial, it is worth noting that Hodges was not always a reliable source. In other areas, comparison of his original notebooks with his published work shows that on occasions he was prone to embellishing drawings of artefacts such as grave slabs. And a recent analysis of his suggestions for original structures at Hexham Abbey has shown that some of them are rather implausible.

Dere Street heads north from Chew Green, and its character changes slightly. Its route from Rochester fits fairly well with the popular image of the Roman Road – long and straight with no corners for nasty natives to hide behind, as readers of *1066 and All That* will remember. But because of the terrain, it negotiates the next section of the Cheviots in a series of doglegs, with the first of these immediately to the north of the camp, where it turns sharply east to cross Chew Sike and traverse the southern slopes of Brownhart Law. From a distance it can be seen that over the centuries several tracks have been cut across this hillside. One result of this multiplicity of routes is that Roy's eighteenth-century map shows the old Chew Green farmhouse to the north of the path, whereas its rectangular outline can now be seen some yards south of the current track. David Dippie Dixon said that quantities of seventeenth-century glasses and pipes had been found here, making it the site of a tavern. He may well have been right, although it is perhaps better thought of as a farm that made money by catering for the needs of passing travellers and traders.

Crossing the Border (Map 8.2)

There are two interesting sites where the track reaches the top of the slope, turns north and crosses briefly into Scotland. The first of these is a cross dyke. This is not immediately obvious from the path because the construction of Dere Street has obliterated some 50 yards of its central section, but longer lengths of the dyke, 120 yards and 130 yards respectively, are clearly visible heading off the ridge to the south-east and the north-west, the latter being on the other side of the fence next to the path (Figure 8.13).

Figure 8.13 Feral goats resting on the western part of the cross dyke bisected by Dere Street at Brownhart Law.

Just beyond the dyke, and again over the fence, is a roughly circular set of earthworks about 90 feet across that is thought be the remains of a Roman signal station, although there's little physical evidence for this. The archaeologist that first made the association was Kenneth St. Joseph, a pioneer of aerial photography who spent almost all his career at Cambridge. His plan of it shows a distinct rectangle with rounded corners and he linked this shape to that of known signal stations. He dug one exploratory trench on the site, but apparently found nothing. Recent aerial photographs, however, show the structure is much less rectangular than he suggested.

However, there are certainly good views to the west; some 13 miles away is the prominent peak of Rubers Law near Hawick, which almost certainly did have a Roman building on top of it, while on a clear day the Eildon Hills above Trimontium can be seen over 20 miles away.

Long-distance Roman signalling must have been rudimentary. There was no word or rank for signaller in the Roman army, and although the Greek historian Polybius described complex communication systems involving forms of semaphore and the use of timed fires to transmit predetermined messages, these would have been impractical

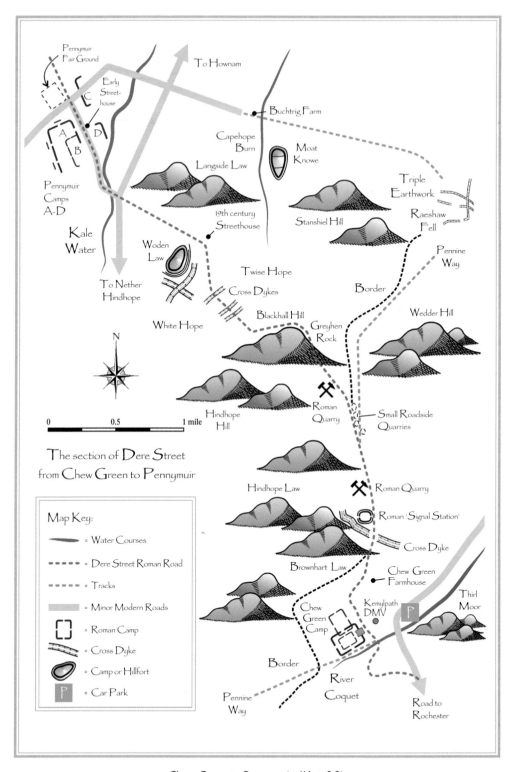

Chew Green to Pennymuir. (Map 8.2)

over the distances here. If Brownhart Law was a signalling station, then it must have relied on the use of fire to convey a single message, in the same way that a network of beacons in the south of England was once used to warn of approaching enemy ships. Indeed, Julius Caesar in his commentary on the Gallic Wars specifically mentions the use of fires to summon troops. A good fire on Rubers Law would be clearly visible from Dere Street, although not, of course, if an astute attacker chose a misty, cloudy day (Figure 8.14).

Figure 8.14 The view north-west from Brownhart Law; Rubers Law is in the distance.

There are, however, no identified signalling sites to the south of Brownhart Law and no line of sight to Chew Green, less than a mile away. Presumably, a runner would have had notify personnel there of any message which might have been ultimately destined for Bremenium. A better approach would have been to build a signal station on top of Brownhart Law, with superior views into Scotland and visiblity from Chew Green. Best of all, a station on top of Thirl Moor, just over a mile away to the south of the Coquet, would still have had views of Trimontium and Rubers Law and could be seen from both Chew Green and Bremenium itself. All this, and the misinterpretation of the structure's shape, suggests that the case for a signal station must be considered not proven.

There are quarries by the side of Dere Street as it continues north, first a large one on the western side of the road about 150 yards north of the cross dyke and then a whole series of smaller ones. These must have been used to keep the road repaired. Parts of the track are very soft and swampy, and it may have been much the same in Roman times; about a mile north of Brownhart Law there's an especially treacherous patch, and just beyond it are the remains of the largest quarry of all. That can't be coincidence.

North of Brownhart Law the road is fairly straight, crossing and recrossing the border but never much more than 100 yards from it until it reaches Blackhall Hill. Here the border heads east and almost immediately Dere Street executes a sharp turn to the west and heads across the northern slopes of the hill. From a footpath higher up, near a large outcrop with the evocative name of Greyhen Rock (the earthenware pots used to transport illicit whisky were called grey hens), you can look down on Dere Street; if the vegetation is not too high you can clearly see the structure of the road, particularly the *agger* (Figure 8.15). Originally raised in the centre for drainage, this was the central part of the road; here it is some 35 feet wide, with ditches on either side. It would have been more than wide enough to accommodate the movement of a Roman legion, described as they were as marching six abreast.

Figure 8.15 Dere Street north-west of Blackhall Hill.

Along this stretch, and after it turns to the north-west towards Woden Law, the road crosses several relatively short cross dykes. It's hard to know what these were for, but they probably predate the Roman construction because Dere Street seems to cut through them; a section of the largest one, right at the foot of Woden Law, has clearly been destroyed by later traffic.

Woden Law

The course of the road leading to Woden Law is interesting. For a few hundred yards it runs along the crest of a ridge which falls away to the Twise Hope to the north-east and the White Hope to the south-west. Dere Street would have had to support both foot and wheeled traffic and here it follows one of the few ways through this part of the Cheviots that does not involve steep climbs or descents. Given they wanted the road to head generally north-west, this was an obvious route for the Romans to choose, but dominated as it is by the Iron Age camp on the top of Woden Law, it seems likely that this was a track through the hills well before the Romans arrived.

Elsewhere in the Cheviots there are Iron Age camps that would be hard to defend because they are built on spurs or slopes. The camp on Woden Law is not like this. Nearly 1,400 feet high, steep inclines surround its hilltop setting, particularly to the west where the ground falls away sharply to Kale Water. Despite this, it boasts

Figure 8.16 Woden Law from the east showing the fort's ramparts, the pair of encircling ramparts down the hill and the remains of another single rampart or dyke further down again.
(Image © RCAHMS).

substantial earthworks, especially to the east where the camp overlooks Dere Street and where the approach, while steep, is slightly more manageable (Figure 8.16).

The camp is at the north end of the summit plateau of the hill and is in the shape of a thin oval about 400 feet long and 140 feet wide. On the east and south sides there are four sets of ramparts, but only three can be seen to the north and west. It may be that there never were any more, but since the steep slopes provide natural protection they may have been small in the first place and more prone to erosion.

The site was excavated in 1950 by two people we've already come across earlier in this chapter, Ian Richmond and Kenneth St. Joseph, but their results were not published until about 1982.

They identified three different phases of development in the camp itself. Clearest on its eastern side, the first consisted of a single rampart originally about nine feet thick, now the second one out from the central area (red in Figure 8.17). Outside that, a later set of double ramparts provided additional defences (blue) and also enclosed two annexes at the south end of the camp. Up to 12 feet thick and separated by a large ditch, the outer of these showed traces of a timber revetment. It seems that they were partially destroyed soon after they were built, because their debris lay on top of only a thin layer of natural silt at the bottom of the ditch.

A final rampart (black) was then built inside the first one – largely of rubble and blocks of stone, some of which are still clearly visible. While preserving access through some of the existing entrances, it ignored others and created a single new one. There are

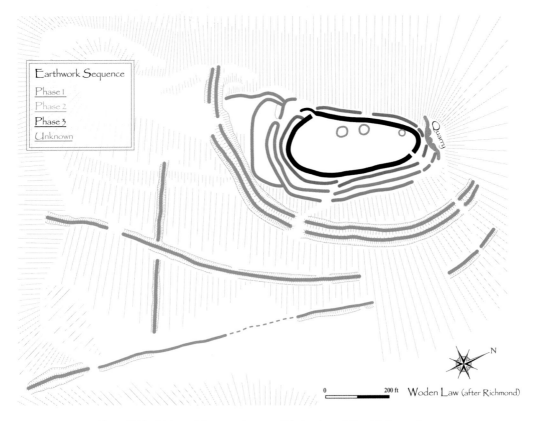

Figure 8.17 A plan of the structures on Woden Law (after Richmond).

few signs of dwellings inside the camp; very hard to see on the ground, aerial photographs show three hut circles on the west side of the camp, close to this innermost rampart. However, it would seem that people did live in the camp or nearby because there are areas of cord rig around the site, particularly to the south.

The excavation uncovered no dateable finds, but Richmond and St. Joseph suggested that the original rampart was built in the late Iron Age, making it contemporary with similar nearby developments such as Hownam Rings[4]. The set of double ramparts may have been built in anticipation of a Roman threat, and were partially destroyed when it materialised. The third, innermost, rampart was identified as being linked to post-Roman re-settlement of the site. This is entirely possible, but some archaeologists have proposed that the original occupation of the site may have been earlier.

The camp's earthworks are not the only structures on Woden Law. Wrapped round its eastern side, at a distance varying from 40 to 100 feet from the outer ramparts,

---

[4] About five miles to the north, and described in the chapter on The Street.

lies a system of two banks and three ditches (green in Figure 8.17). Further out, to the east and south-east there are two more ditched banks (also green). At their closest these are 80 and 100 feet respectively from the inner system, but they are not concentric with it, and the outer one ends up over 800 feet away. These two also cut across an earlier linear bank that runs away to the south-east from a point about 250 feet beyond the camp's outer rampart.

Richmond and St. Joseph observed that these banks appeared to be built in discrete sections and in parts were unfinished. Exploration of the inner system revealed that the outer of the two banks was ballasted; in other words, it did not consist of material just piled up from the adjacent ditch. Had this been the case, then the lighter topsoil would have been at the bottom, with heavier, stonier material from the bottom of the ditch at the top. In fact, the opposite was the case; this method of construction led Richmond and St. Joseph to suggest that the works were Roman, with the flat-topped, outer bank acting as a base for siege engines. They also proposed that the works had not been built in order to capture the camp on the hilltop, but were instead used for training and practice, with the camp already overrun and the troops involved being based about a mile away at Pennymuir.

It is an attractive theory, but Richmond and St. Joseph found no other evidence for this and they did not explain how a siege engine would be configured to sit on top of what is actually a relatively narrow bank (Figure 8.18). Nor did they investigate the other earthworks around the camp, and more recently archaeologists have suggested they are all Iron Age rather than Roman. This possibility has added weight because Roman siege sites, real or practice, are very rare in the British Isles. The only other certain example is that at Burnswark, near Lockerbie, where two Roman camps were built on either side of an Iron Age fort. Long thought to be a practice ground, it now

Figure 8.18 The alleged Roman earthworks to the east of the fort. At this point they are about 150 feet from the outer ramparts.

seems likely that it was the site of an actual military campaign. Unlike Woden Law, specific ballista platforms have been identified and a project led by the Trimontium Trust and Dumfries and Galloway Museums has found large numbers of ballista bolts and sling shot missiles around the Iron Age structure. Richmond and St. Joseph found nothing comparable in the trenches they opened, and this absence must raise doubts about their diagnosis.

As it passes Woden Law, Dere Street turns to the north for a short distance and runs up to a small deserted building, which because of the prevailing winds has no windows or doors on three of its sides. Surrounded by stock pens it is now used for storage, but maps from the mid-nineteenth century identify it as *Streethouse* or *Woaden Street House*. The 1861 census shows a family called Turnbull living there, but there seem to be no records after that. By the 1920s the building's name had been transferred to another one, now demolished, about 500 yards to the east. Interestingly, neither of them was the first Streethouse; that honour goes to a farm further along Dere Street, opposite the Roman camps at Pennymuir and shown on William Roy's survey of the mid-eighteenth century (Figure 8.21).

Leaving the nineteenth-century Streethouse, Dere Street heads north-west, drops down into the valley, crosses Kale Water at Towford, and leaves the main body of the Cheviots. Once over the river it makes a turn to the north, its last serious bend for about six miles, and passes the Pennymuir camps. But before we deal with these, there is one more site to be described.

Moat Knowe

Back on Blackhall Hill, before reaching Woden Law and looking north towards Buchtrig Farm, there is a view along the Capehope Burn between Langside Law and Stanshiel Hill. Between the two of these is a smaller and apparently insignificant hill called Moat Knowe. On top of it, however, is something rather unusual (Figure 8.19).

Almost every hilltop camp in the Cheviots predates the Romans, although some were probably still used after they left the area. Moat Knowe, however, was almost certainly built in what are sometimes called the Dark Ages. Although never excavated, it bears a strong resemblance to sites like Dunadd in Argyll where finds have revealed occupation between the sixth and ninth centuries. Known as nuclear forts, such structures consist of a central stronghold – the nucleus – surrounded by fortified enclosures or courtyards at lower levels.

Moat Knowe is elongated in form, with its long axis running north-south. The central stronghold is on the top of the hill and the two courtyards on each side are defined by the remains of rubble walls which combine to make a continuous barrier on the east of the fort. A narrow street runs along the western side of the whole length of the structure, linking the courtyards. These may have been separated from the street by a series of large edge-on stones; six of these are still standing next to the southernmost courtyard, while others lie on the grass. The central stronghold exploits natural stone outcrops to form a number of terraces, and stone quarried from the summit area has clearly been used elsewhere on the site. Apart from a few faint hollows, there are no obvious signs of buildings, but excavations at Dunadd revealed the remains of wood and turf structures.

Figure 8.19 The fort on Moat Knowe from the west. The 'street' runs the length of the near side of the structure and the nucleus with its natural terracing is in the centre. There are two courtyards on each side; the southern one (on the right) has the remains of a stone wall dividing it from the street. There are more remains at the north (left) end and a large circular enclosure beyond.

In general, the usable space inside nuclear forts was substantially less than in their Iron Age counterparts. It has been suggested that they acted as strongholds for local chieftains as they maintained their authority by progressing around their territory.

There are two other adjacent structures. Below the hill to the east of the fort is a large circular enclosure; thick-walled and with an entrance on the south side, it's impossible to date without excavation and even its function is unclear. And at the north end of Moat Knowe, again on lower ground, ruined walls form an enclosure containing courtyards and the indistinct outlines of some buildings. Again, this cannot be dated but the style of construction suggests it may be later than the fort.

Moat Knowe is less than a mile from Dere Street and is well worth a visit.

Pennymuir

The Roman camps at Pennymuir are the other major archaeological sites of interest in the immediate area. Near the road from Hownam, there were originally four of them, two to the west of Dere Street as it headed north after crossing Kale Water, and two to the east (Figure 8.20). These latter two, Camps C and D, were first identified by air photography in the 1940s. Camp C was shaped like a parallelogram and measured about 900 by 600 feet, lying across the Hownam road between Towford Farm and the junction with Dere Street. A keen-eyed person standing about 100 yards east of that junction can just see the remains of a bank running away to the south of the road, and in the right light that same bank can also be seen from Dere Street itself. Longer stretches of ramparts were reportedly visible 70 years ago, but all other traces have been lost to cultivation.

Camp D is even more ephemeral. Until the 1960s, a low earth bank that may have formed part of the north and east sides of a camp was visible on the ground some way to the south of Camp C. The fact that it was older than the cultivation which had damaged it (Kale Water had removed other parts) and the presence of a rounded

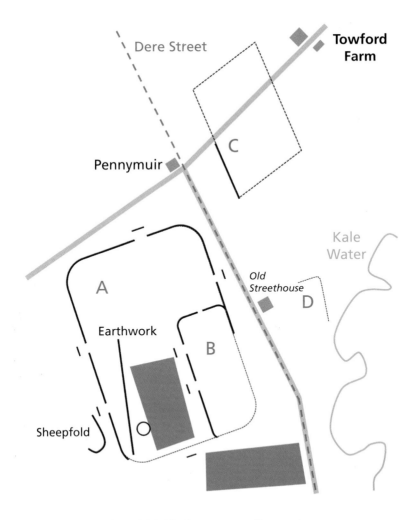

*Figure 8.20 **The four camps at Pennymuir.***

corner, led archaeologists to believe that it was Roman. This may be so, but modern drainage ditches and other works seem to have removed all sign of it.

Camps A and B on the west side of Dere Street are a different story. The larger and earlier one, Camp A, covers some 42 acres. Most of the southern rampart and the southern part of the eastern rampart have vanished through cultivation and erosion. The rest of them are well-preserved, up to four feet high in places and surrounded by a substantial ditch. Four of the probable six gates survive, one on the north side, two on the west and one on the east – the second one here being lost to farming. Each gate has its *titulus*. There is also a *titulus* on the south side of the camp next to some forestry, and it shows where the southern gate was, even though it and the ramparts around it have been lost – perhaps eroded by the sike running between the *titulus* and the site of the gate.

Camp B was constructed in the south-eastern quadrant of Camp A and covers just nine acres. It was clearly built later because at its north-east corner its rampart overlies the ditch around Camp A. Like Camp A, most of its southern and eastern ramparts have disappeared; indeed, it may well have re-used those of the earlier camp. It has three obvious surviving gates, two on the west and one on the north. The two western gates have *tituli*, even though they are inside the earlier camp. Roy's

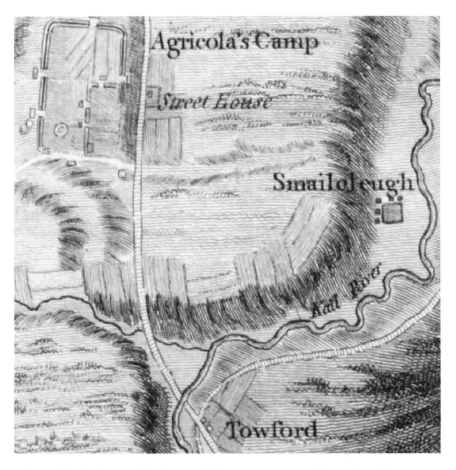

Figure 8.21 Roy's map of the two main Pennymuir camps and the eighteenth-century Street House opposite them. It includes details such as the tituli in front of each gate.

eighteenth-century map (Figure 8.21) shows one at the northern gate as well, but this is now very hard to see – its presence possibly being marked by grass of a slightly different colour.

There are some post-Roman remains in the area as well. Next to the modern gate leading to the camps from the road are the clear remains of a dyke outlining a rectangular field. Opposite, on the east side of Dere Street, is a platform on which the original Street House stood. Just south of it is another enclosure, and the whole represents the remains of a once active post-medieval farm that was probably abandoned in the early nineteenth century.

In the south-west corner of Camp A, next to some modern buildings, is a circular enclosure that is also shown on William Roy's map, as is another smaller enclosure and curved dyke just outside the camp. Both are probably related to stock management; the enclosure outside the camp has no obvious entrance and may be the remains of a stack stand.

More puzzling is a long ditch and dyke that runs north across the interior of Camp A from its south-west corner. On a line diverging slightly from the western rampart, it is clearly visible on the ground as far as the north end of the modern tree plantation, by which time the western rampart is some 150 feet away (Figure 8.20). Aerial photographs show that it probably continued to the northern rampart, meeting it 200 feet from the north-west corner of the camp. It presumably represents some form of medieval or post-medieval boundary, but it's hard to see why whoever built it did not exploit the Roman rampart nearby.

With no excavation at Pennymuir there are no artefacts to provide dating evidence. Most people believe that, like Chew Green, the larger Camp A was built during Agricola's campaign in the north, while Camp B is indicative of later activity, either supporting the construction of the Antonine Wall, or the Severan campaign of the early third century (see Chapter 3).

Pennymuir is 12 miles from Bremenium and between 17 and 18 miles from the fort at Trimontium. Even allowing for the crossing of the Cheviots, these distances are no more than a day's march for a legion and it is tempting to suggest that the original camp was large because of the occasional need to accommodate several bodies of troops, some going north and some going south. Of course, it's probably more complicated than that; other camps were available, especially between Chew Green and Bremenium, and if Richmond and St. Joseph were right with their theory about Woden Law being used for training in siege tactics, then some troops would have been stationed at Pennymuir for extended periods. All these scenarios, though, mean that the term 'marching camp' is not strictly suitable for the structures at Pennymuir – or indeed Chew Green. They might not have been occupied permanently by the same people, but they were not built by legionaries after a day's march and for periods would have been used regularly by troops in transit.

Just north of the Pennymuir camps, Dere Street crosses a modern road. Predating the large lightweight building at the junction, a cottage here served as an inn until the late nineteenth century. Agricultural fairs were held in the adjacent field twice a year – in August and October; in 1835 the *Farmer's Magazine* reported that one of them handled more than 9,000 sheep.

This activity supports the tradition that, especially in post-medieval times, Dere Street was a major route for stock movement and droving. Cattle and sheep destined for markets in England would be brought across the border at many points, and this route was well positioned to take animals from Jedburgh. Descriptions of the markets there in the 1830s mention cattle being bought and taken to Yorkshire.

Although it was a well-defined track, the drovers did not follow Dere Street religiously. They were anxious to avoid obstacles such as tolls and difficult river crossings; at Featherwood, for example, the track to the south-east offered easier access to the major droving centre at Elsdon and the market at Stagshaw Bank above Corbridge.

Pennymuir to Whitton Edge (Map 8.3)

North of Pennymuir, Dere Street follows a straight line, slightly west of north, for about half a mile and then embarks on a long gradual curve which takes it round the eastern flanks of the high ground of Braid Knowe and Cunzierton Hill[5]. The latter is higher at 1,100 feet but the countryside around is much less harsh than anything before, with extensive arable and pasture fields; clear and plentiful signs of rig and furrow show that this land has been cultivated for a long time. The modern track follows the Roman road almost exactly; often bounded by widely separated drystone walls, it was clearly well-suited for moving stock. In places the cambering of the original *agger* is still visible, with a low central mound between 20 and 25 feet across. Every

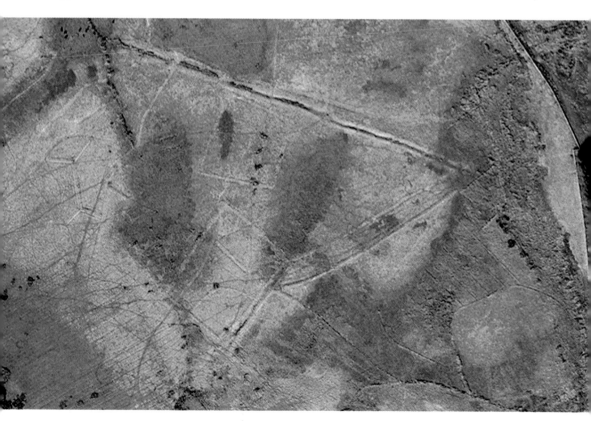

Figure 8.22 **The stock-related structures at Pennymuir** (Image © 2016 Google, Getmapping plc).

---

[5] There seem to be several different ways of pronouncing this. Some possibilities include 'Kinnerton' or 'Kunyerton', with the 'nz' sounding like the Spanish ñ. The most common, though, is 'Kunston'. There are medieval references to *Cuniardon*, and the name may come from Middle English and Scottish words like *cuningar*, meaning rabbit warren.

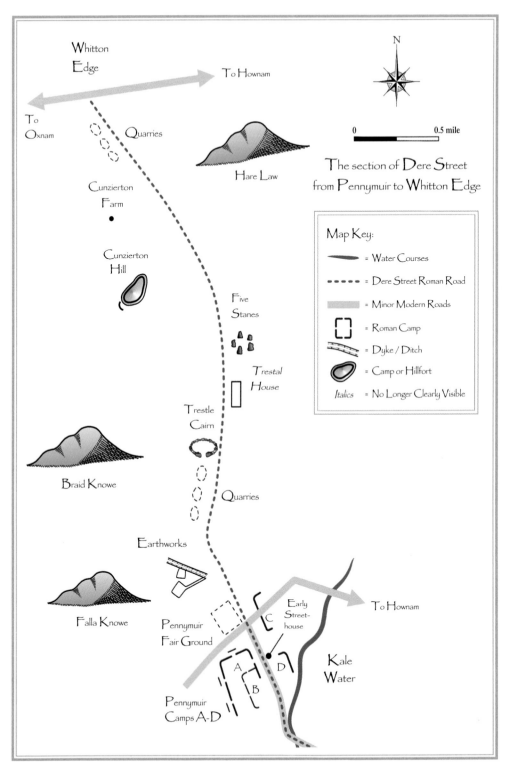

Pennymuir to Whitton Edge. (Map 8.3)

so often, the walker will see small hollows on either side of the path; these are the remains of yet more Roman quarries for material used to build and maintain the road.

About half a mile north of Pennymuir, there are some interesting structures in a field to the west of Dere Street. The most prominent of these is a well-defined earthen dyke and ditch that runs on a slight diagonal for about 300 yards. Its eastern end is about 100 yards from the path, and at this point two other dykes head back in a south-westerly direction (Figure 8.22). Over 50 feet apart in places, and roughly parallel, they form boundaries to a broad track that eventually opens out into a rectangular enclosure of more than an acre. There are other earthworks nearby as well; none of them are shown on any map and it's not clear what their purpose is. The most likely explanation is that they were built to hold animals for the nearby fair or corral them while the drovers enjoyed the hospitality of Pennymuir. It could have been both.

Figure 8.23 The Trestle Cairn.

About a mile further on are two stone structures by the road that are marked on almost every map. The first of these is the Trestle Cairn, lying about 50 yards west of Dere Street and just north of a set of quarries. Badly damaged, a very low section of ridge on its western edge suggests that it was once 50 to 60 feet across (Figure 8.23). Close to it are two stones that are probably in their original position, but all the others – and there are now about 15 of them – have been upended, moved or broken. There is no record of when this happened; the 25-inch Ordnance Survey map of 1859 qualifies the name *'Trestle Cairn'* with the description *'Druidical Circle (remains of)'* and draws 18 stones in a neat circle, but this may have been wishful thinking. Because of the damage, it's impossible to date it properly. However, its position is of some significance, being on the highest point of the track north of Pennymuir.

Half a mile beyond Trestle Cairn and close by Dere Street on the east are the Five Stanes (Figure 8.24). Arranged in a rough circle about 20 feet across, three of these

Figure 8.24 The Five Stanes.

are still standing while two are prone; none of the vertical ones is more than three feet high. About 50 feet further east there are more small stones; some of these are now barely visible but they may have come from the original grouping.

Midway between the Trestle Cairn and the Five Stanes, just to the east of the path, a set of low earth banks defines a rectangular enclosure about 180 feet long and 90 feet wide. A nearby mound to the south has been described as a possible cairn and is so marked on some modern maps. There is rig and furrow close by and an 1808 map of the estate of Over Chatto, a farm a mile to the north-east now called Upper Chatto, shows that this enclosure once contained a farm called *Trestal House*. The Ordnance Survey map of the 1860s has it marked as *'Threstle (ruins of)'*, so it seems to have been abandoned in the first half of the nineteenth century. There have been reports of an outline of a rectangular building some 50 feet long and 20 feet wide, but nothing is now clearly visible on the ground.

Half a mile beyond the Five Stanes, Dere Street passes east of Cunzierton Hill and the farm of the same name. Occupying the top of the hill is a camp about 500 feet long (from north-east to south-west) and half that across. Most of the main rampart is low and eroded and only one or two of the original facing stones can still be seen. The source of the stone seems to have been a set of quarries both inside and outside the structure, and if there ever was one, no external ditch has survived. There are places, particularly at the north-east and south-west ends, where there appear to be additional ramparts. These might have been defensive, but they overlook steep slopes and the most vulnerable area would have been the south-east side, where there is an entrance at the top of a gentler gradient. The interior of the camp is on two levels, one on a lower plateau towards the south-west and the other on the north-east peak of the hill; there are no traces of houses or huts. The whole thing probably dates from the Iron Age, but it's never been excavated.

Figure 8.25 Three jadeitite Neolithic axeheads. The central one was found at Cunzierton and comes from Monte Viso. The one on the left, also from Cunzierton, comes from Monte Beigua. (Image courtesy National Museum of Scotland).

However, the main reason Cunzierton is interesting is not because of this camp, but because of nearby finds. In the late nineteenth century, two axe heads made from a mineral called jadeitite were discovered on land belonging to the farm; these are now in the National Museum of Scotland (Figure 8.25). The presence of these axes shows that people have been active in the area for nearly 6,000 years, from the Neolithic to the present day.

Jadeitite is hard and dense with a colour typically ranging from pale to dark green, although traces of elements such as chromium or iron can result in other hues. Found in several places around the world, it's been used to produce decorative objects by civilisations as diverse as the Chinese and the Mayans.

Although the mineral is not native to the British Isles, nearly 200 jadeitite axe heads have been found here. They are typically over six inches long, thin and triangular; highly polished, it's been estimated that they took hundreds of hours to make, and they show no signs of ever having been used.

Research into these, and 2,000 counterparts from mainland Europe, has revealed that they were traded across a Neolithic, continent-wide network that extended from Ireland in the west to Bulgaria in the east. Most of this activity seems to have happened in the fourth millennium BC and the source of the jadeitite has been tracked down to mountainous locations in northern Italy. Analysis of an axe found near Dunfermline has pinpointed its source to a specific block of jadeitite over 7,000 feet up on the slopes of Monte Viso, high in the western Italian Alps near the French border. Three other axes found in northern Germany came from exactly the same block. One of the Cunzierton axes originated from this area, while the source of the other was about 100 miles to the east, on Monte Beigua near Genoa.

Early versions of these tools seem to have been actually used, and then abandoned near where they were quarried. But an export trade developed for higher quality blades, with Morbihan in southern Brittany becoming a centre for reworking, thinning and polishing objects that may have been ceremonial in nature. The only secure dating for such an axe in Britain is for one found near the Sweet Track in Somerset (see Chapter 1) which puts it at around 3800 BC. Such objects could have been first brought to this country by early Neolithic farming immigrants, for whom they were already treasured heirlooms.

The British equivalents of these axes are those from the slopes of the Langdale Pikes in the Lake District. Probably mined later than the Alpine jadeitites, they consist of a rock known as greenstone, were traded widely and have been found across Britain and Ireland. It is tempting to draw social parallels between the two types of axe; both came from high, inaccessible locations, both came in similar colours and both were apparently treated as valuable.

Once past Cunzierton, Dere Street continues to the north-west, passing between expanses of rig and furrow to the east and a line of quarry pits to the west. At a junction about a mile further on, the grass-covered path meets a minor road and the Roman route turns abruptly to the west. Although its destination was Trimontium, and a change of direction was inevitable at some stage, the sharp nature of this turn suggests that the Romans may have been exploiting earlier paths. However, they fairly soon reverted to type. From various points along the route from Pennymuir, on a clear day a legion marching north would have been able to see the Eildon Hills, and after a short stretch of western travel, the road now takes off directly towards them to the north-west, barely changing direction for 11 or 12 miles.

And so, well and truly out of the Cheviots, this is where we leave Dere Street – and our Border Roads.

Afterword

This book is just one of the planned publications resulting from Coquetdale Community Archaeology's project on the Border Roads that started in 2014.

There is a companion website at www.border-roads.org. This is continually evolving and being updated; it typically contains more details than we could fit into this book, and presents information in ways that cannot be done on paper.

Finally, we will be producing a book of self-guided archaeology walks, with options ranging from those for the serious walker to others that are suitable for families or those with limited time. The publication of this book will be announced on the website.

Glossary

This glossary covers a number of unusual or dialect terms, but is not intended to be exhaustive. Items are often explained in more detail in Chapters 1 to 3.

Andesite	a volcanic rock.
Angles	a tribe from around Schleswig-Holstein; a source of early medieval immigrants to Britain.
Anglo-Saxon	a cultural reference to the complete set of early medieval, Germanic immigrants.
Archaeomagnetic dating	a technique for dating once-heated objects from their magnetic alignment.
Ard	a light plough that uses a sharp stick to dig a shallow furrow without inverting the soil.
Auroch	an extinct variety of large wild cattle.
Barmkin	a substantial, defensive stone wall surrounding a building such as a bastle.
Bastle	a defendable building for both people and stock.
Bell Pit	an early form of coal mine without lateral galleries.
Bigg or bere	an ancient variety of barley.
Bronze Age	a period from around 2200 BC to 750 BC when bronze was the main metal in use.
Bucht	a fold or building primarily for milking sheep.
Camps	also hillforts. Iron Age structures often covering an acre or more enclosed by ramparts.
Chartulary	a manuscript containing transcriptions of an establishment's legal and business documents.
Cist	a small stone coffin-like box used to hold dead bodies or body parts.
Clavicula	a protective, curved extension of a rampart at the side of a gate into a Roman camp.
Cord Rig	an early form of rig and furrow that is close-set and created by hand ploughing.
Cross Dyke	a dyke built across a ridge, but whose precise purpose is unknown.
Crow Steps	rectangular stone blocks along the top of a gable.
Dark Ages	the period from the fall of the western Roman empire to the first millennium.
Dendrochronology	analysis of tree ring patterns used to determine the age or felling date of wood.
DMV	Deserted Medieval Village.
Droving	the movement of stock over long distances for commercial reasons.
Earning	a term for the rennet used in cheese-making.
Einkorn	an ancient variety of wheat.
Elk	a large species of the deer family.
Emmer	an ancient variety of wheat.

Fell Sandstone	thick sandstone layers found in the Northumbrian landscape.
Garth	a yard or rectangular enclosure adjoining a building.
Gauger	a customs officer and collector of excise taxes who might also track down smugglers.
Granite	a hard, often light-coloured rock with visible grains. Formed by the crystallisation of magma.
Greywacke	a coarse-grained sandstone possibly formed as a result of underwater avalanches.
Guild	a medieval fraternity of craftsmen; both a professional association and a trade union.
Head Dyke	a dyke separating arable land from moorland.
Hollow-ways	deeply eroded tracks formed by heavy traffic.
Ice Age	a period in which Arctic ice covered significant areas of Europe.
Inquisition *post mortem*	a medieval tax assessment on a dead person's estate.
Iron Age	a period from around 750 BC to the arrival of the Romans in AD 43.
Kiln	a chamber for drying (e.g. barley) or burning (e.g. lime).
Lay Subsidies	a form of medieval taxation.
Lazy Beds	small-scale hand-crafted rig and furrow, usually for horticulture not agriculture.
LiDAR	a laser-based technology used to capture information about landscape profiles.
Longhouse	a medieval or post-medieval rectangular building that housed both people and stock.
Lynchets	cultivation terraces that run across a slope.
Lynx	a wild cat up to four feet long (in Eurasia).
Marches	the medieval and early modern Anglo-Scottish border area, divided into East, Middle and West.
Marching camps	camps used by Roman troops in transit.
Medieval	a period also called the Middle Ages.
Early	from the fall of the Roman empire to the first millennium.
High	from the first millennium to around AD 1300.
Late	from *circa* AD 1300 to around the end of the 15th century.
Medieval Warm Period	a warm period in the North Atlantic area from about AD 950 to 1250.
Mesolithic	in the British Isles, a period from around 8000 BC to 4000 BC.
Muster Rolls	lists of actual troops or the potential troops an area might supply.
Neolithic	in the British Isles, a period from the introduction of farming around 4000 BC to 2200 BC.
Nuclear fort	a defensive site from the Dark Ages with courtyards around a central nucleus.
Palaeolithic (Upper)	the final period of the Stone Age, from about 50,000 BC to 8000 BC.

Palisade	a wooden 'wall' built for defence. Two concentric ones form a double palisade.
Peat Bog	a wetland in which plant debris accumulates to form peat.
Pele	a defensive tower usually built by authorities or high-status individuals.
Poitín	an Irish distilled drink, sometimes produced illegally; best made from malted barley.
Poll tax	a medieval fixed-rate tax levied regardless of the ability to pay.
Post-medieval	a term used to describe activities from the sixteenth century onwards.
Quarter Sessions	local courts held quarterly from the fourteenth century.
Quern	a simple hand mill for grinding corn, typically consisting of two circular stones.
Quoin	an external angle of a wall or building.
Radiocarbon dating	using radioactive decay in carbon to assess the date of an organic object.
Reivers	raiders often involved in cattle theft and other illegal activities.
Rig and Furrow	sets of ridges and furrows produced by ploughing a field in a regular pattern.
Romano-British	used to describe native British activities during the period of Roman occupation.
Rooing	the process of removing a sheep's fleece by pulling the wool off by hand.
Roundhouse	an early form of circular house, built from wood and perhaps stone with a conical roof.
Scooped Settlement	a settlement on a platform dug back into a slope.
Shale	a soft stratified sedimentary rock that was originally consolidated mud or clay.
Sheep stell	a circular structure used for sheep management and shelter.
Shieling	a poorly built dwelling typically used during upland summer pasturage.
Sike	a small stream, often in marshy ground.
Spelt wheat	an ancient, but still cultivated, variety of wheat.
Stack stand	a place where fodder could be stored and protected from stock.
Steading	a farm and its buildings.
Still	a site or building used for the production of spirits.
Tenterhooks	hooks used to attach newly-fulled cloth to tentering frames for drying and bleaching.
Titulus	a bank outside a gate of a Roman camp, built to protect the opening from direct attack.
Transhumance	the movement of stock to uplands for summer grazing.
Wedder	a castrated male sheep.

Further Reading

This book on the Border Roads has not been written like a paper in an archaeological journal, nor is it aimed at an academic audience, so we have not provided citations for every piece of information presented, or every conclusion drawn. As far as possible, however, we have based our material on what we've found in primary sources as well as on our own observations. In the course of the project we've found many useful references; some of these have already been mentioned in Chapter 2, so this section lists some additional sources.

A few are specifically archaeological in nature, while others cover human and economic history. As we implied in the Introduction, it's rarely useful to try to split the two. The reader of this book who wants to know more about the Border Roads, and the archaeology and the history of the Cheviots in general, should find these sources fascinating.

We start with archaeological journals, of which there are two whose focus includes the border area. These are *Archaeologia Aeliana*, published annually by the Society of Antiquaries of Newcastle upon Tyne (SANT), and the History of the Berwickshire Naturalists Club. The former was first published nearly 200 years ago; copies can be consulted in specialist libraries and there is an index of contents and authors on the SANT website. The Society is in the process of digitising the journal; all nineteenth-century copies are now available on *archive.org* and a start has been made on the twentieth century[1].

Despite its name, the History of the Berwickshire Naturalists Club carries a high proportion of papers on archaeology and history. Almost as old as *Archaeologia Aeliana*, most editions up to the 1970s are also on *archive.org*.

There are many archaeological websites. The most comprehensive and authoritative include *Canmore*, a site compiled and managed by Historic Environment Scotland. It holds information from many sources, and there are sets of search tools to help locate archaeological sites. On the English side of the border, there is *Pastscape*, a comprehensive website maintained by Historic England. Back over the border, *ScotlandsPlaces* is a subscription site that integrates information from several different databases. One of these is *Canmore*, but there is additional material covering tax rolls, estate and church records and government archives. Finally, there are websites that are even more specialised. A particularly interesting one, although its scope extends far beyond our area, is ORBIS. Created by Stanford University and based on detailed information about Roman transport systems, it simulates movement along the Roman network of roads, rivers and sea routes, reconstructing the duration and financial cost of travel in antiquity.

There are specialist books as well as specialist websites. A very useful one is *The Iron Age in Northern Britain*, by Dennis Harding. With a similar focus, *Hillforts* by Al Oswald, Stewart Ainsworth and Trevor Pearson provides detailed coverage of these structures in the Northumberland National Park. A book with an even tighter geographic focus, but which covers every period, is *Fifty Centuries of Peace and War* by Beryl Charlton, which examines the archaeology of the Otterburn Training Area. North of the border, a similar approach was taken by the Royal Commission on the Ancient Monuments of Scotland, which published a two-volume study of the archaeology of Roxburghshire in 1956. A lot of the material in this work has been republished on the *Canmore* website.

Then there are books that cover particular social aspects of the Border Roads. These include *Drove Roads of Northumberland* by Ian Roberts, Alan Rushworth and Richard Carlton. A book on the same subject but covering the whole of the country is *The Drovers* by Kenneth Bonser.

These are all books that were published in the twentieth century or later; some earlier books were discussed in Chapter 2 in its coverage of archives and records. The information their

---

[1] Rather than supply long and cumbersome URLs which the reader would have to retype, the best way to find these (and other) publications is to Google "archive.org" together with the name of the item wanted.

authors presented and the conclusions they drew sometimes have to be treated carefully, although they can provide valuable insights into contemporary thoughts and practice. On occasions they can be very useful in directing the reader towards even older primary sources. These include publications such as the *State Papers of Henry VIII*, which hold material about the border conflicts of the sixteenth century. Even earlier than that are the chartularies of monastic orders such as those at Newminster (Morpeth), Melrose and Kelso (Calchou), which provide information on medieval landholdings, deals and disputes. Images of transcripts of these are available on the web, but the only problem is that, as far as we know, there are no full translations into modern English. This means the researcher has to battle with medieval Latin, helped only by the occasional English gloss.

More accessible is a website on the *People of Medieval Scotland* – a database of all the people of the country between 1093 and 1314 that were mentioned in over 8,000 contemporary documents, together with the transactions or events associated with them. It includes references from the Scottish chartularies mentioned above.

In England, the Surtees Society is dedicated to transcribing and publishing historical material relevant to Northumberland and Durham. With its first publication in 1835, they have now produced over 200 books, a full list of which can be found on their website.

As described in Chapter 2, maps can be an important source of historical information. The National Library of Scotland's website has an excellent collection; not only does this include digital versions of old Scottish county maps, but also a complete set of early Ordnance Survey maps for both Scotland and England at a scale of 6 inches to the mile. Other old maps are available at libraries, such as Newcastle Central, and in the extensive holdings of archive and research centres.

Of these, the most useful ones for the areas covered in this book are Hawick's Heritage Hub and the Northumberland Archives at Woodhorn. Both have on-line catalogues of the material they hold, as do the National Archives in Kew and the National Records of Scotland in Edinburgh. On occasions, the catalogues of these national bodies will direct users to holdings in regional archives and libraries.

Census information is readily available online at subscription sites such as those offered by *Ancestry* and *Findmypast*; archive centres and local libraries will very often have subscriptions that facilitate public access to these sites. *ScotlandsPeople* offers similar services north of the border. These sites also maintain sets of parish registers, although they are not complete. Family History Societies can also be a good source for these, although sometimes the transcriptions they hold omit useful information such as farm names and occupations. If they have microfilm or microfiche copies of the originals, those are better. Some transcriptions of specific parish registers are on *archive.org*.

Durham University maintains an online system called the *North East Inheritance Database*. This holds probate material for Northumberland and Durham such as wills and inventories that were drawn up prior to 1858. Searchable by name and parish, these can provide invaluable insights into wealth, landholdings and family relationships, and many images of original documents are available. These are the kind of things that can make archaeology come alive, but the older the documents are, the harder they can be to read. As a final recommendation, therefore, there are online tutorials on old handwriting from places like the National Archives, Cambridge University and the National Records of Scotland, as well as books such as *Palaeography* by Hilary Marshall.

Site Type Index

This index, and the one that follows, are not exhaustive.
Rather, the intention is to help the reader dip into the book to find where there is most information
on particular sites or places along the Border Roads.

Place Name Index